P9-BIH-752

COLUMBIA BRANCH
RECEIVED

AUG 05 2017

NO LONGER PROPERTY OF
SEATTLE PUBLIC LIBRARY

4 pages 16 bars

a visual mixtape

VOL. 3: DOIN' OUR OWN THANG

BLAXIS

VOL. 03 PLAYLIST

number 13

globalists

bayne

trailblazers

PUBLISHER - JIBA MOLEI ANDERSON
DIRECTOR OF MARKETING - ROCHON PERRY
ART DIRECTOR - LA MORRIS RICHMOND
COPY EDITOR - JUDE W. MIRE

e.p.i.c.

4 Pages 16 Bars: A Visual Mixtape Volume Three: Doin' Our Own Thang is published by Blaxis Publishing, an imprint of Cedar Grove Books, Inc. 3500 West Armitage Avenue #2R Chicago, IL, 60647, USA. On the internet: http://www.griotenterprises.com; all artwork, the distinct likenesses thereof, and all related indicia are TM and © 2016 their respective creators, all rights reserved. The stories, characters and incidents presented in this publication are fictional. Any resemblance to persons living or dead is purely unintentional. All other material, except where noted, is TM and © 2016 Blaxis Publishing. Except for purposes of review, no portion of this publication may be reproduced or reprinted in any way without the express written permission of the copyright holder(s). Printed in the USA.

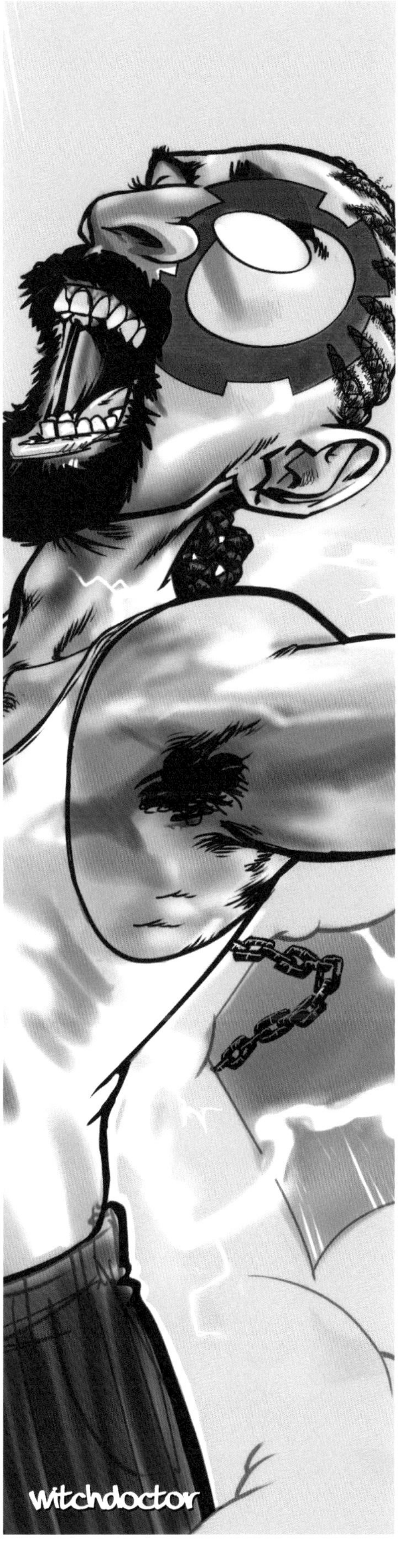
witchdoctor

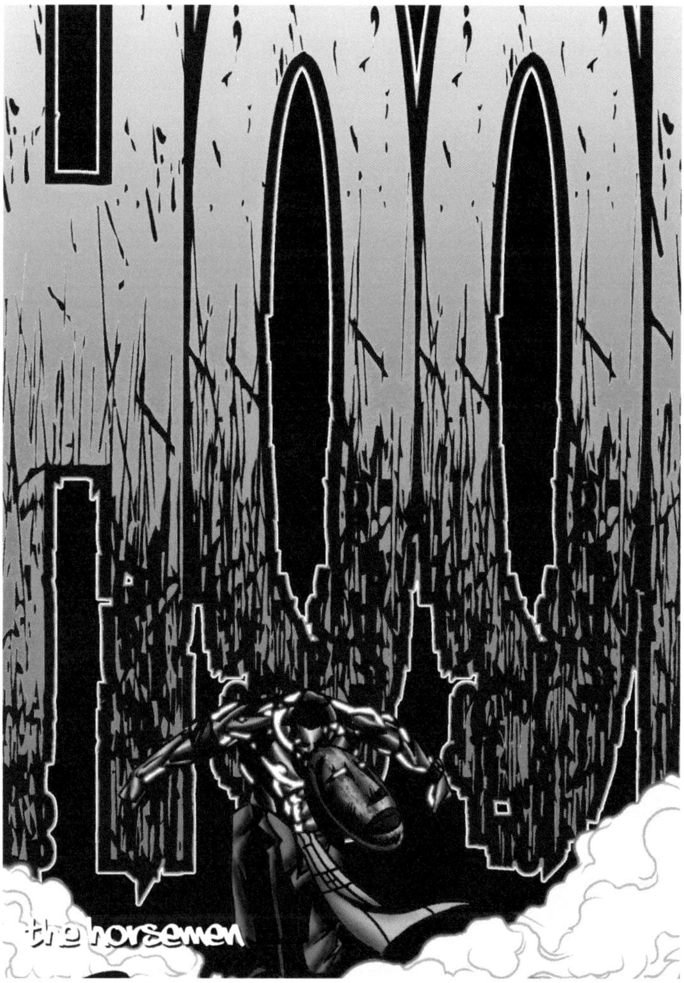
the horsemen

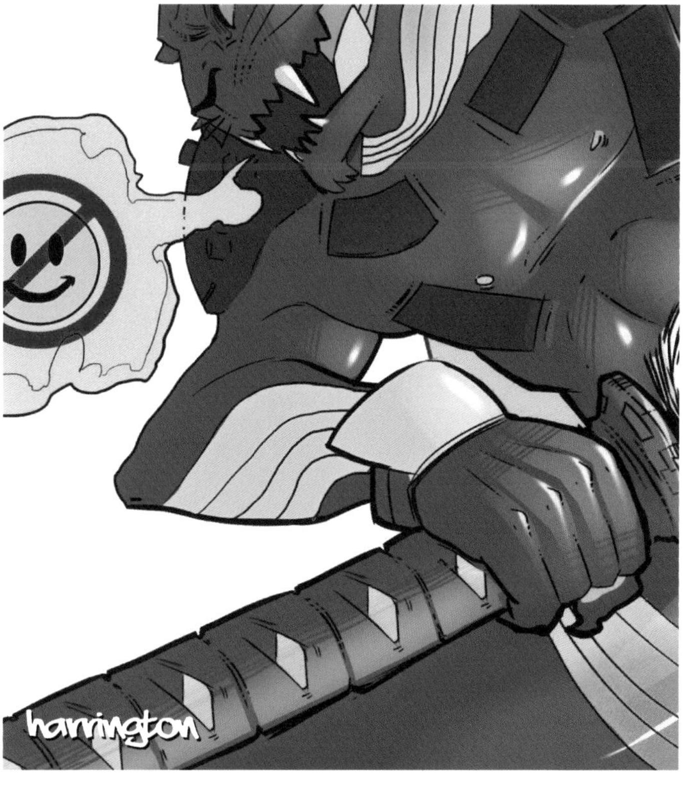
harrington

for dwayne mcduffie
THE MAN WHO INSPIRED A GENERATION
CO-CREATOR OF THE MILESTONE UNIVERSE (1962 - 2011)

mind your surroundings
BY JIBA MOLEI ANDERSON

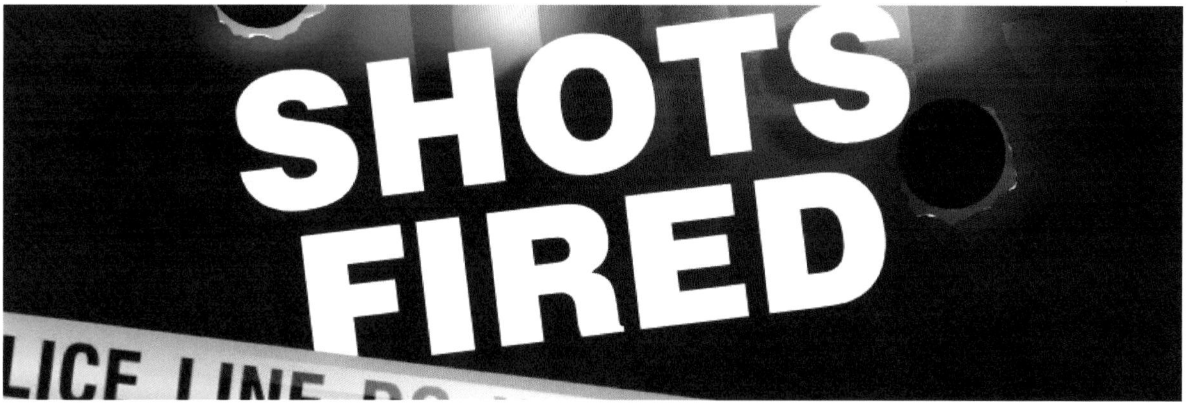
SHOTS
FIRED
LICE LINE

"The only weapon the uninformed has in a debate against an informed opponent is the circular argument..."

- Jib Tzu – The Art of Verbal War

It's interesting to be responded to, and referenced as a solution, simultaneously...

A follower of mine on Facebook had a response to my article concerning the return of **Milestone Media**. Here are a couple of excerpts:

"Its not that black people don't want these comics or minorities in general, its the lack of authenticity in most minority creators approach to selling the books based on our needs and behavior as a group of minorities in America. As someone who substitutes at schools where I have shown minority comics with excitement, I've witnessed from the shining eyes of children from 5th -8th grade school I know they want it.

Too many Minority-owned companies competing in an industry where there is not enough mainstream established creators for it to have meaning. As in this industry is so dominated by Caucasians that each time a minority creator is so called competitive that they are not building more ground to establish themselves, but rather are really lessening their appeal for its numbers that decide who is successful and a hot commodity in an industry.

And Milestone is only repeating a common practice by most Blacks when it comes to success, that its not understood to maintain it that you have to grow it from the community you are trying to represent instead of obtaining success and not spreading it."

Wow.... That response pissed a number of my fellow creators off. Here's an excerpt of a response from ***T.A.S.K.*** creator **Damion Gonzalez**:

"You called Dwayne McDuffie, Denys Cowan, Derek Dingle and Michael Davis sellouts. You accused them of not hiring minorities. I think that Joseph Illidge, Ivan Velez, Jr., ChrissCrossX, Jason Scott Jones, Robert Washington (RIP), Eric Battle and Micheline Hess would beg to differ. Those are just the people ***I know****. Also Michael Davis would go on to mentor and tutor scores of other* ***including*** *N Steven Harris!!! You can talk all the businesses talk you want to talk but calling those men sellouts and ignoring what they* ***actually*** *did to foster your lack of knowledge about what they did will not fly."*

Wildfire creator **Quinn McGowan** also offered this as a counter to the argument posed by the commentator:

"Perhaps doing some actual research (as has been suggested to you before) and being informed before criticizing and tagging other people in your argument based in emotion (not in fact) would behoove someone considering themselves offering suggestions to people doing the work (And clearly already offering real and workable suggestions) in this industry..."

E.P.I.C. creator **Lonnie Lowe Jr.** came at my man straight no chaser with his response:

"Ok, until you create or contribute something with at least 1/16 of the importance of what Milestone did for creators of color and minority creators you need to chill.

You're way too heavily opinionated for someone who hasn't done one thing to push the culture forward yet you have all the answers and solutions. You lack tangibility. You have no physical evidence. You haven't done anything creator wise other than talk and make these long-ass posts about what someone else should be doing."

I feel what some can do is share the article on his wall to spread the word as opposed to preaching to the choir with his manifesto.

One of the points in my article is that the activation of fandom is also crucial in this equation.

For example, instead of explaining the Creator's responsibility (which as the name of this group suggests, most of us are), you could share this article on your wall in addition to other walls thereby spreading the message. Active fandom is an essential part of the cause. People do it for **DC** and **Marvel** all the time. Why not for us doing the good work as well?

In the 20 years since Milestone ceased regular publication, this is what happened:

Griot Enterprises
Rosaruim Publishing
Gettosake Entertainment
Ravenhammer Entertainment
133Art
The Operative Network
Black Comix
ONYXCON
The Glyph Awards
MECCA Con
Genius
Concrete Park
Blackjack
Wildfire
4 Pages 16 Bars
T.A.S.K.
Exo: The Legend of Wale Williams
Trill League
Cannon Busters
Legend of the Mantamaji

And, that's just the tip of the iceberg...

The point I am making is that your solutions are in practice... **right now**. As stated, the widespread awareness of diversity in comics in its infancy (in your estimate, only 20 years when in actuality it's almost 30). It takes not only time, but also an active word-of-mouth audience who purchases our work and promotes it for all to succeed.

We do the promotion. We're active on social media and have been getting exposure on mainstream and independent media outlets. We've got the conventions established. We're doing our part. What we need are active, not passive, consumers.

With Print On Demand outfits like **Ka-Blam**, Amazon's **Createspace**, **IngramSpark**, etc., there is no need to spend extra money to print books in all 50 states to increase awareness or availability... Anyone can buy our books, in print and digital formats, anywhere in the world. One doesn't even have to go to the comic book store to get their books. One goes to the comic book store for a sense of community, kinda like the barbershop.

In terms of marketing, social media takes care of the wide net awareness approach (i.e. articles, posts, etc.) while conventions (if one could afford the cost of travel, housing, booth space, meals and product) handle the personal interaction and direct sales to potential fans...

In short, we as creators don't have to reinvent the wheel.

What the consumer needs to do is click on that post, read that article, come to the cons to see cats who look like them doing this thing well and purchase the books that speak to them. Then, they need to tell their people about it and support the movement in their way.

We do it for others, but we don't do it for ourselves. Instead of blaming the creators, why not take your fellow consumers to task? Why not shout from the rooftop about that new book you picked up that no one is hip to yet?

Why is it so hard for the consumer of color to do their part in making this grow? They do it for less... Why they scared?

With ***4 Pages 16 Bars: A Visual Mixtape***, each contributor gets access to order print copies of the book through my printers at MY printing costs. In addition, they also receive a copy of the digital issue **for free** to sell on their websites. I've already implemented what you proposed... It ain't new. That's cross promotion 101.

4 Pages 16 Bars: A Visual Mixtape is Cross Promotion 101, a place for those who don't know to sample what we have to offer with links to the websites of those participating so that we continue to build on the community... Emphasis on **continue**.

The simple fact is, everything you say Black Indie Creators should be doing, we are doing. What you, the fans, need to do is stop and take a look.

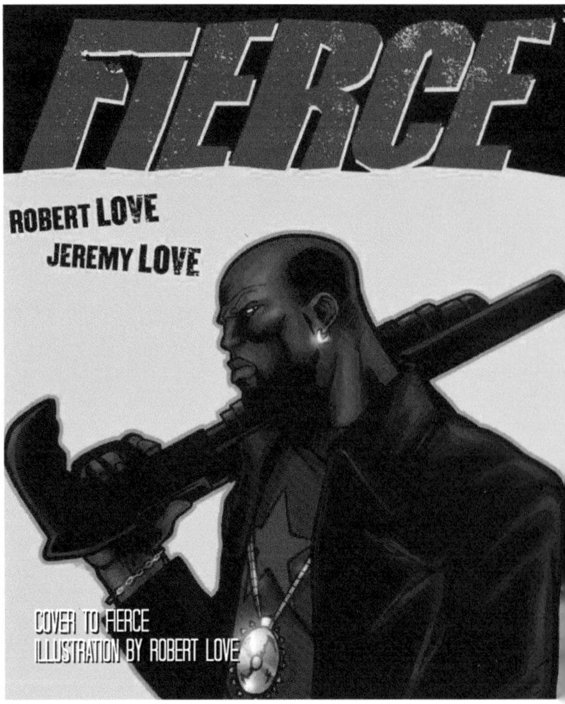
FIERCE
ROBERT LOVE
JEREMY LOVE
COVER TO FIERCE
ILLUSTRATION BY ROBERT LOVE

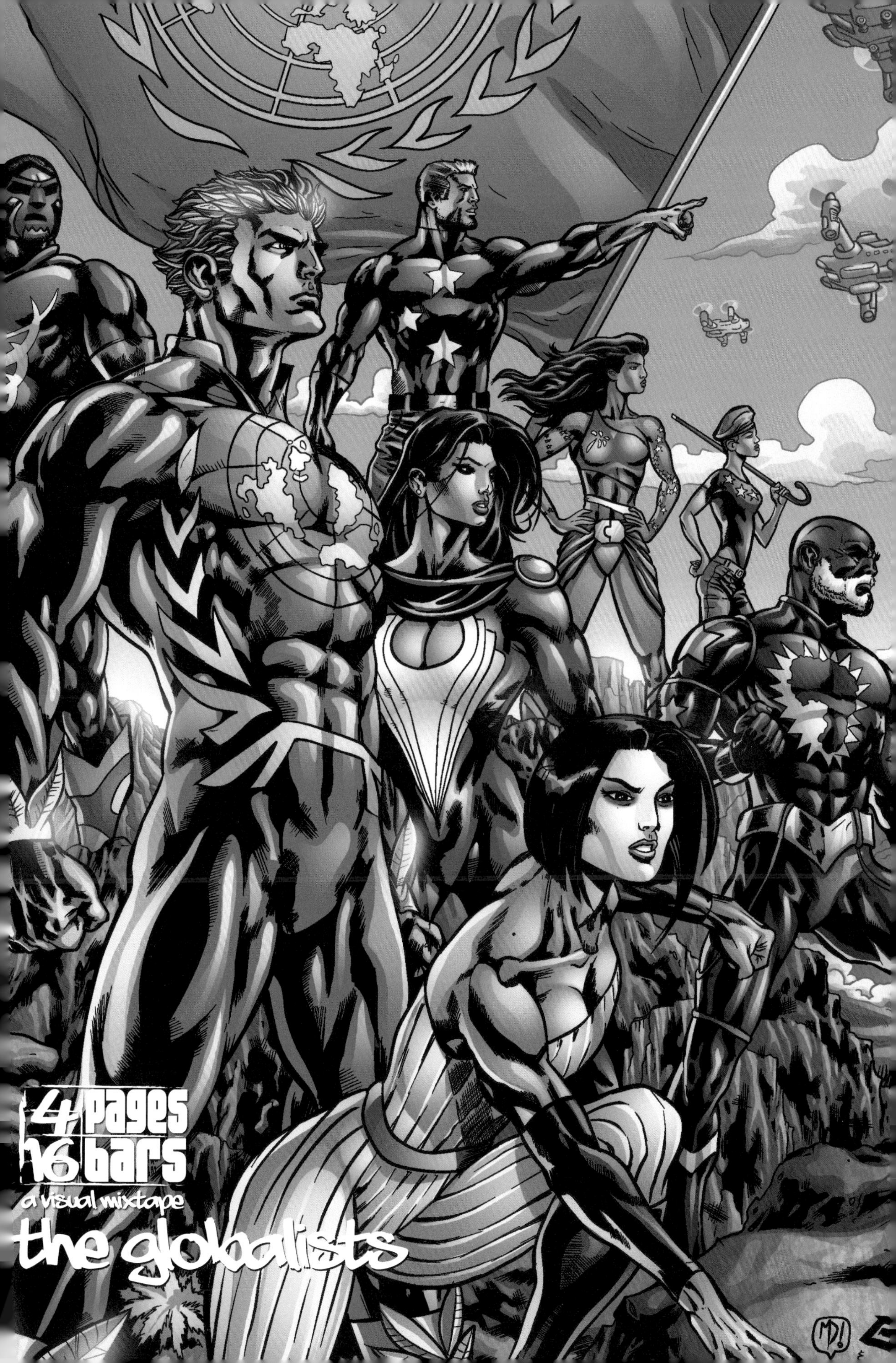
4 pages
16 bars
a visual mixtape
the globalists

ART BY
KEVIN KEANE & MALFLY TANAKA

Nigel Flood is a comic book writer residing in the grand country of Ireland and publisher of **Punt Press**. Married to a Nigerian women with two lovely girls (the "Afrocelts" as we have to call them), Nigel is at the forefront of the growing independent Irish comic book scene. His first project, the **Celtic Clan**, is a superhero team in the model of **The Avengers**, with a strong connection to Irish culture, mythology and politics.

Keeping in the political vein, Flood has created **The Globalists**.
The Globalists are worshiped like celebrities as they have put an end to global conflict and turned the world into a Utopia, crime and world hunger have all mostly been eliminated. The Globalists are a team that rule the world, each of them control a continental union but they are all answerable there supreme leader the United Nationalist, his word is law, he has the final say on every decision. In his world religion is outlawed, all native languages are outlawed, there is one global language spoken and that is Esperanto.

However, the world of the Globalists is not so rosy as they will soon feel push back from the likes of the **Resistance**, the **Swiss** and the **Individual**...

website: twitter.com/thecelticclan

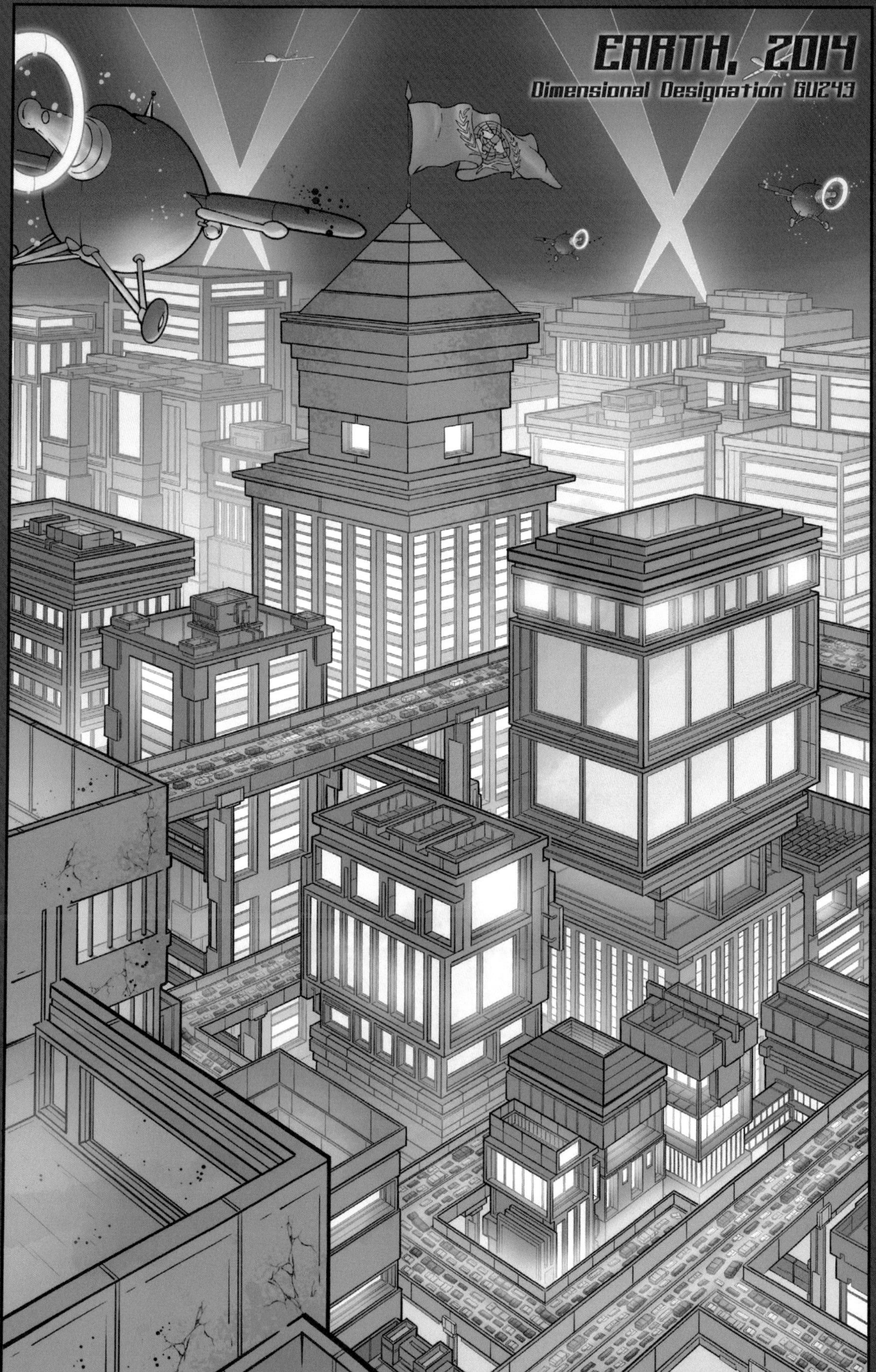
EARTH, 2014
Dimensional Designation 6U243

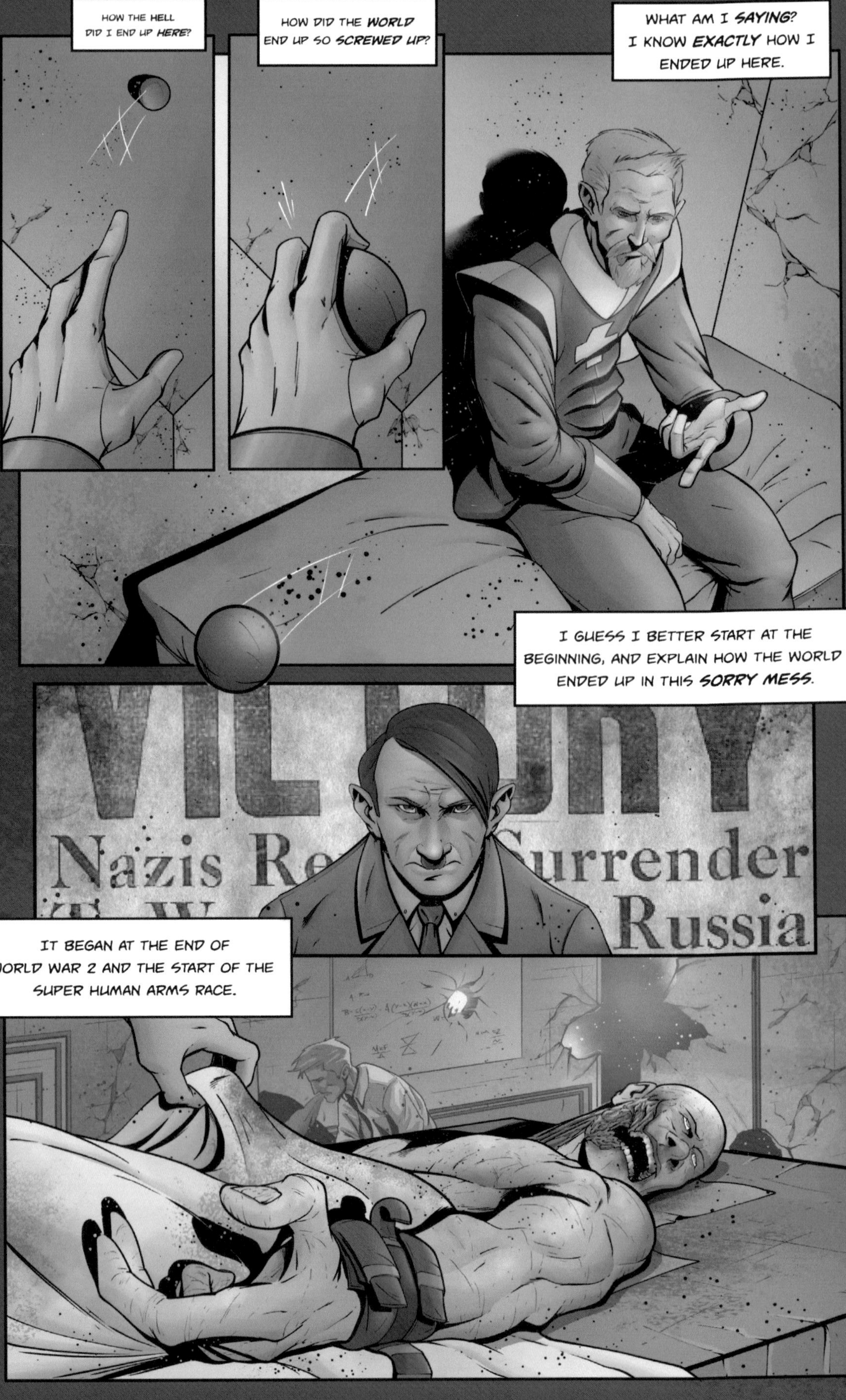
HOW THE HELL DID I END UP HERE?
HOW DID THE WORLD END UP SO SCREWED UP?
WHAT AM I SAYING? I KNOW EXACTLY HOW I ENDED UP HERE.
I GUESS I BETTER START AT THE BEGINNING, AND EXPLAIN HOW THE WORLD ENDED UP IN THIS SORRY MESS.
Nazis
Russia
IT BEGAN AT THE END OF WORLD WAR 2 AND THE START OF THE SUPER HUMAN ARMS RACE.

THE ALLIES HAD HEARD **RUMOURS** OF THE NAZI SCIENTISTS WORKING ON THEIR WUNDERWAFFES AND THEIR QUEST FOR THE UBERMENCH.

BUT THEY HAD NO IDEA THEY WERE SO CLOSE TO **SUCCEEDING**. THIS WAS THE SPARK THAT STARTED THE FIRE.

THE ALLIES SEIZED THE FILES AND THE KNOWLEDGE. BETWEEN THEM, THEY TRIED TO KEEP THE SOVIETS OUT, BUT LITTLE DID THEY KNOW THAT STALIN HAD BEEN WORKING ON HIS **OWN** SUPER HUMANS.

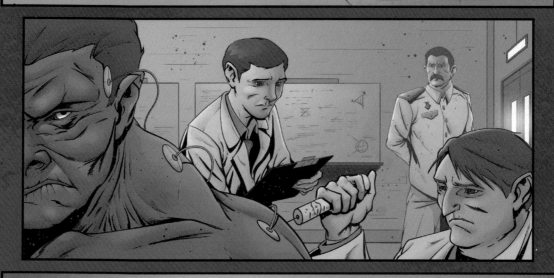

THE SUPER HUMAN ARMS RACE SPREAD LIKE WILD FIRE.

SOME OF THE NAZI SCIENTISTS HAD ESCAPED TO SOUTH AMERICA AND BEGAN, ANEW, THEIR EXPERIMENTS ON CREATING A **NEW BREED** OF SUPER HUMANS WITH THE FUNDING AND SUPERVISION OF THEIR NEW MASTERS.

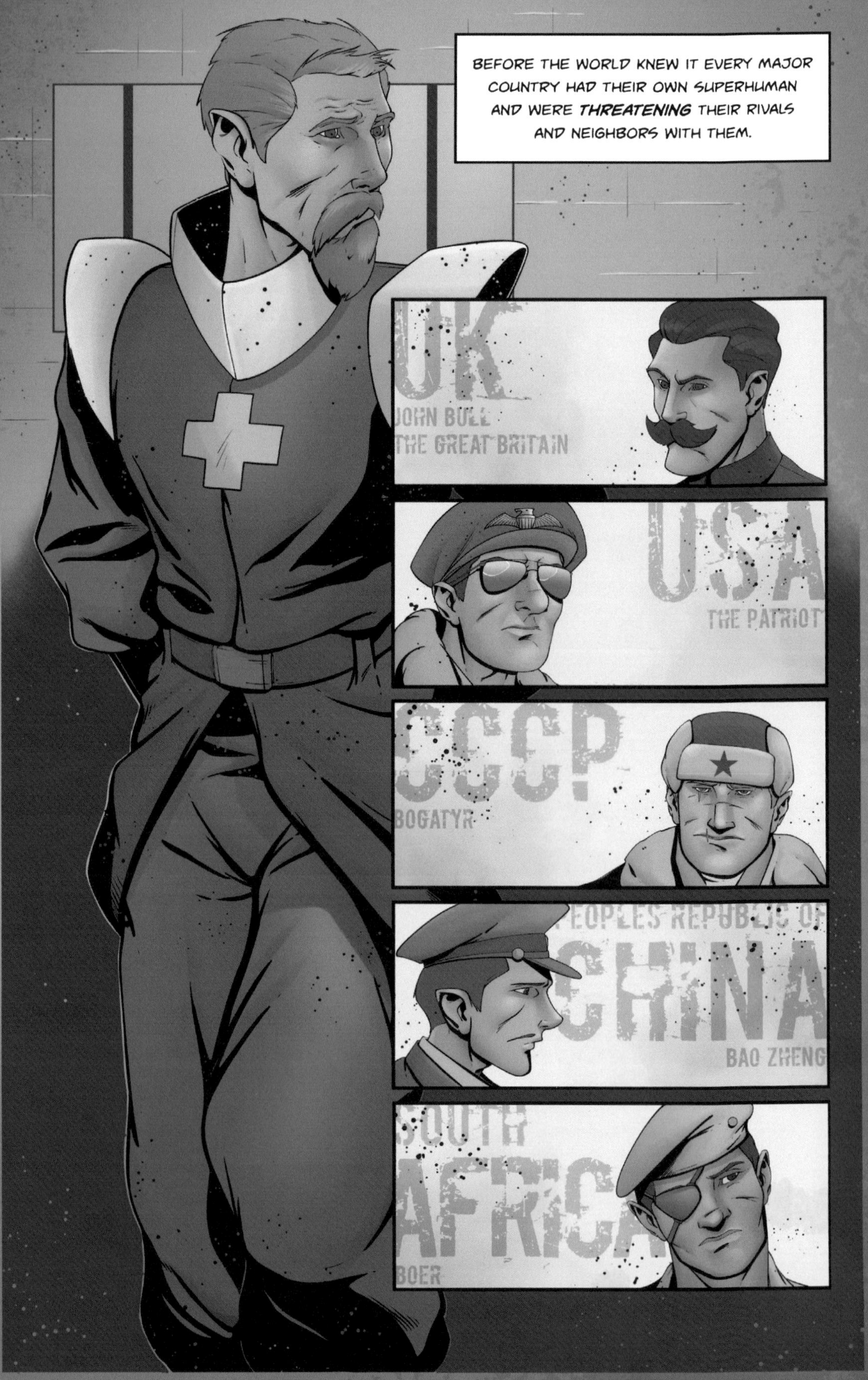
BEFORE THE WORLD KNEW IT EVERY MAJOR COUNTRY HAD THEIR OWN SUPERHUMAN AND WERE ***THREATENING*** THEIR RIVALS AND NEIGHBORS WITH THEM.
UK
JOHN BULL
THE GREAT BRITAIN
USA
THE PATRIOT
СССР
BOGATYR
EOPLES REPUBLIC OF
CHINA
BAO ZHENG
SOUTH
AFRICA
BOER

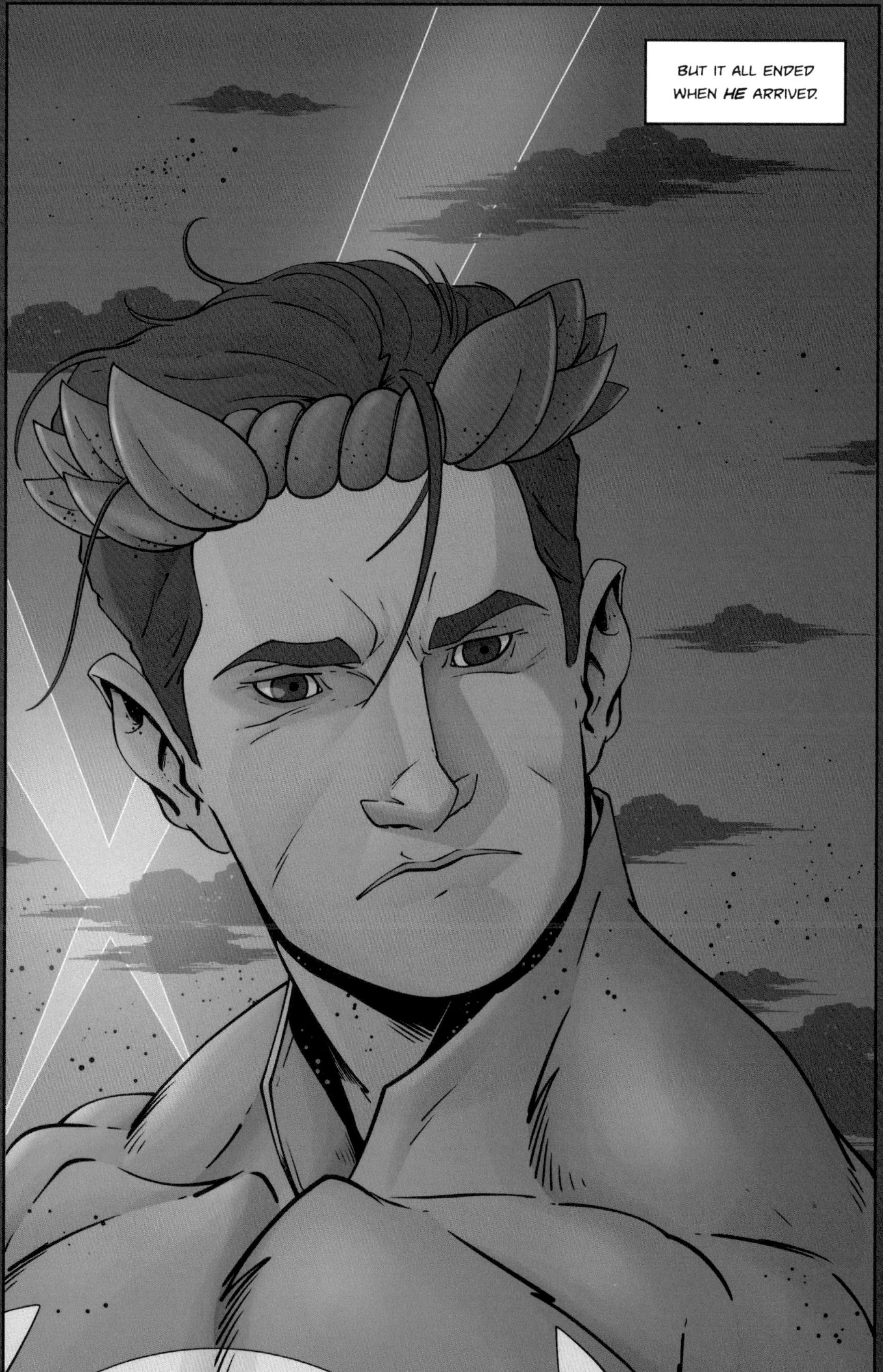
BUT IT ALL ENDED WHEN HE ARRIVED.

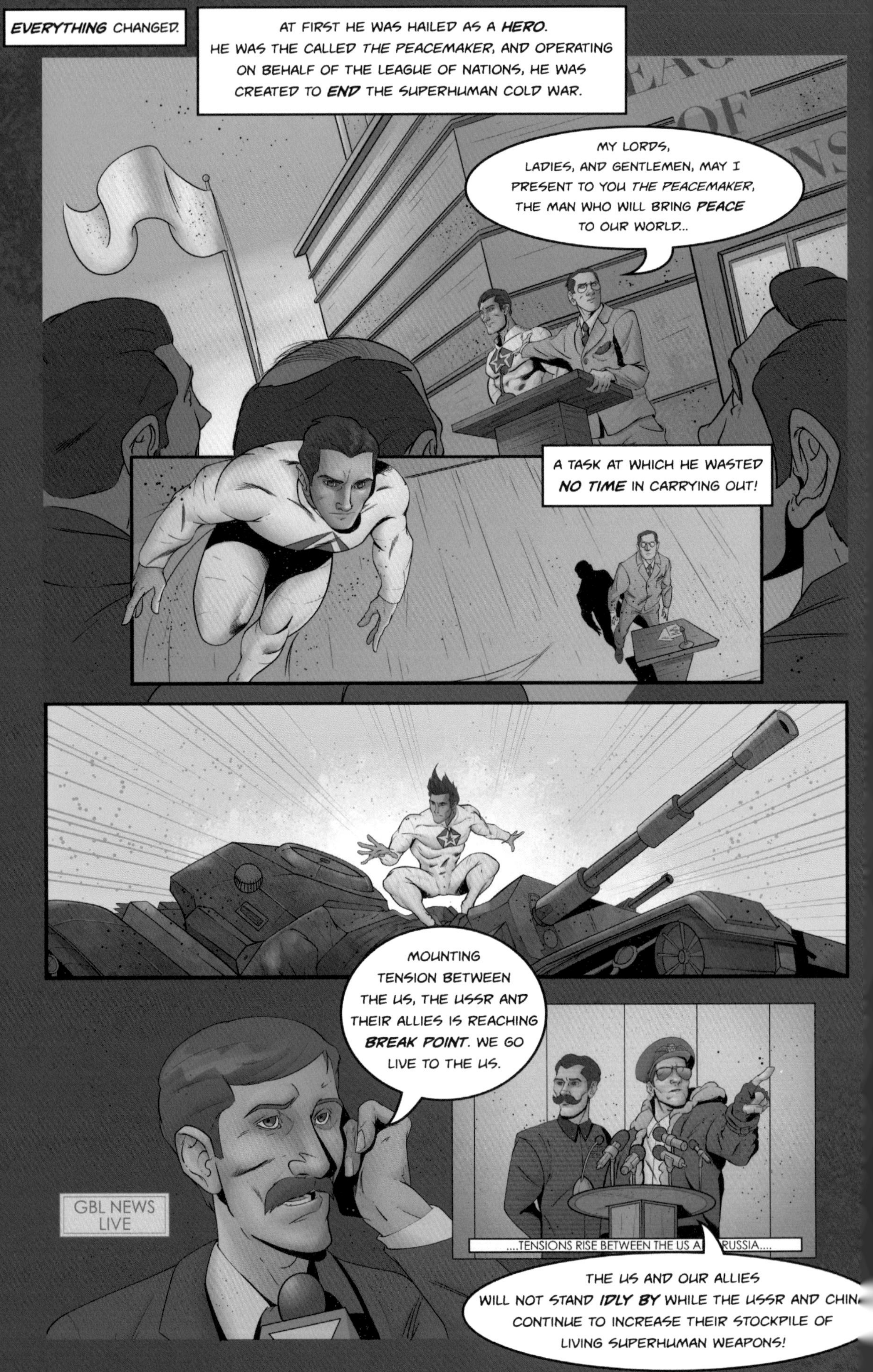
EVERYTHING CHANGED.
AT FIRST HE WAS HAILED AS A HERO. HE WAS THE CALLED THE PEACEMAKER, AND OPERATING ON BEHALF OF THE LEAGUE OF NATIONS, HE WAS CREATED TO END THE SUPERHUMAN COLD WAR.
MY LORDS, LADIES, AND GENTLEMEN, MAY I PRESENT TO YOU THE PEACEMAKER, THE MAN WHO WILL BRING PEACE TO OUR WORLD...
A TASK AT WHICH HE WASTED NO TIME IN CARRYING OUT!
MOUNTING TENSION BETWEEN THE US, THE USSR AND THEIR ALLIES IS REACHING BREAK POINT. WE GO LIVE TO THE US.
GBL NEWS LIVE
....TENSIONS RISE BETWEEN THE US A RUSSIA....
THE US AND OUR ALLIES WILL NOT STAND IDLY BY WHILE THE USSR AND CHIN CONTINUE TO INCREASE THEIR STOCKPILE OF LIVING SUPERHUMAN WEAPONS!

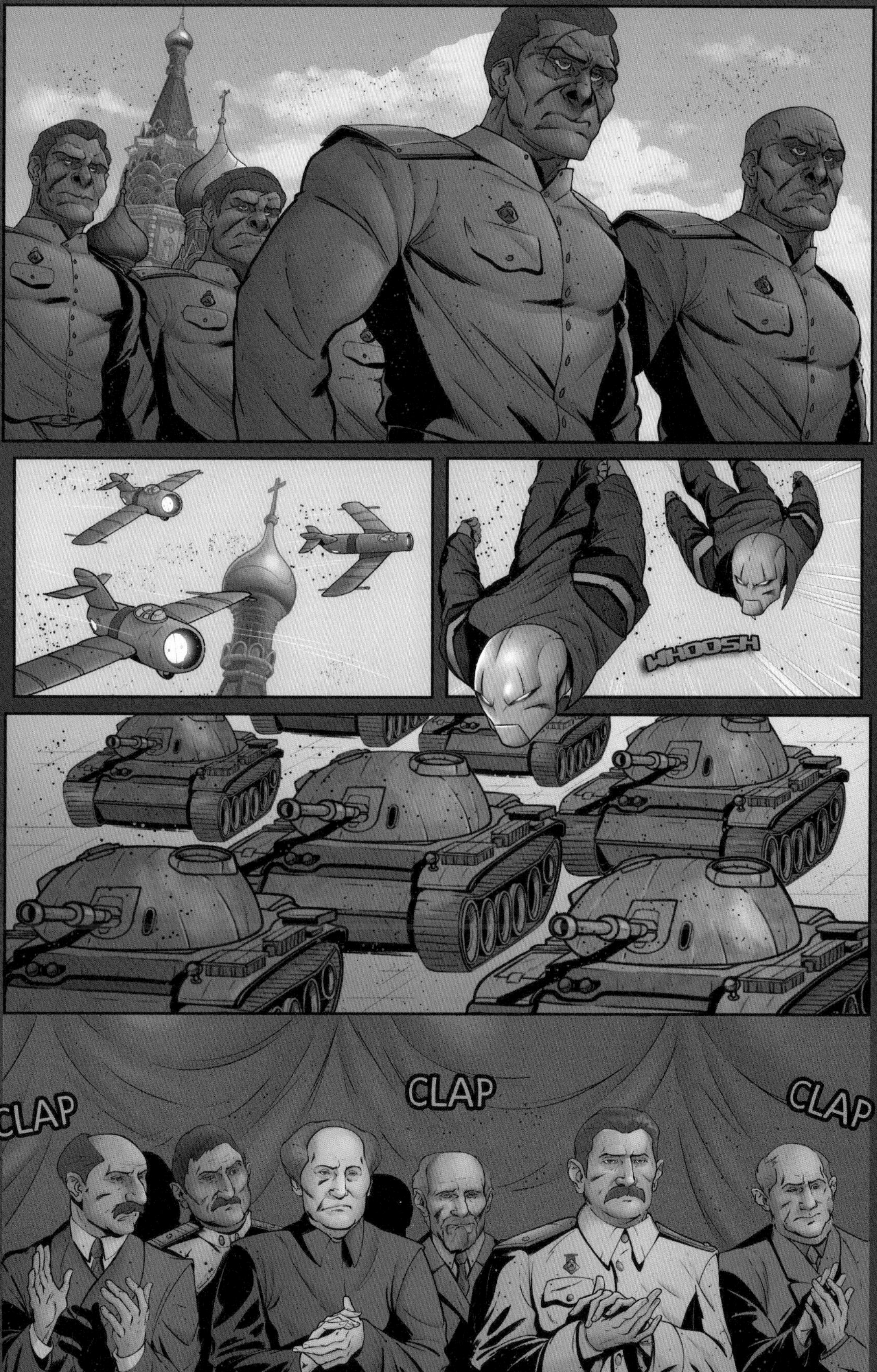
WHOOSH
CLAP
CLAP
CLAP

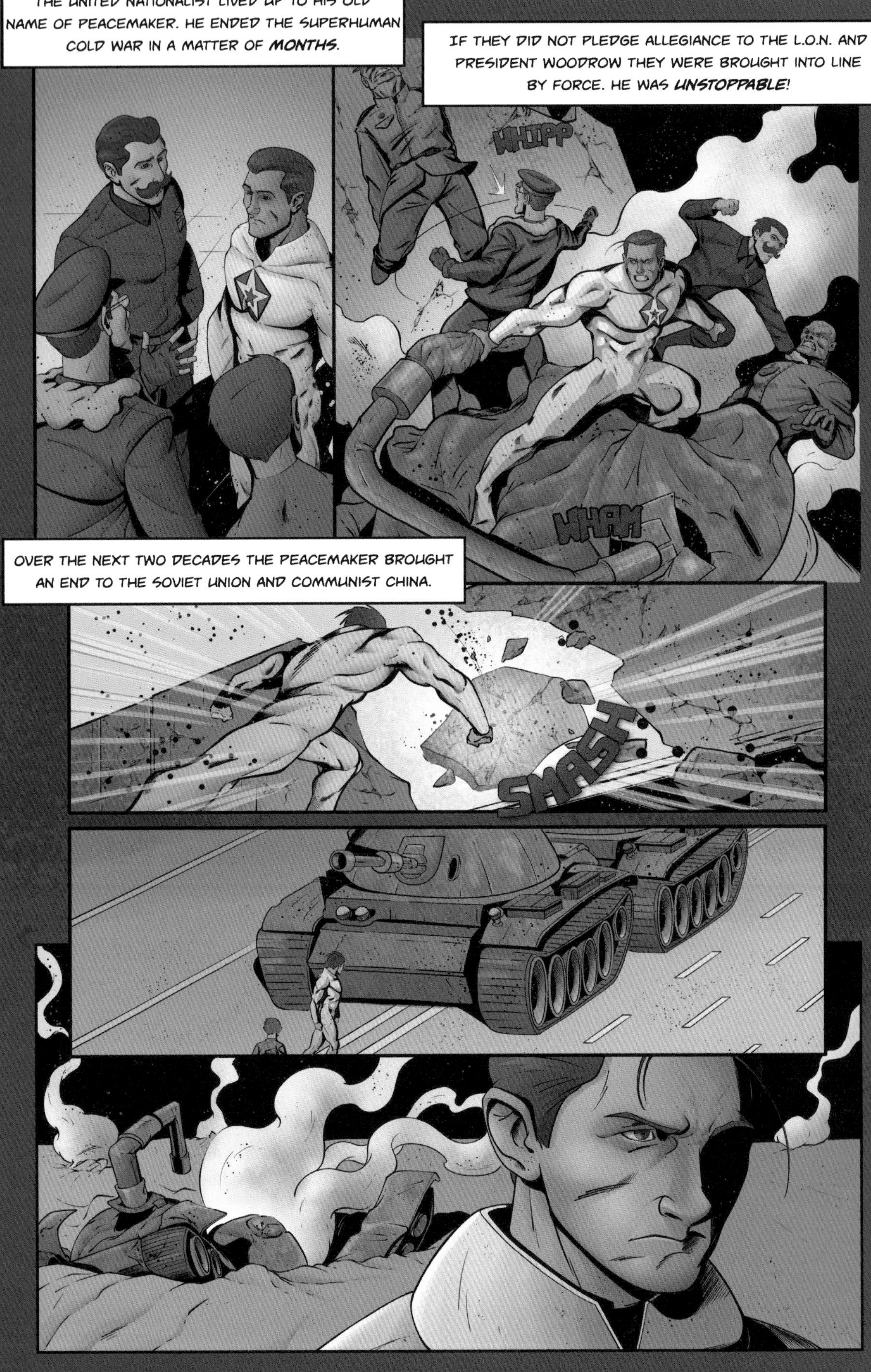
THE UNITED NATIONALIST LIVED UP TO HIS OLD NAME OF PEACEMAKER. HE ENDED THE SUPERHUMAN COLD WAR IN A MATTER OF MONTHS.
IF THEY DID NOT PLEDGE ALLEGIANCE TO THE L.O.N. AND PRESIDENT WOODROW THEY WERE BROUGHT INTO LINE BY FORCE. HE WAS UNSTOPPABLE!
WHIPP
WHAM
OVER THE NEXT TWO DECADES THE PEACEMAKER BROUGHT AN END TO THE SOVIET UNION AND COMMUNIST CHINA.
SMASH

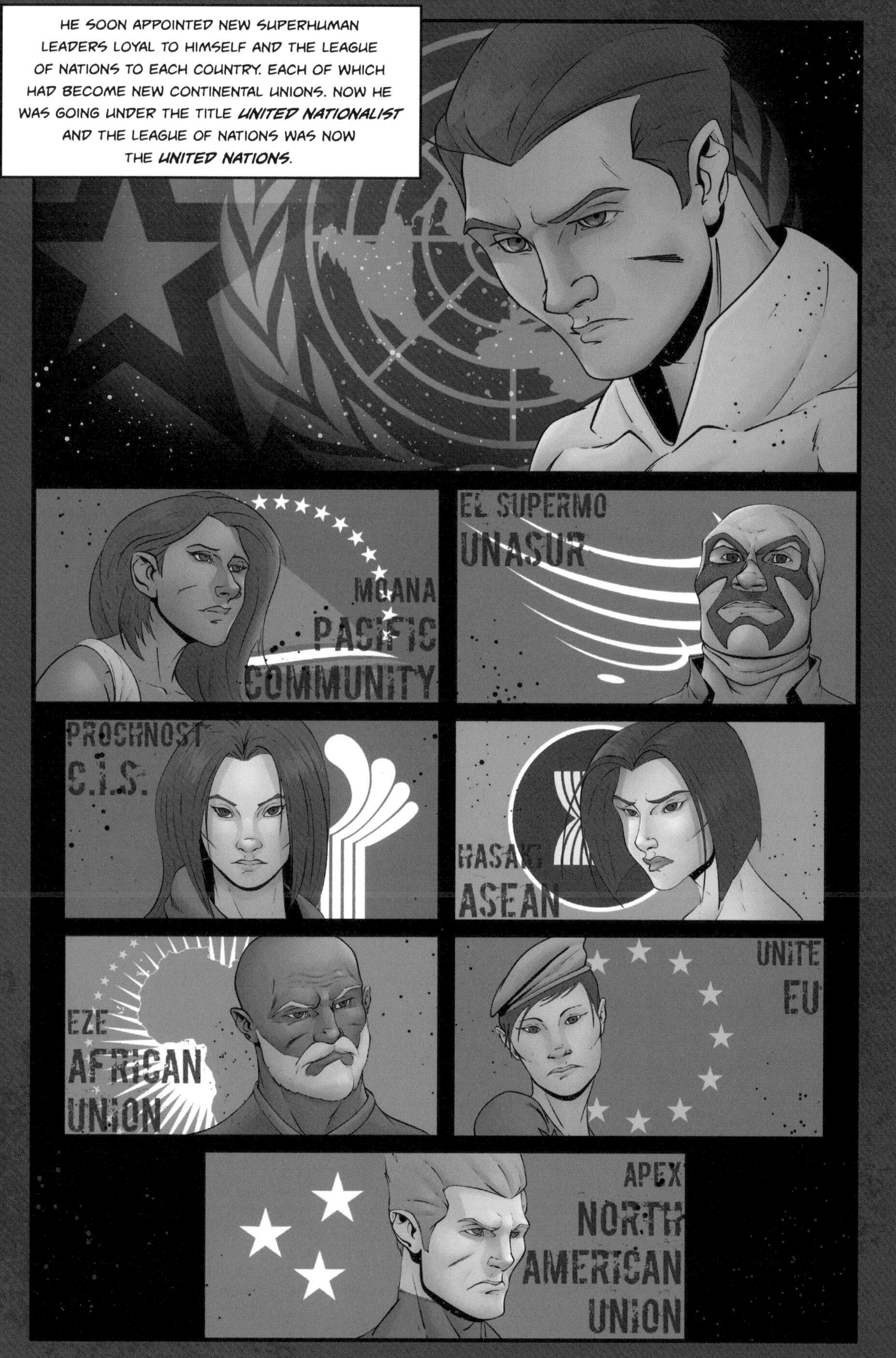
HE SOON APPOINTED NEW SUPERHUMAN LEADERS LOYAL TO HIMSELF AND THE LEAGUE OF NATIONS TO EACH COUNTRY. EACH OF WHICH HAD BECOME NEW CONTINENTAL UNIONS. NOW HE WAS GOING UNDER THE TITLE *UNITED NATIONALIST* AND THE LEAGUE OF NATIONS WAS NOW THE *UNITED NATIONS*.
MOANA
PACIFIC COMMUNITY
EL SUPERMO
UNASUR
PROCHNOST
C.I.S.
HASAK
ASEAN
EZE
AFRICAN UNION
UNITE
EU
APEX
NORTH AMERICAN UNION

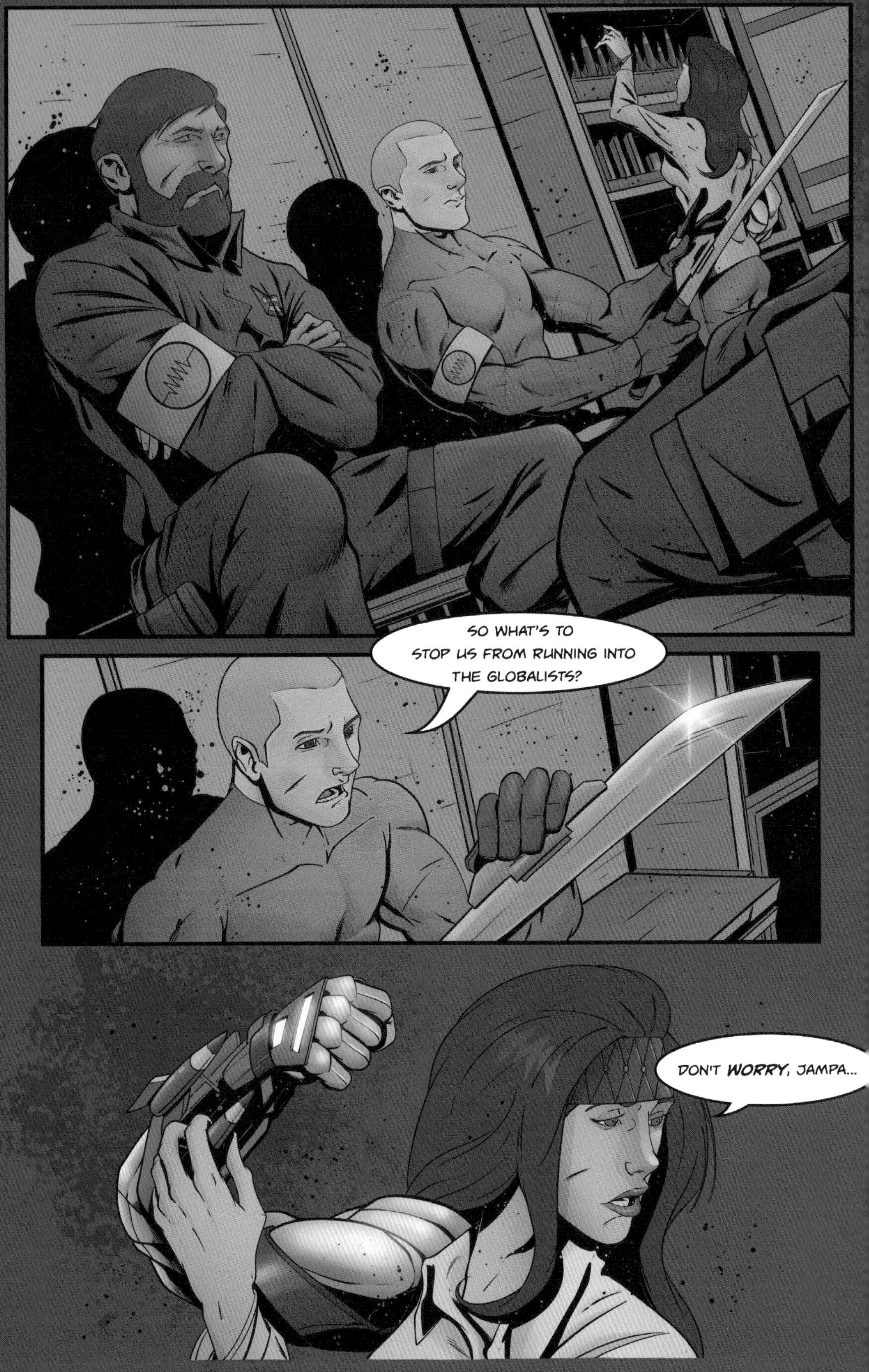
SO WHAT'S TO STOP US FROM RUNNING INTO THE GLOBALISTS?
DON'T WORRY, JAMPA...

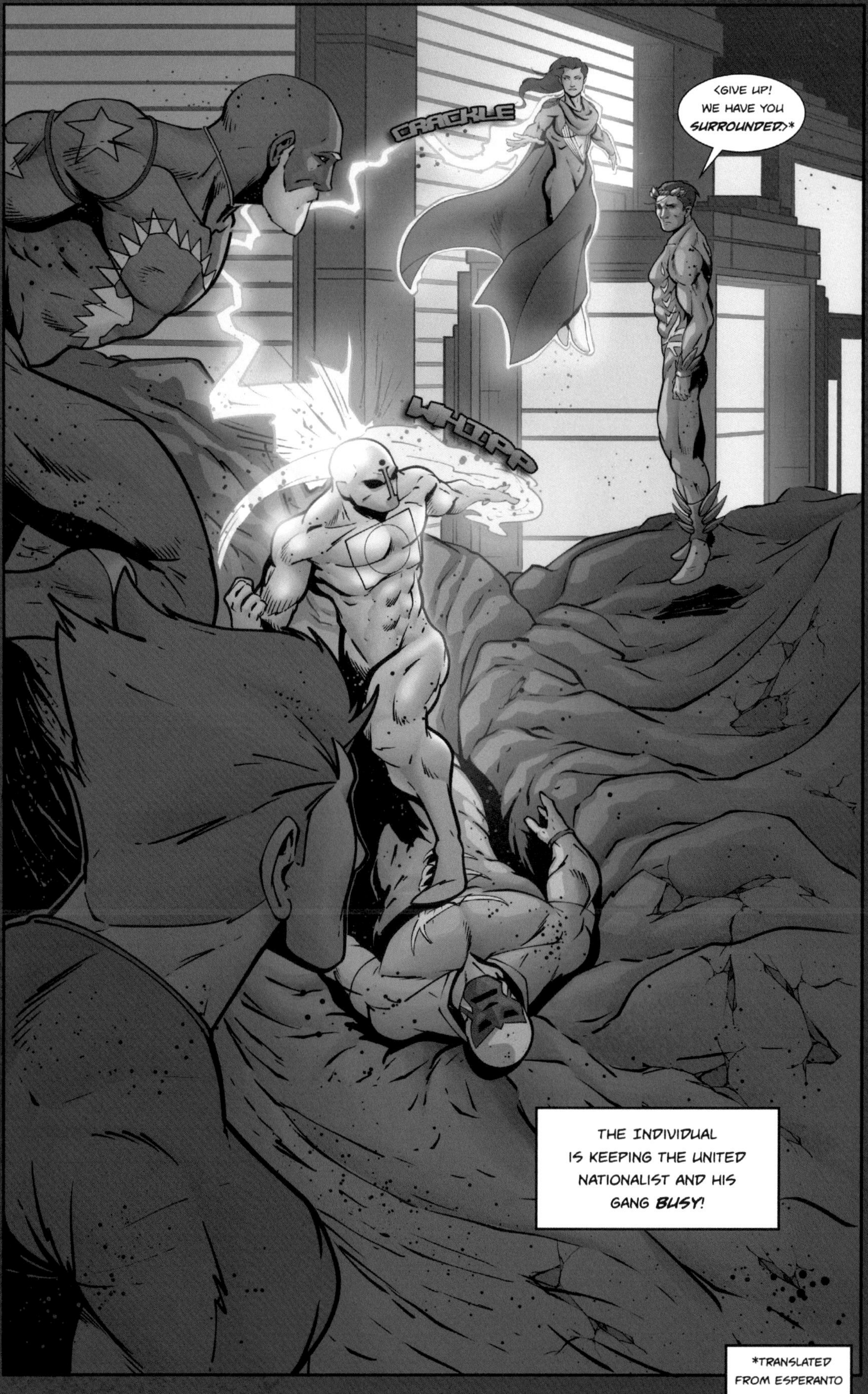
CRACKLE
<GIVE UP! WE HAVE YOU **SURROUNDED.**>*
WHIPP
THE INDIVIDUAL IS KEEPING THE UNITED NATIONALIST AND HIS GANG ***BUSY***!

*TRANSLATED FROM ESPERANTO

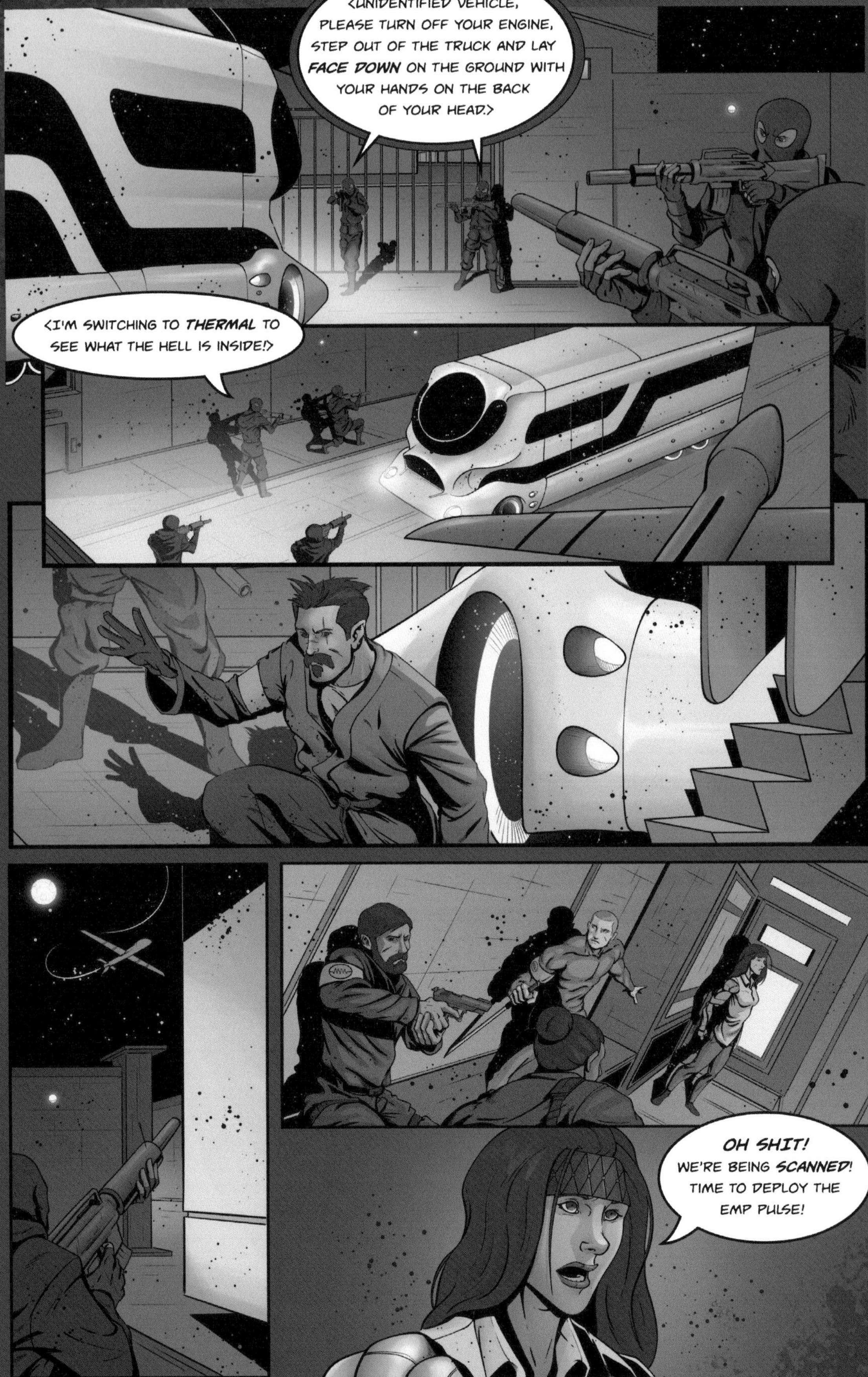
<UNIDENTIFIED VEHICLE, PLEASE TURN OFF YOUR ENGINE, STEP OUT OF THE TRUCK AND LAY FACE DOWN ON THE GROUND WITH YOUR HANDS ON THE BACK OF YOUR HEAD.>
<I'M SWITCHING TO THERMAL TO SEE WHAT THE HELL IS INSIDE!>
OH SHIT! WE'RE BEING SCANNED! TIME TO DEPLOY THE EMP PULSE!

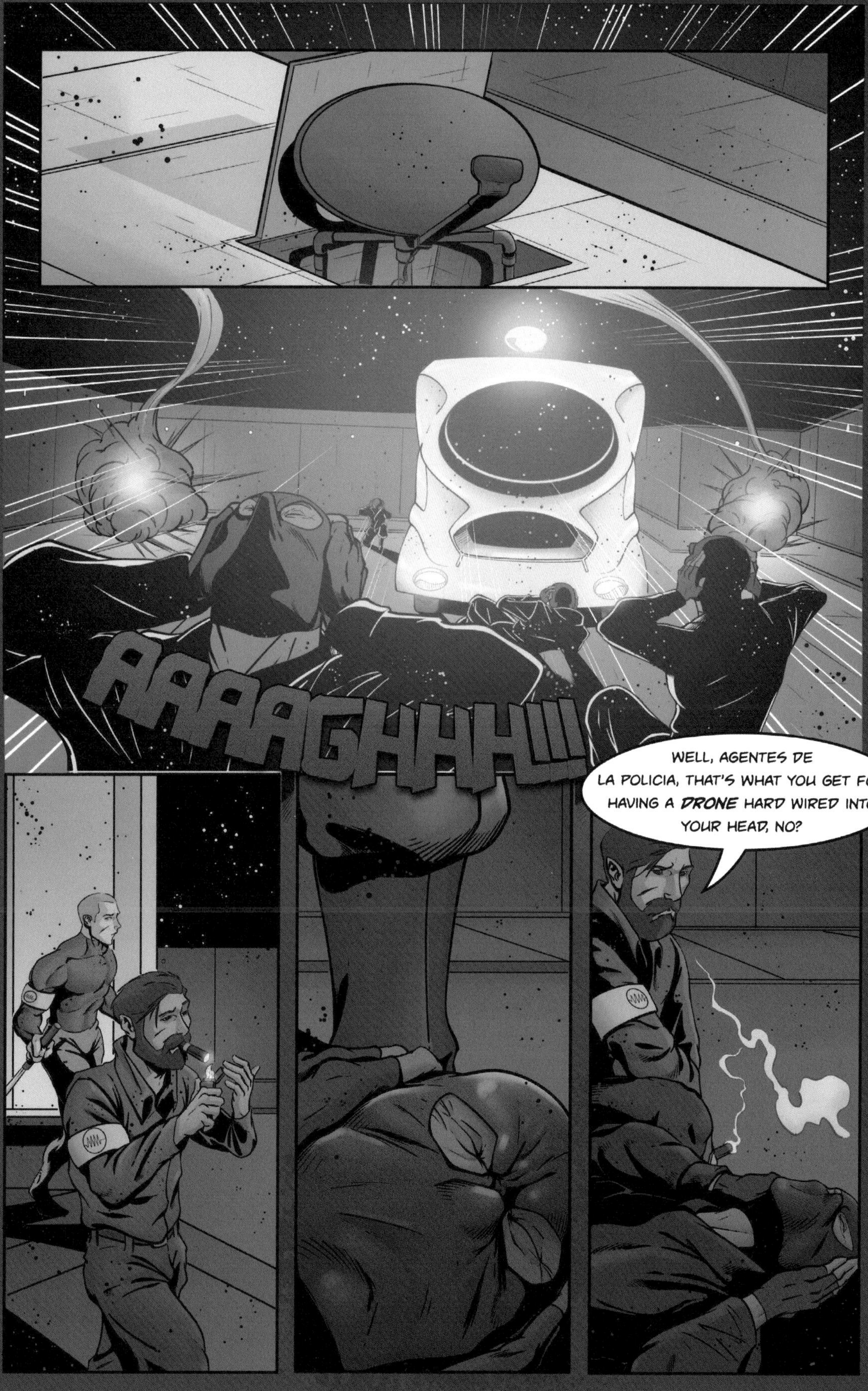
AAAAGHHHH!!!!
WELL, AGENTES DE LA POLICIA, THAT'S WHAT YOU GET FOR HAVING A *DRONE* HARD WIRED INTO YOUR HEAD, NO?

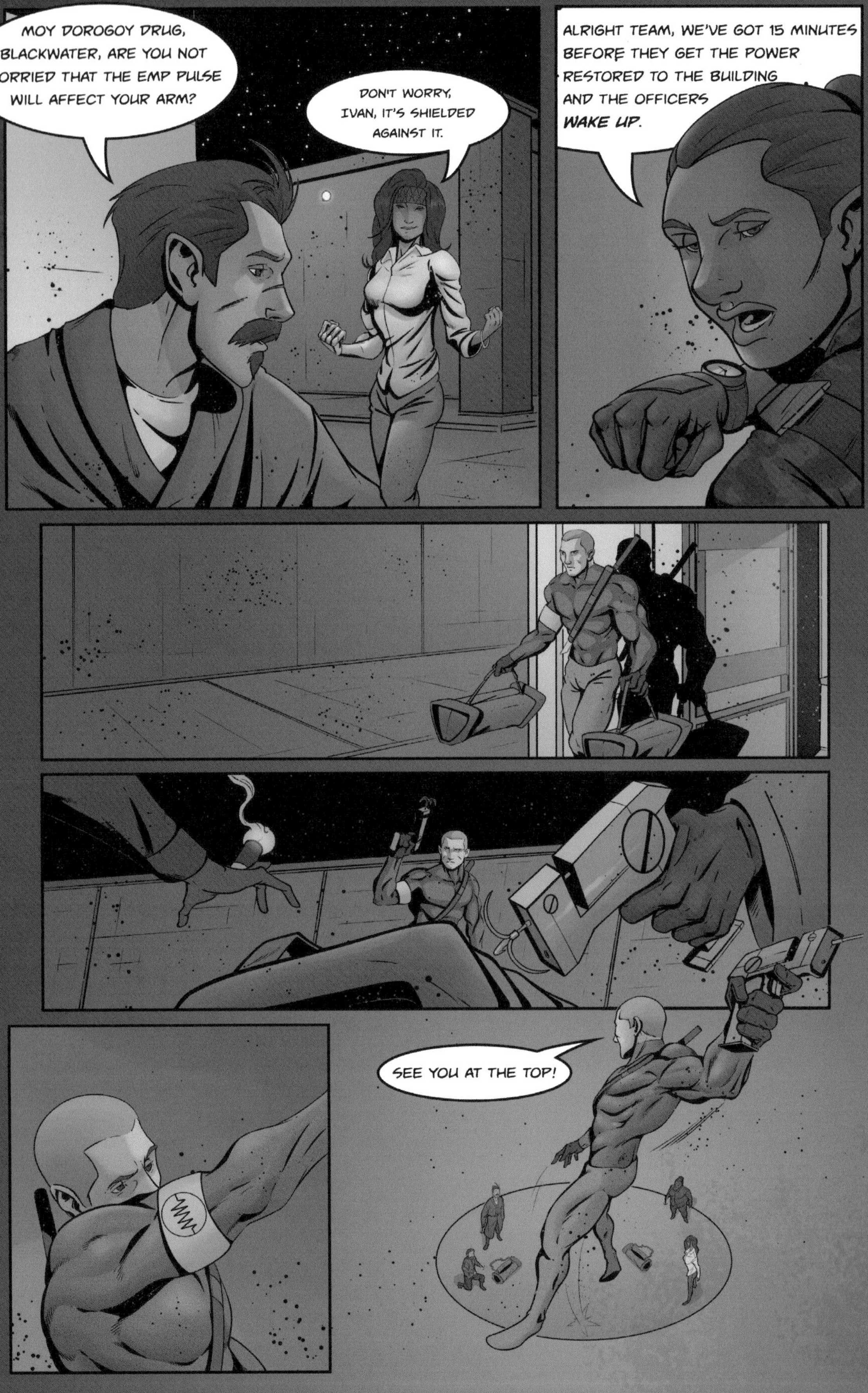
MOY DOROGOY DRUG, BLACKWATER, ARE YOU NOT WORRIED THAT THE EMP PULSE WILL AFFECT YOUR ARM?
DON'T WORRY, IVAN, IT'S SHIELDED AGAINST IT.
ALRIGHT TEAM, WE'VE GOT 15 MINUTES BEFORE THEY GET THE POWER RESTORED TO THE BUILDING AND THE OFFICERS **WAKE UP**.
SEE YOU AT THE TOP!

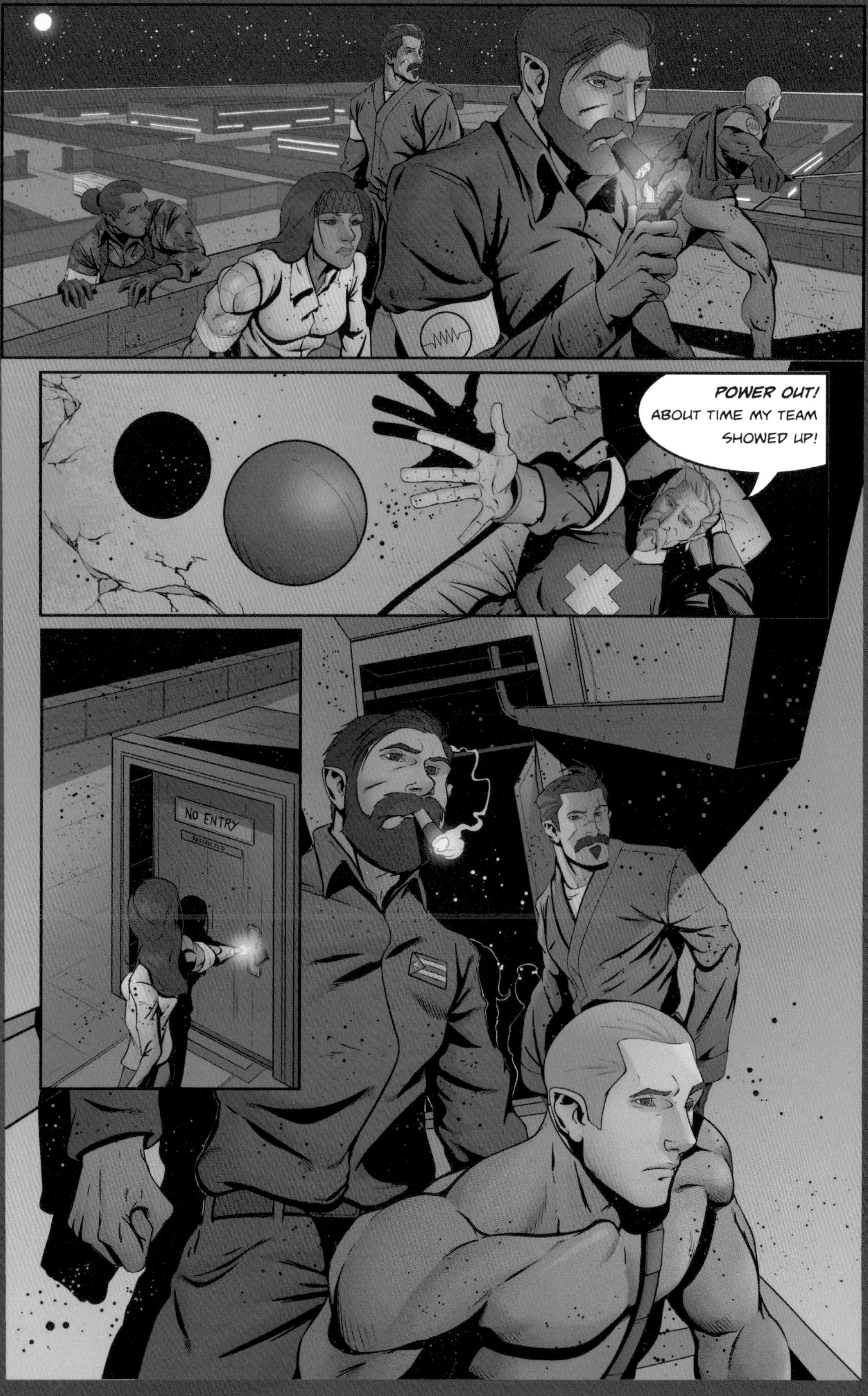
POWER OUT!
ABOUT TIME MY TEAM SHOWED UP!
NO ENTRY
RESTRICTED

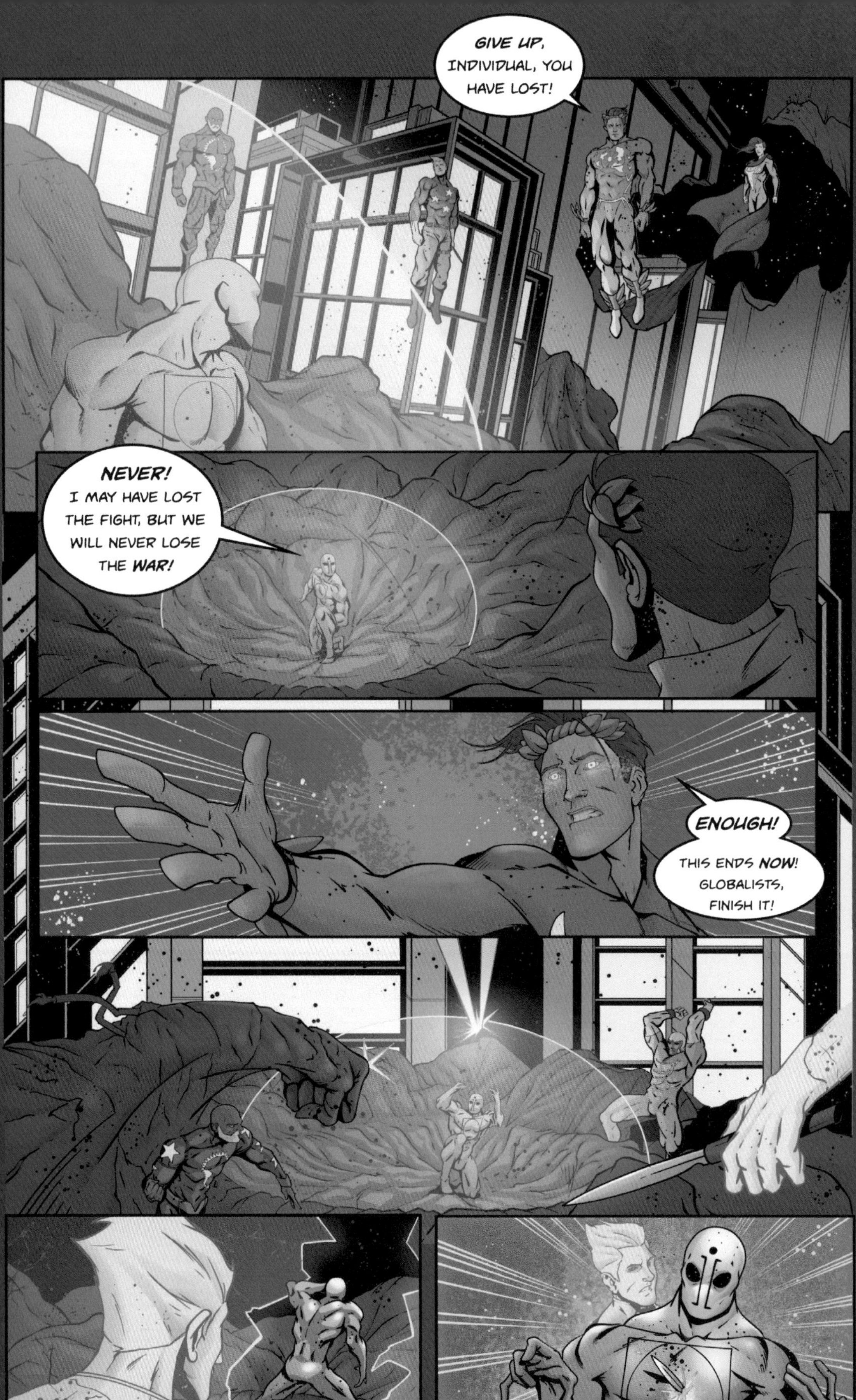
GIVE UP, INDIVIDUAL, YOU HAVE LOST!
NEVER! I MAY HAVE LOST THE FIGHT, BUT WE WILL NEVER LOSE THE WAR!
ENOUGH!
THIS ENDS NOW! GLOBALISTS, FINISH IT!

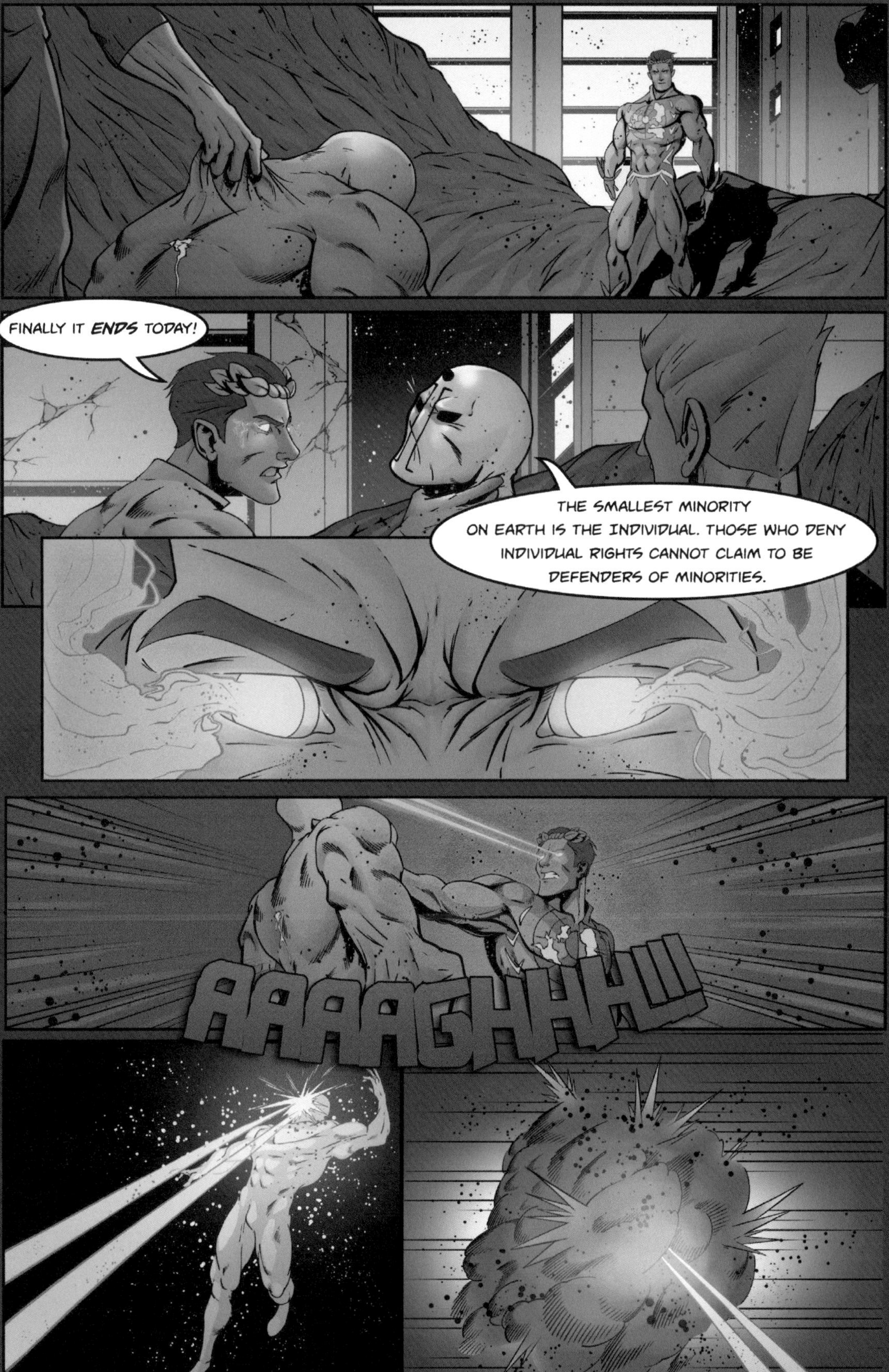
FINALLY IT ENDS TODAY!
THE SMALLEST MINORITY ON EARTH IS THE INDIVIDUAL. THOSE WHO DENY INDIVIDUAL RIGHTS CANNOT CLAIM TO BE DEFENDERS OF MINORITIES.
AAAAGHHH!!!

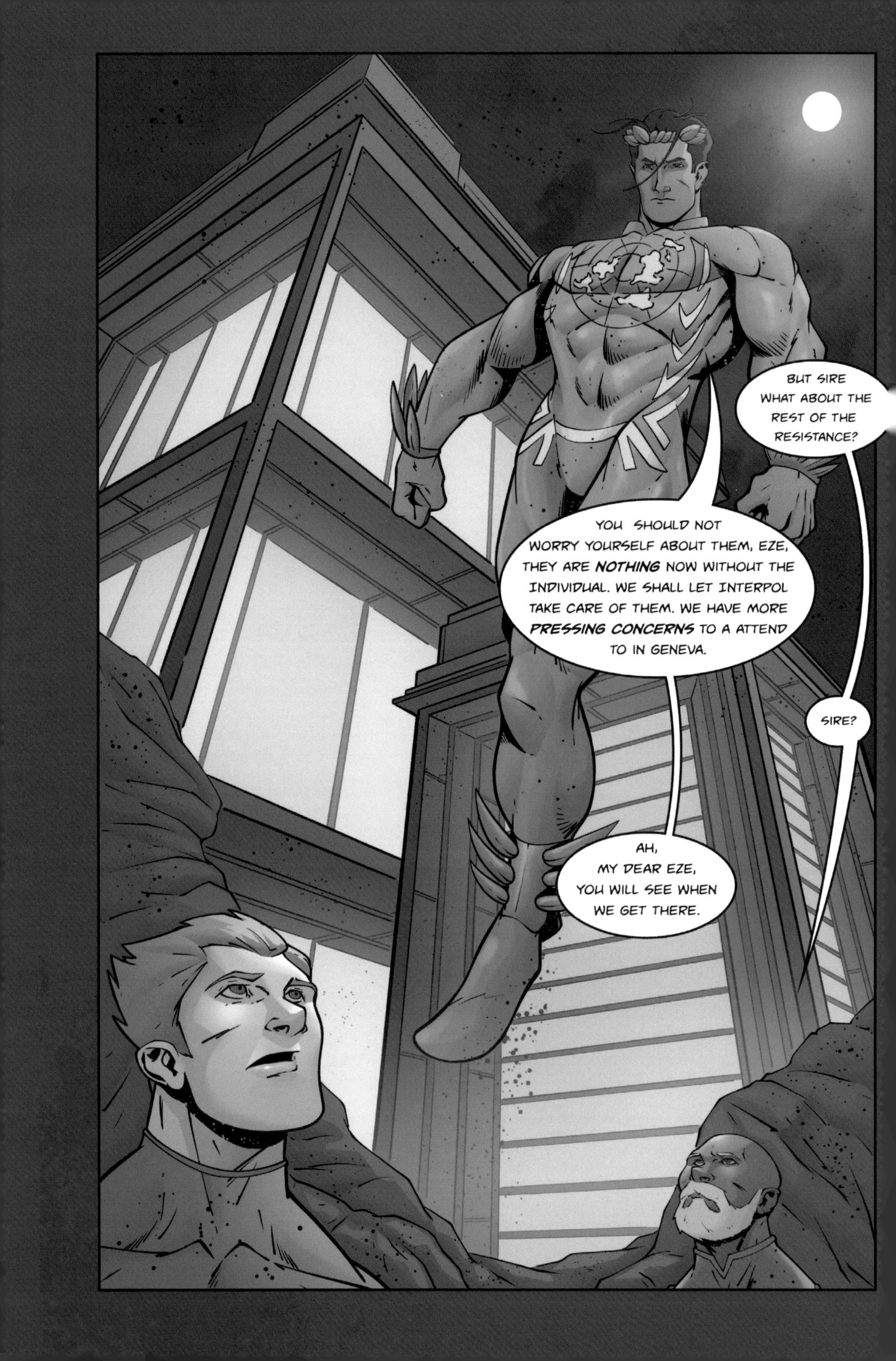
BUT SIRE WHAT ABOUT THE REST OF THE RESISTANCE?
YOU SHOULD NOT WORRY YOURSELF ABOUT THEM, EZE, THEY ARE **NOTHING** NOW WITHOUT THE INDIVIDUAL. WE SHALL LET INTERPOL TAKE CARE OF THEM. WE HAVE MORE **PRESSING CONCERNS** TO A ATTEND TO IN GENEVA.
SIRE?
AH, MY DEAR EZE, YOU WILL SEE WHEN WE GET THERE.

THE SOUNDTRACK OF BLACK SCI-FI

GHETTO**OF**THE**MIND**
ACROSS THE POND

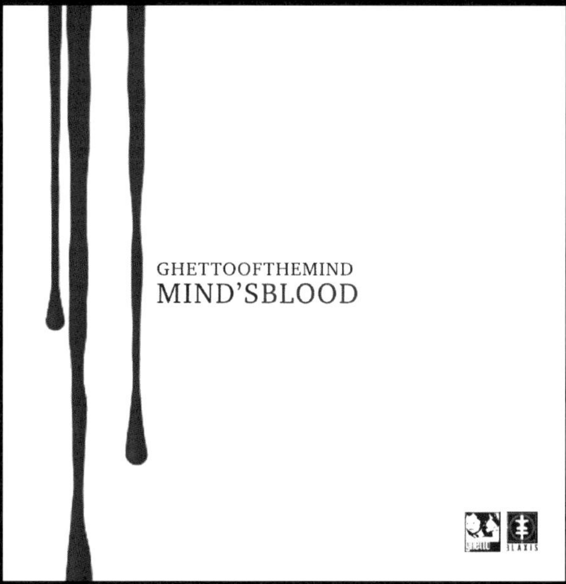

GHETTOOFTHEMIND
MIND'SBLOOD

GHETTO**OF**THE**MIND**
GRACE

I battle the forces of mediocrity on a daily basis.

I walk the Eightfold Path of righteousness seeking the Universal Truth.

I stand on the rooftop with my barbaric yawp calling to the tribe.

I scream at the top of my lungs to the heavens letting them know that warriors have entered the celestial plane.

I change the world in my own way, with passion, with panache, and with style...

Episodes available now on Itunes

j a z i n t e l l e c t . p o d o m a t i c . c o m

ghetto

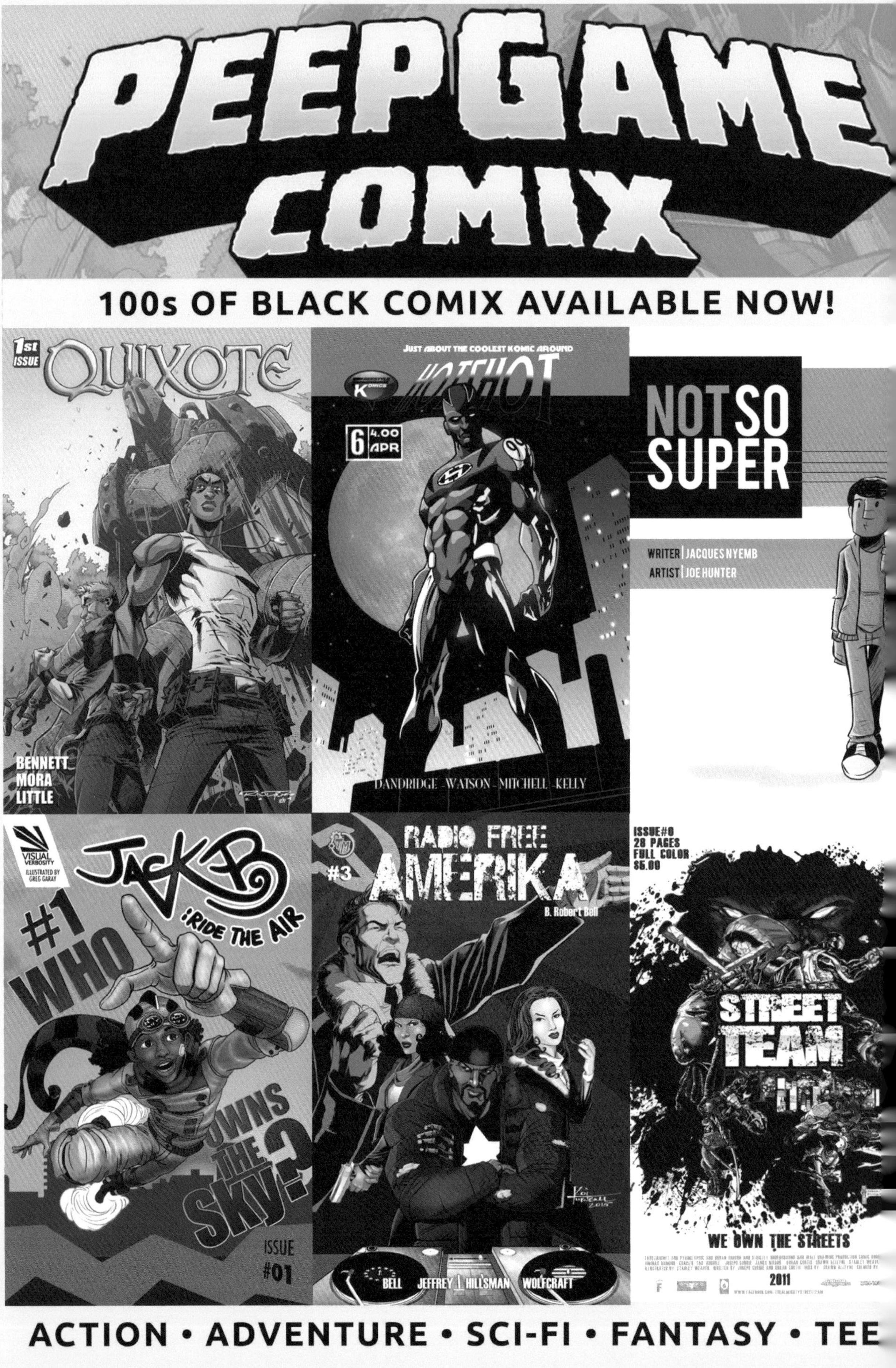
PEEP GAME COMIX
100s OF BLACK COMIX AVAILABLE NOW!
1st ISSUE
QUIXOTE
BENNETT
MORA
LITTLE
JUST ABOUT THE COOLEST KOMIC AROUND
HOTSHOT
6 4.00 APR
DANDRIDGE WATSON MITCHELL KELLY
NOT SO SUPER
WRITER | JACQUES NYEMB
ARTIST | JOE HUNTER
VISUAL VERBOSITY
ILLUSTRATED BY GREG GARAY
JACK B
:RIDE THE AIR
#1
WHO OWNS THE SKY?
ISSUE #01
RADIO FREE AMERIKA
#3
B. Robert Bell
BELL JEFFREY | HILLSMAN WOLFCRAFT
ISSUE#0
28 PAGES
FULL COLOR
$5.00
STREET TEAM
WE OWN THE STREETS
2011
ACTION • ADVENTURE • SCI-FI • FANTASY • TEE

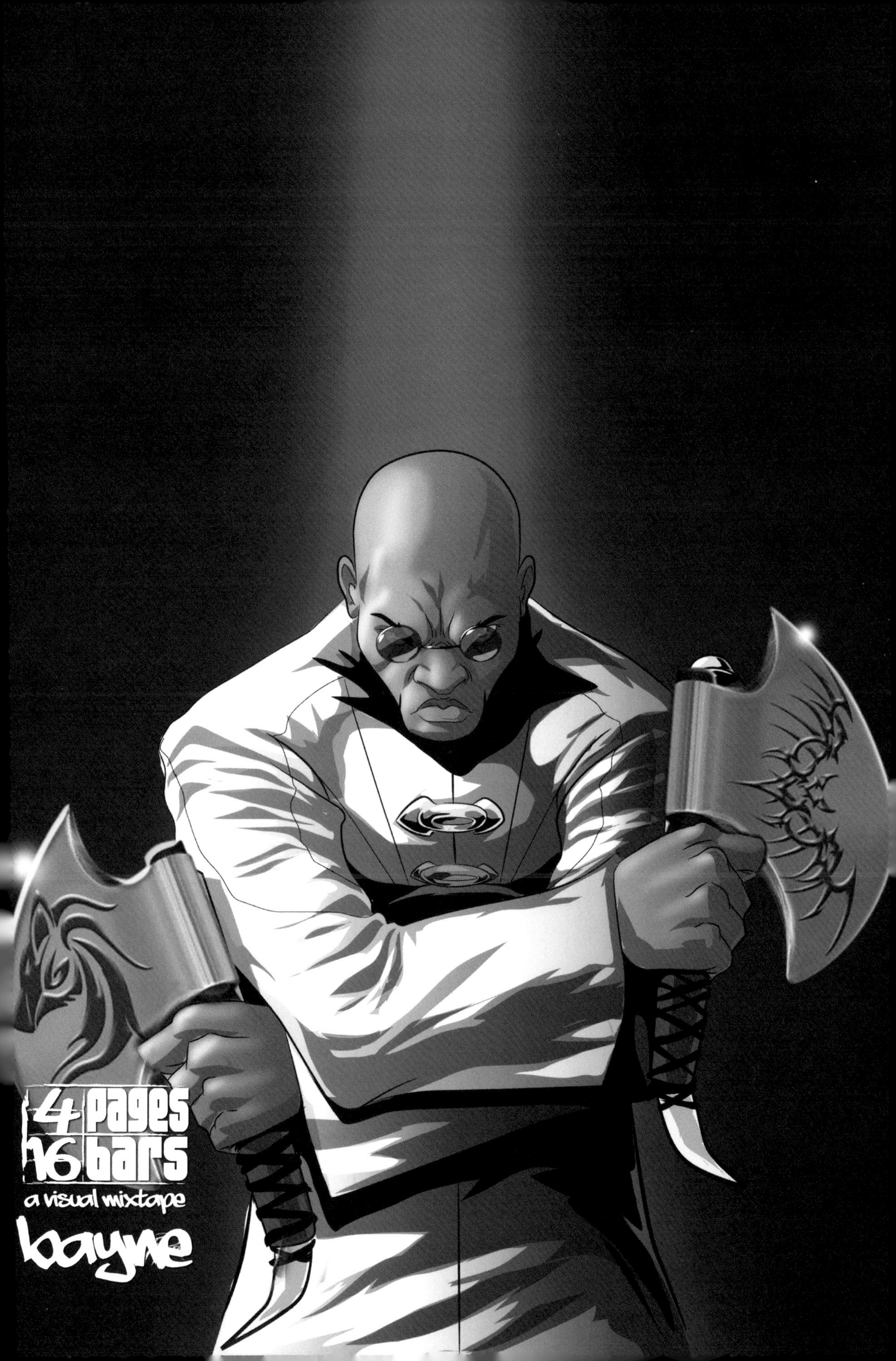
4 pages
16 bars
a visual mixtape
bayne

ART BY
JAY REED

Created by **Chyna McCoy** and heavily influenced by Marvel Comics' **Blade**,
Bayne was born in Siberia in 1620 AD, Bayne was the unfortunate result of a
still-born birth due to a sudden and vicious assault on his pregnant mother by
an Elder Vampire known as Lord Damascus the First. Seeing what his blood-
lust has wrought, Damascus decided to solidify his cruelty by unleashing the
savage Warwolves upon the dying mother-to-be. The genetic mixture of Lord
Damascus' blood with the feral beasts under his boot heel served to ensure
the child's survival, and a powerful Werewolf Dhampir was born – Bayne.

website: baynelegacyapocalypse.weebly.com

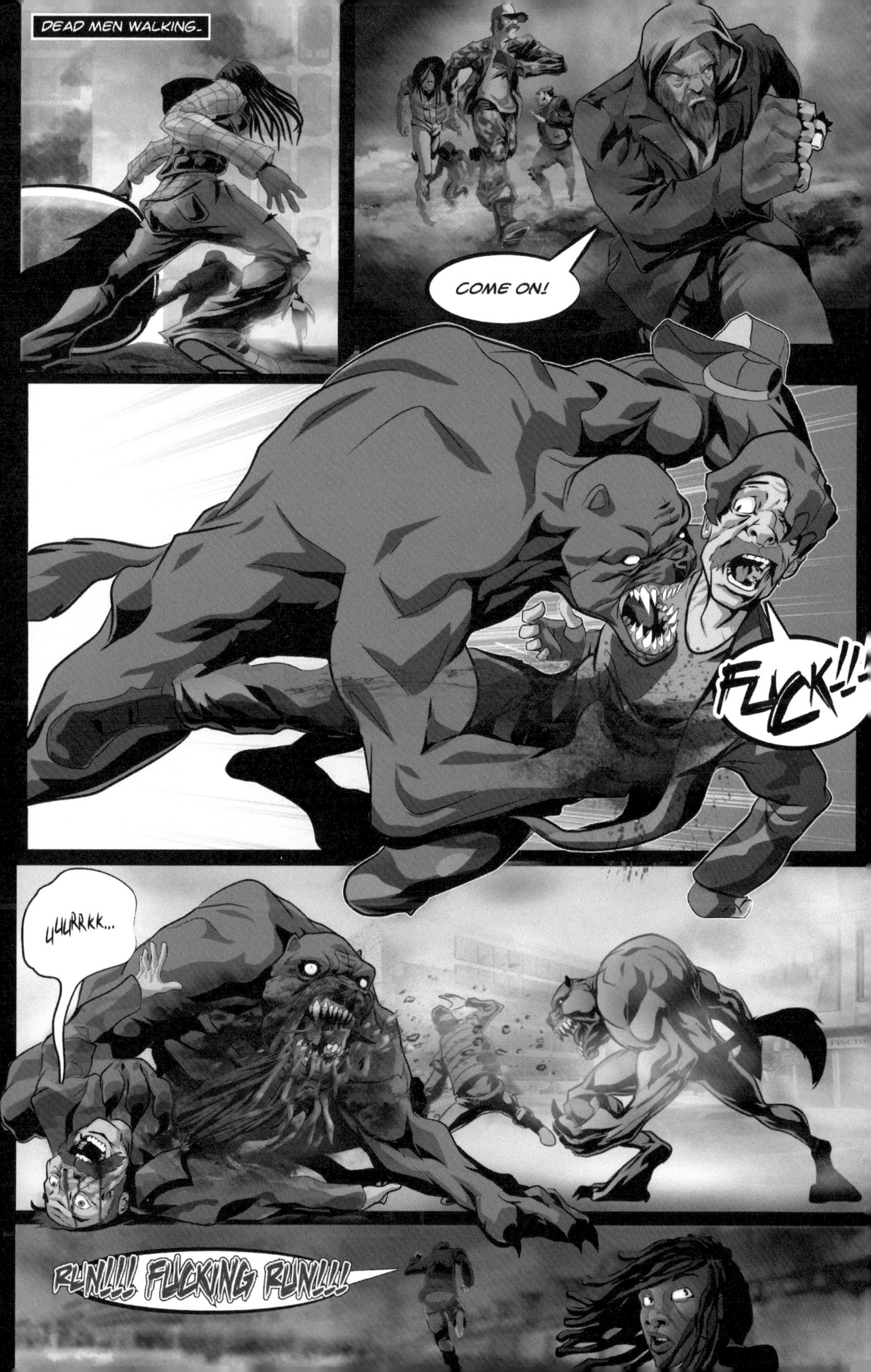

DEAD MEN WALKING...
COME ON!
FUCK!!!
UURRKK...
RUN!!! FUCKING RUN!!!

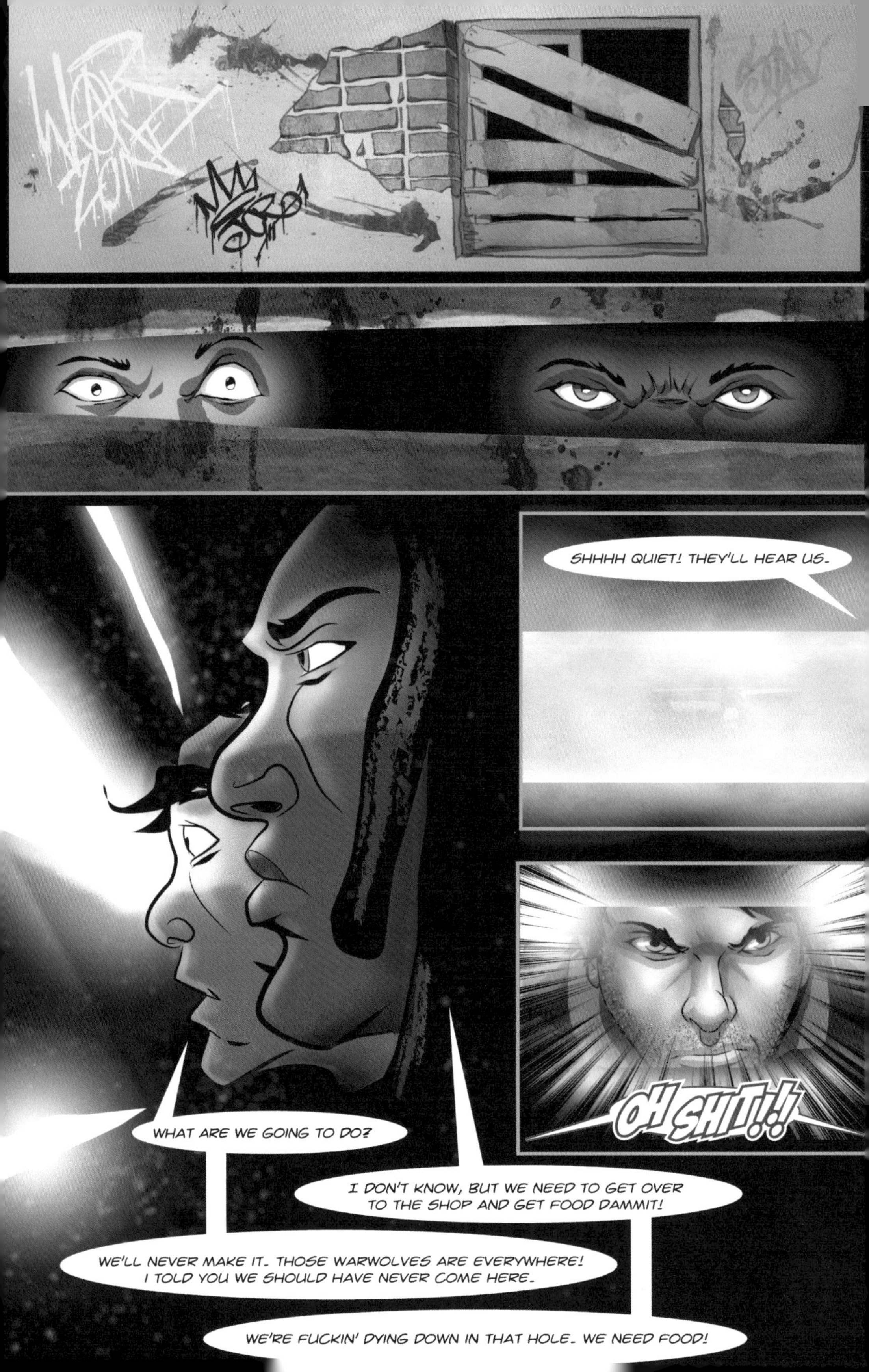

WAR ZONE
SHHHH QUIET! THEY'LL HEAR US.
OH SHIT!!!
WHAT ARE WE GOING TO DO?
I DON'T KNOW, BUT WE NEED TO GET OVER TO THE SHOP AND GET FOOD DAMMIT!
WE'LL NEVER MAKE IT. THOSE WARWOLVES ARE EVERYWHERE! I TOLD YOU WE SHOULD HAVE NEVER COME HERE.
WE'RE FUCKIN' DYING DOWN IN THAT HOLE. WE NEED FOOD!

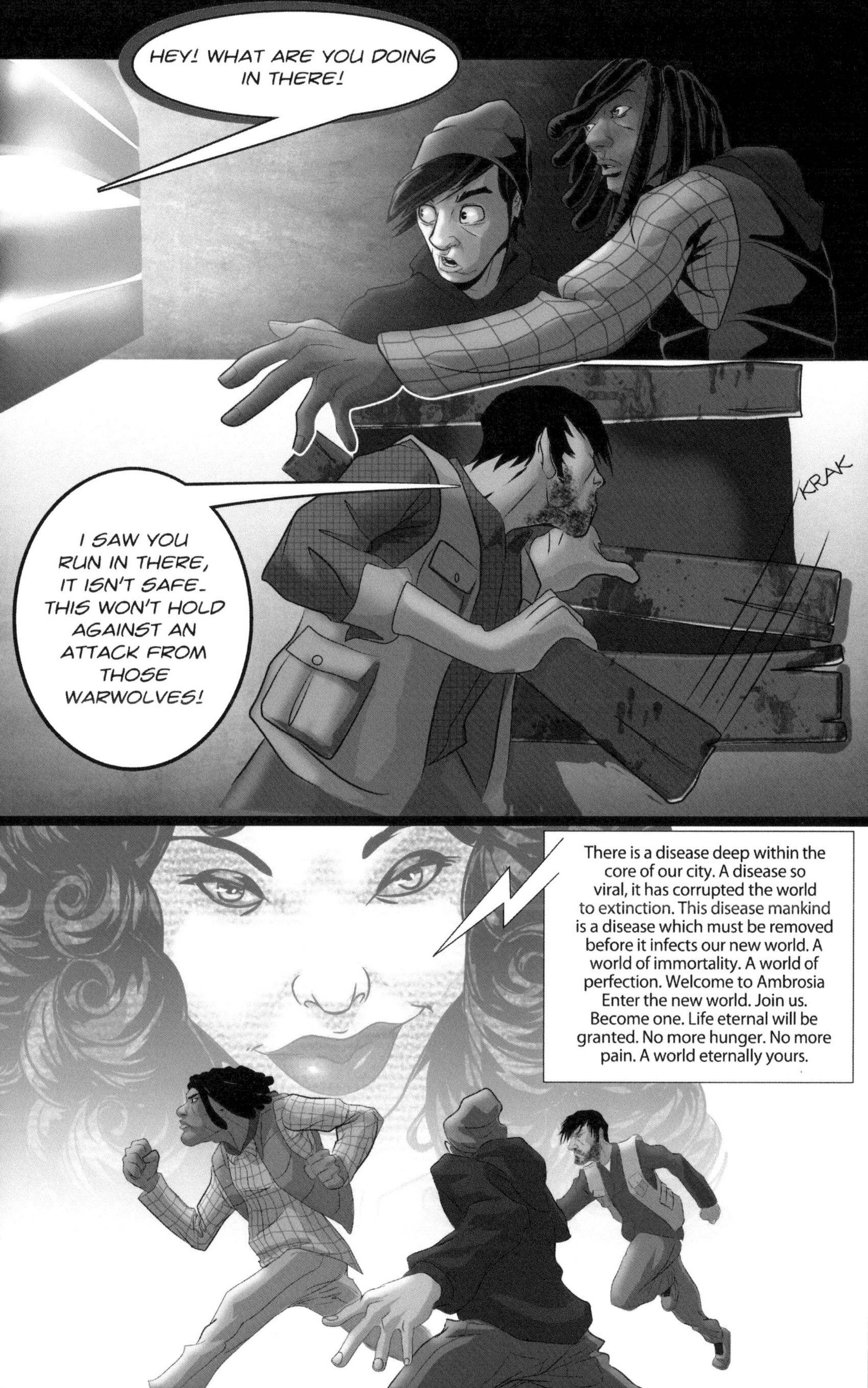
HEY! WHAT ARE YOU DOING IN THERE!
I SAW YOU RUN IN THERE, IT ISN'T SAFE. THIS WON'T HOLD AGAINST AN ATTACK FROM THOSE WARWOLVES!
KRAK
There is a disease deep within the core of our city. A disease so viral, it has corrupted the world to extinction. This disease mankind is a disease which must be removed before it infects our new world. A world of immortality. A world of perfection. Welcome to Ambrosia Enter the new world. Join us. Become one. Life eternal will be granted. No more hunger. No more pain. A world eternally yours.

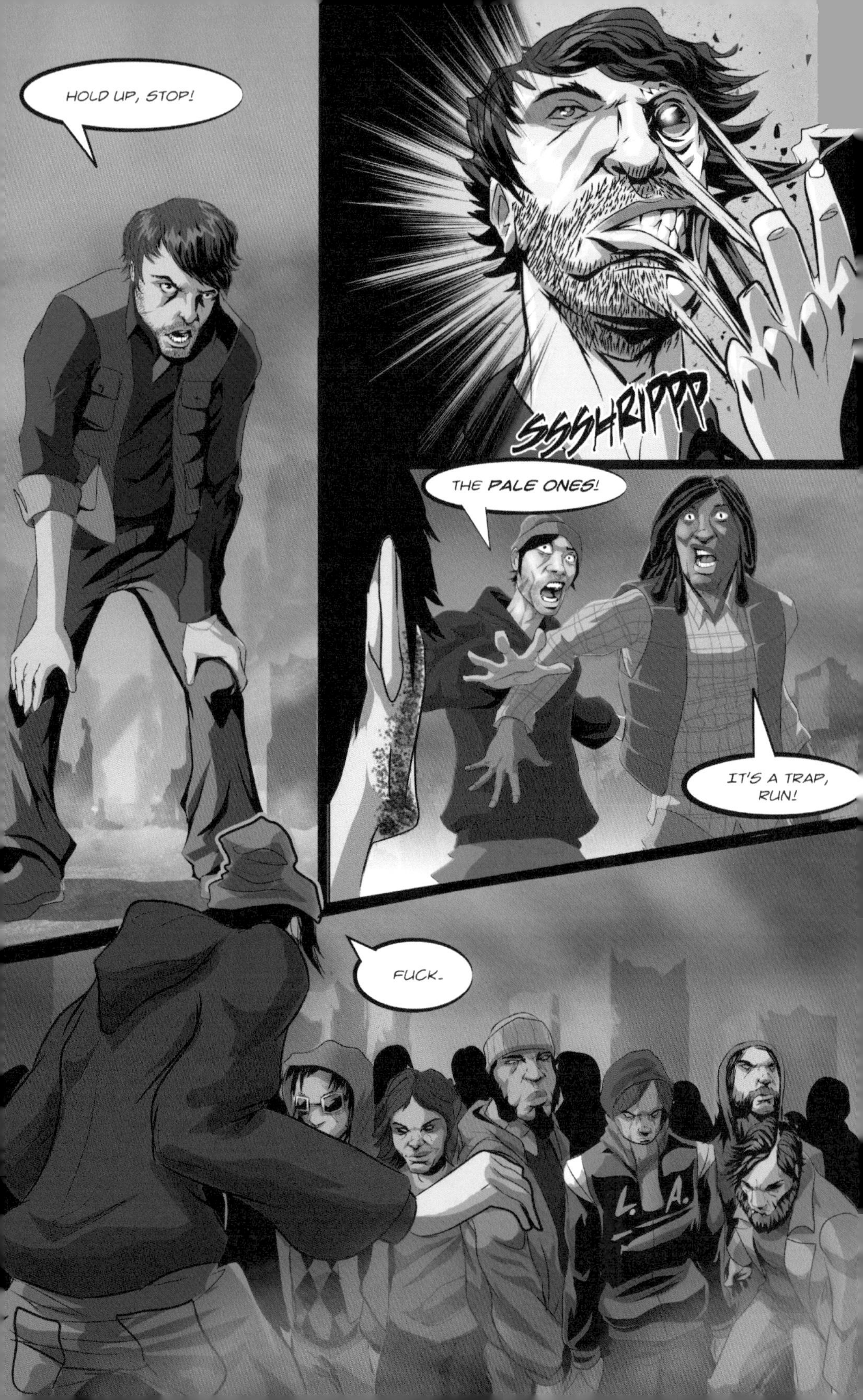
HOLD UP, STOP!
SSSHRIPPP
THE PALE ONES!
IT'S A TRAP, RUN!
FUCK.
L.A.

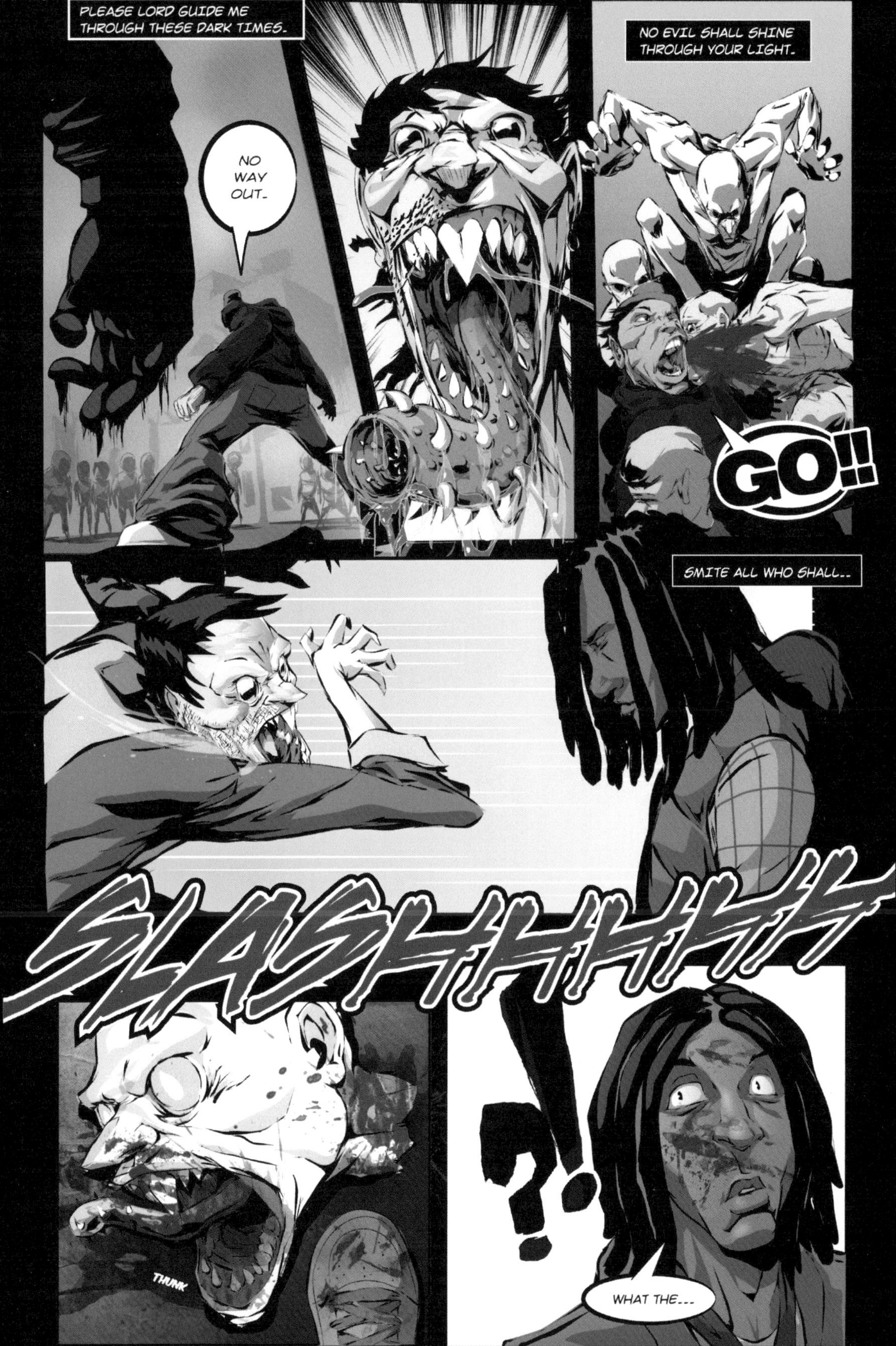
PLEASE LORD GUIDE ME THROUGH THESE DARK TIMES.
NO WAY OUT.
NO EVIL SHALL SHINE THROUGH YOUR LIGHT.
GO!!
SMITE ALL WHO SHALL...
SLASHHHHH
THUNK
WHAT THE...

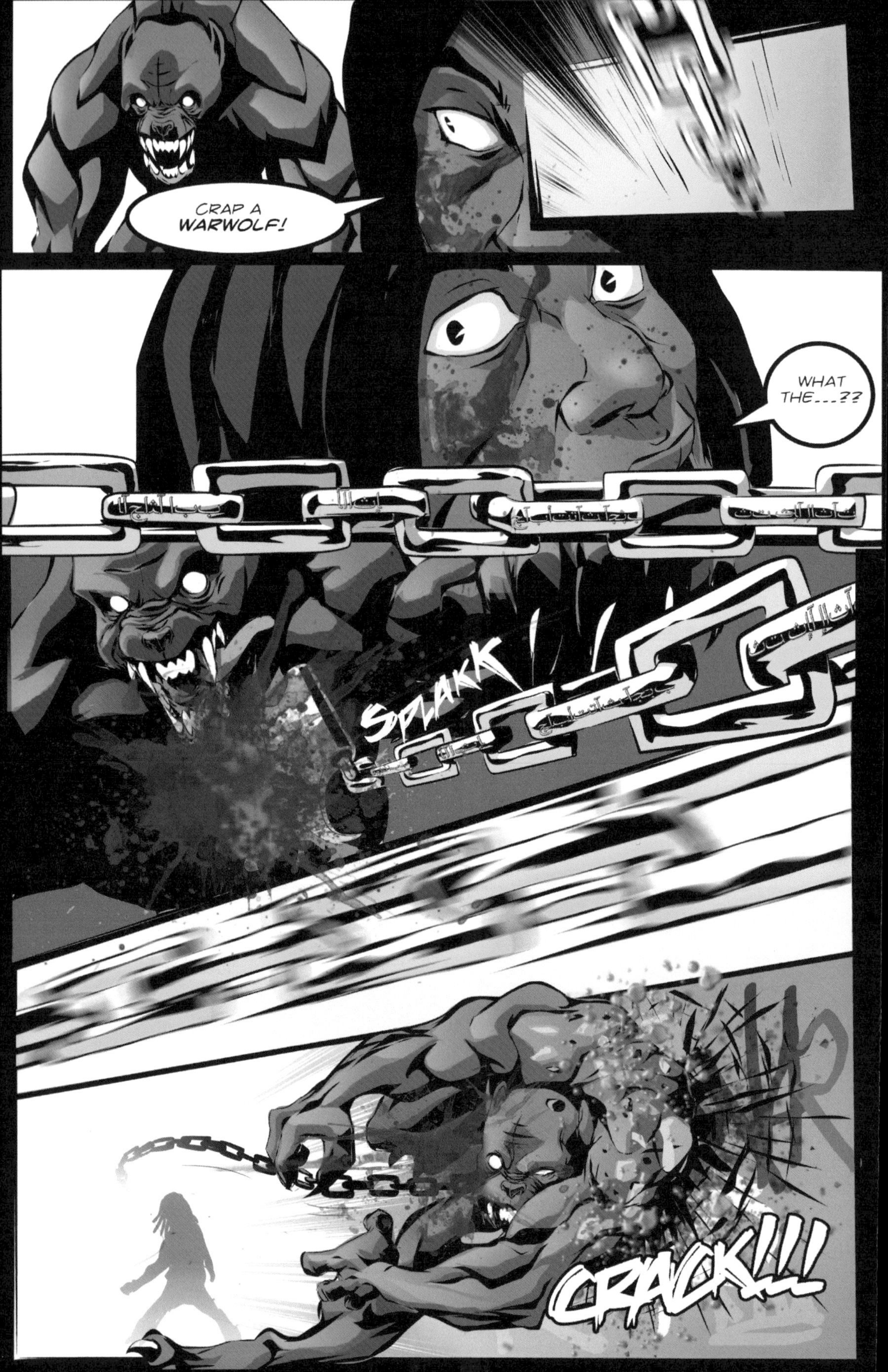
CRAP A WARWOLF!
WHAT THE...??
SPLAKK
CRACK!!!

APB

ARTISTS against POLICE BRUTALITY

A COMIC BOOK ANTHOLOGY

EDITED BY BILL CAMPBELL / JASON RODRIGUEZ / JOHN JENNINGS

ON SALE NOW EVERYWHERE

trailblazers

BY JIBA MOLEI ANDERSON

Comics are a unique construction. They are the definitive synthesis of an ancient form of expressing thoughts and ideas (images) with a modern form (text), which performs the same function.

Before the invention of the written language, ancient Man expressed their thoughts through the creation of images. These images could be seen on cave walls, on the tools that they crafted in order to aid in their daily survival, so on and so forth. Indeed, the first known written language was nothing more than miniature illustrations. Perhaps, the most well known form of "picture writing" would be Egyptian hieroglyphics. As these images became more refined and more abbreviated, they would be the basis for what we know today as the written word.

However, the use of representational images for the purposes of creating a narrative, still held a place in the development of communication. Though humanity created the written word, most humans could not manipulate (neither read nor write) this new invention. So, images still held an integral part in expression. For example, in order to spread the word of Christianity, Monks spent many years "illuminating" bibles (the text would be lovingly handcrafted and illustrated by these holy men). The Japanese would often have text accompanying their beautiful silk paintings (which may help explain the popularity and mainstream acceptance of Japanese manga). Even the fabled Kama Sutra is heavily illustrated, showing various sexual positions along with written instruction. However, because these texts were handmade, they were also extremely expensive. The average Joe on the street at the time could never hope to possibly own any one of these tomes. Therefore, only the rich could afford the luxury of being able to read or write.

With the creation of the Guttenburg Press in 1440, books became more readily available to the masses. The synthesis of image and text went along for the ride. With the emergence of the cartoon in various European newspapers, the common man could laugh along with the artist as they poked fun at the events of the day. These cartoons could also spark fear, anger, or any variety of emotions that the newspaper publisher wanted his audience to feel and experience in order to get his agenda across to the people. The elegance of the cartoon is this: not everyone would understand the words under the picture, but everyone would get the message from the picture.

When Europeans journeyed to the "New World," they brought the printed word along with them. Indeed, as more and more people learned how to read, the newspaper was instrumental in linking the various European ethnic groups together, thereby aiding in the creation of the persona known as "The American." Cartoons helped to unite this country against the British during the Revolutionary War. Cartoons helped to create the American identity. However, since these Europeans also brought along their notions of division through the exercise of class distinction (which would later evolve into a caste system based on skin color), not everyone would be considered "good enough" to partake in the American experiment. Indeed, when African slaves were brought to this new country in the 1700s and 1800s, they were forbidden to learn how to read, for reading might put ideas such as equality and freedom into their heads. Nevertheless, many Africans did learn to do just that, and the construction of the cartoon helped them to do so.

After the Civil War, more and more people immigrated to this new country. Increasingly, more and more of these new Americans did not hail from France, England, or Spain. They began to arrive from "undesirable" European countries like Italy and Ireland. Many of them were of different hue than Europeans like the newly arrived Chinese who, along with the Africans, the South Americans, and the indigenous people who were living in this country, all wanted to experience the American Dream. The American commentary, the cartoon, would express the fears and prejudices of the aristocrat and common alike, thereby giving birth to a medium, the comic strip and later, its sibling, the comic book.

Now, Forget everything you know about the African-American presence in comic books...because it probably isn't much.

Documentation on the subject is sketchy at best. Much like the African American experience is either ignored or merely given lip service in the study of American history so too has the African American presence has been treated in the discussion of comics.

Some would say, "There are not enough 'Black' comics characters, or creators, to warrant an examination of the subject."

As the British would say, "bollocks."

Simply put, the African American presence has been evident in comics since the inception of the medium. Granted, for most of the medium's history, the portrayal of African American culture has, at its best been skewed and, at its worst, offensive. But it cannot be denied that the African American character has always had a place in comic strips and comic books, and the African American comics' creator has had a hand in developing the art form.

We have been here from the beginning and every day, there is another person of color, with nothing more than a pencil and imaginations, creating sepia-toned superheroes to right wrongs and provide inspiration to future comic book fans.

This is a celebration of the African American contribution to a uniquely American art movement, one, that at over 100 years and counting, has lasted longer than any modern artistic movement in history.

Here now are some of the trailblazers who paved the way for all of us from Milestone to Ania to Gettosake to Griot Enterprises and so many more of us making comics today.

We salute you.

KRAZY KAT

George Herriman's premise of the series goes a little something like this: **Krazy Kat** is in love with **Ignatz Mouse**. Ignatz Mouse rebuffs Krazy Kat's affections by throwing bricks at Krazy's head. Krazy takes the brick throwing as a sign of affection from Ignatz Mouse and continues the pursuit. In this abusive situation comes **Offissa Pupp**, who is love with Krazy Kat, locks Ignatz Mouse up in order to show his feelings for the Kat who is totally oblivious to the good Offissa's intentions.

Krazy Kat is, unmistakably, a Black comic strip. Through Herriman's cultural chameleon-like way approaching life and work, he was able to bring his African American viewpoint on life and love to the masses…and the masses ate it up.

TORCHY

Created by **Jackie Ormes**, *Torchy Brown in Dixie to Harlem*, starring Torchy Brown, was a humorous depiction of a Mississippi teen who found fame and fortune singing and dancing in the Cotton Club. Ormes became the first African-American woman to produce a syndicated comic strip.

Torchy presented an image of a black woman who, in contrast to the contemporary stereotypical media portrayals, was confident, intelligent, and brave.

MATT BAKER

Clarence Matthew Baker is the first known African-American artist to find success in the comic-book industry. He entered comics through the Jerry Iger Studio, one of the 1930s to 1940s "packagers" that provided outsourced comics to publishers entering the new medium. Baker's first confirmed comics work is penciling and inking the women in the 12-page **Sheena, Queen of the Jungle** #69.

His other artwork for comic books includes the light-humor military title **Canteen Kate**, **Tiger Girl**; **Flamingo**, **South Sea Girl**, **Glory Forbes**, **Kayo Kirby**; and **Risks Unlimited**. Baker illustrated **Lorna Doone** for **Classic Comics** in December 1946, and others.

Baker was inducted into the **Will Eisner Comic Book Hall of Fame** in 2009.

THE BLACK PHANTOM

Published in 1964, created by Steve Perrin and Ronn Foss for **Mask and Cape** #4, The Black Phantom pre-dates Jack Kirby's **Black Panther** appearance in th Fantastic Four by two years. This fact makes the Black Phantom the *first* Black costumed superhero.

The Black Phantom was Lafayette Jefferson, an engineer and soldier who worked with the N.A.A.C.P. to address racial injustice in the southern United States. While traveling, he meets a young whit man and orphan named Joey Trager. Together, they become the **Black Phantom** and the **Wraith** to battle the likes of the Ku Klux Klan and other opponents of tolerance and change.

DATELINE: DANGER!

Inspired by the television series *I Spy*, the first TV dramatic show to co-star an African-American in a lead role, writer **John Saunders** and artist **Al McWilliams** created the adventure comic strip Dateline: Danger! for the **Publishers-Hall Syndicate**. Introduced as both a daily and a color Sunday strip i November 1968, it similarly was the first in this mediu with an African-American lead character, Danny Rave As in the TV show, the two protagonists were Americ secret agents who globetrotted to trouble spots und the cover of another profession.

FRIDAY FOSTER

Friday Foster was an American newspaper comic strip, created and written by **Jim Lawrence** and later continued by **Jorge Longarón**. It ran from 1970 to 1974 and was notable for featuring the first African American woman as the titular character in a comic strip.

Early on, Lawrence's story lines had a harder edge showing the contrast of Friday's family with her stree wise brother trying to accept her newfound success in the world of magazine publishing. But soon its episodes changed focus to showcase more soap-ope thrills of romance and travel for the gorgeous African-American.

POWERMAN

Powerman was a British comic book series written by **Don Avenall** (aka Donne Avenell) and **Norman Worker**, and illustrated by **Dave Gibbons** and **Brian Bolland** that was initially distributed in Nigeria in the early 1970s. The series starred a superhero named Powerman. When the comics were re-published in the United Kingdom the character's name became Powerbolt.

An executive from a Nigerian advertising agency approached Bardon Press Features to discuss the ide of making a series with a black superhero; the man a his wife saw that in Nigeria, the comics available wer imported and had White protagonists. Gibbons said that he remembered asking why Africans did not wo on the strips and hearing that the African artists wou likely emerge once comics become popular in Africa

Oh, man... How they have emerged...

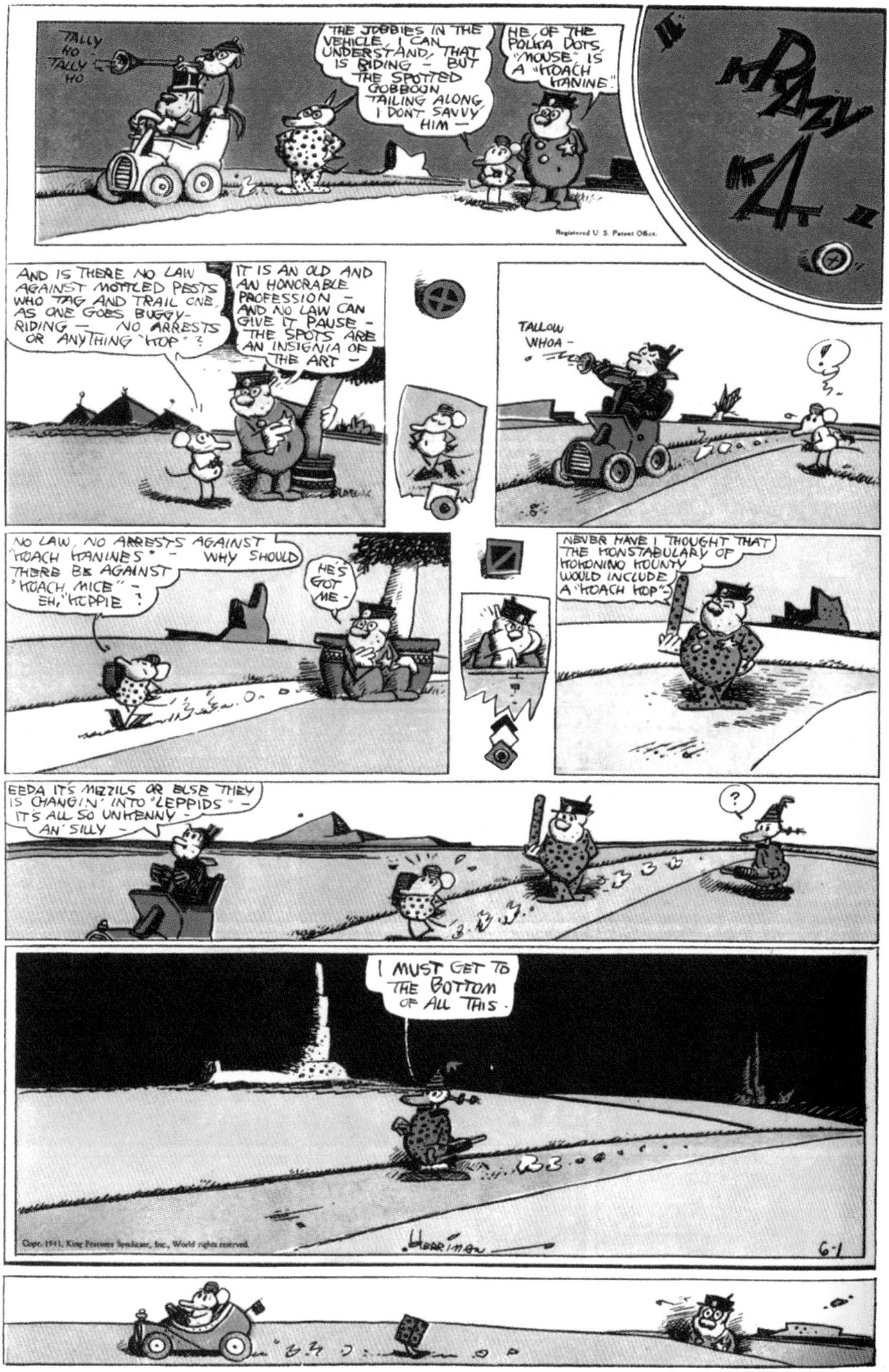
KRAZY KAT
Registered U. S. Patent Office.
TALLY HO TALLY HO
THE JOBBIES IN THE VEHICLE, I CAN UNDERSTAND, THAT IS RIDING - BUT THE SPOTTED GOBBOON TAILING ALONG I DON'T SAVVY HIM -
HE, OF THE POLKA DOTS, "MOUSE" IS A "KOACH KANINE".
AND IS THERE NO LAW AGAINST MOTTLED PESTS WHO TAG AND TRAIL ONE, AS ONE GOES BUGGY-RIDING — NO ARRESTS OR ANYTHING "KOP"?
IT IS AN OLD AND AN HONORABLE PROFESSION — AND NO LAW CAN GIVE IT PAUSE — THE SPOTS ARE AN INSIGNIA OF THE ART —
TALLOW WHOA -
!
NO LAW, NO ARRESTS AGAINST "KOACH KANINES" - WHY SHOULD THERE BE AGAINST "KOACH MICE" - EH, "KOPPIE"?
HE'S GOT ME -
NEVER HAVE I THOUGHT THAT THE KONSTABULARY OF KOKONINO KOUNTY WOULD INCLUDE A "KOACH KOP".
EEDA IT'S MIZZILS OR ELSE THEY IS CHANGIN' INTO "LEPPIDS" - IT'S ALL SO UNKENNY - AN' SILLY -
?
I MUST GET TO THE BOTTOM OF ALL THIS.
Copr. 1941, King Features Syndicate, Inc., World rights reserved.
Herriman
6-1

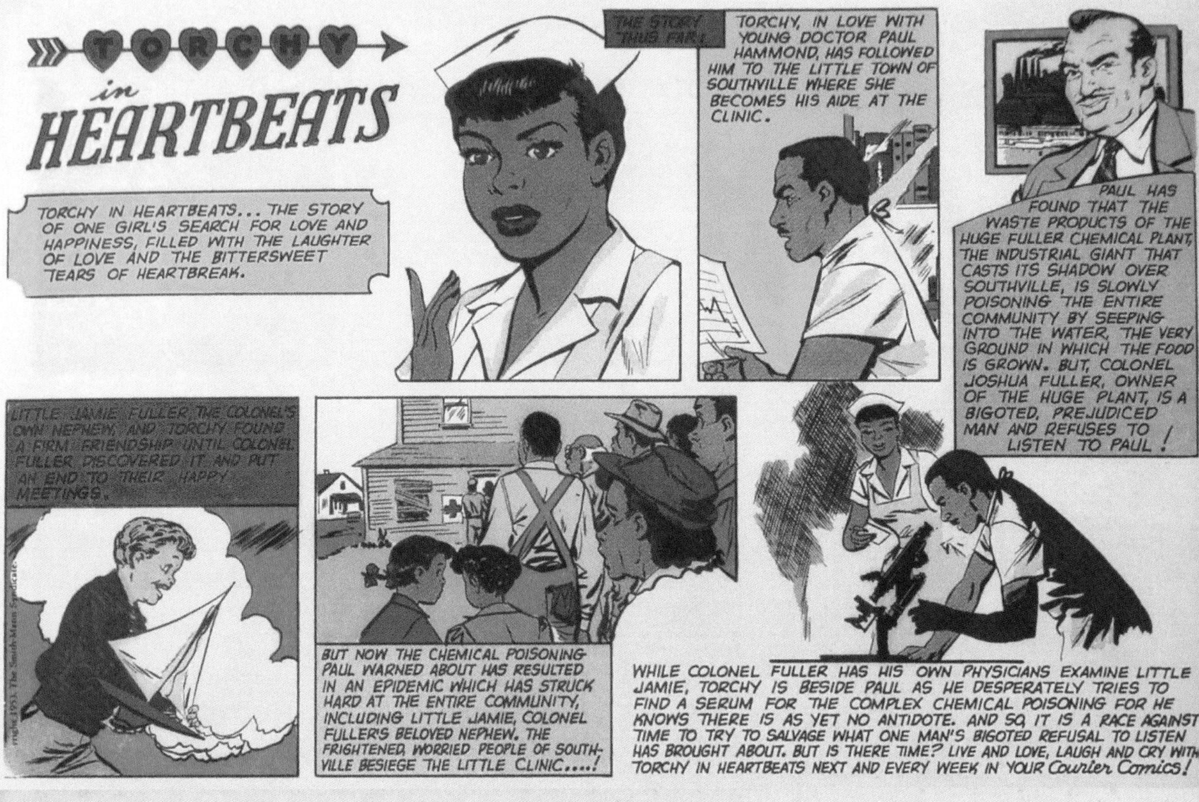
TORCHY
in
HEARTBEATS
TORCHY IN HEARTBEATS... THE STORY OF ONE GIRL'S SEARCH FOR LOVE AND HAPPINESS, FILLED WITH THE LAUGHTER OF LOVE AND THE BITTERSWEET TEARS OF HEARTBREAK.
THE STORY THUS FAR,
TORCHY, IN LOVE WITH YOUNG DOCTOR PAUL HAMMOND, HAS FOLLOWED HIM TO THE LITTLE TOWN OF SOUTHVILLE WHERE SHE BECOMES HIS AIDE AT THE CLINIC.
PAUL HAS FOUND THAT THE WASTE PRODUCTS OF THE HUGE FULLER CHEMICAL PLANT, THE INDUSTRIAL GIANT THAT CASTS ITS SHADOW OVER SOUTHVILLE, IS SLOWLY POISONING THE ENTIRE COMMUNITY BY SEEPING INTO THE WATER, THE VERY GROUND IN WHICH THE FOOD IS GROWN. BUT, COLONEL JOSHUA FULLER, OWNER OF THE HUGE PLANT, IS A BIGOTED, PREJUDICED MAN AND REFUSES TO LISTEN TO PAUL!
LITTLE JAMIE FULLER THE COLONEL'S OWN NEPHEW, AND TORCHY FOUND A FIRM FRIENDSHIP UNTIL COLONEL FULLER DISCOVERED IT AND PUT AN END TO THEIR HAPPY MEETINGS.
BUT NOW THE CHEMICAL POISONING PAUL WARNED ABOUT HAS RESULTED IN AN EPIDEMIC WHICH HAS STRUCK HARD AT THE ENTIRE COMMUNITY, INCLUDING LITTLE JAMIE, COLONEL FULLER'S BELOVED NEPHEW. THE FRIGHTENED, WORRIED PEOPLE OF SOUTHVILLE BESIEGE THE LITTLE CLINIC....!
WHILE COLONEL FULLER HAS HIS OWN PHYSICIANS EXAMINE LITTLE JAMIE, TORCHY IS BESIDE PAUL AS HE DESPERATELY TRIES TO FIND A SERUM FOR THE COMPLEX CHEMICAL POISONING FOR HE KNOWS THERE IS AS YET NO ANTIDOTE. AND SO, IT IS A RACE AGAINST TIME TO TRY TO SALVAGE WHAT ONE MAN'S BIGOTED REFUSAL TO LISTEN HAS BROUGHT ABOUT. BUT IS THERE TIME? LIVE AND LOVE, LAUGH AND CRY WITH TORCHY IN HEARTBEATS NEXT AND EVERY WEEK IN YOUR Courier Comics!

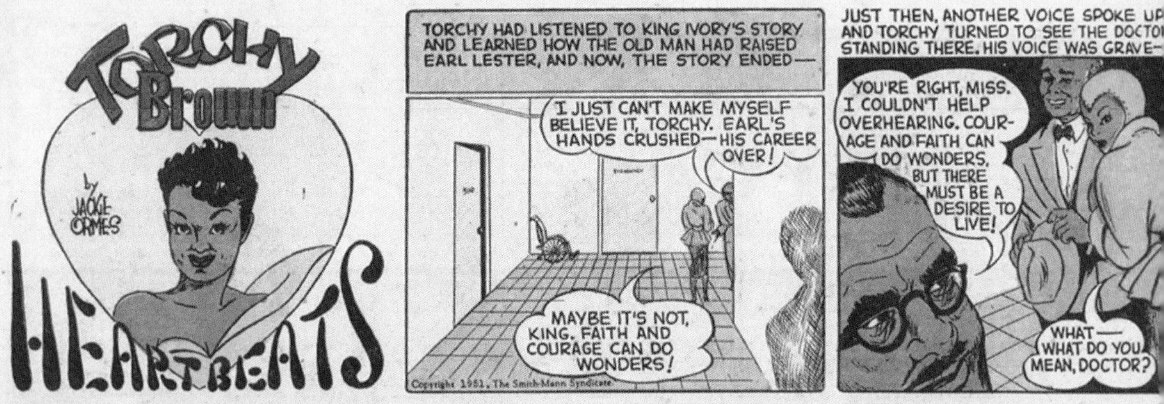
Torchy Brown
by JACKIE ORMES
HEARTBEATS
TORCHY HAD LISTENED TO KING IVORY'S STORY AND LEARNED HOW THE OLD MAN HAD RAISED EARL LESTER, AND NOW, THE STORY ENDED—
I JUST CAN'T MAKE MYSELF BELIEVE IT, TORCHY. EARL'S HANDS CRUSHED—HIS CAREER OVER!
MAYBE IT'S NOT, KING. FAITH AND COURAGE CAN DO WONDERS!
Copyright 1951, The Smith-Mann Syndicate.
JUST THEN, ANOTHER VOICE SPOKE UP AND TORCHY TURNED TO SEE THE DOCTOR STANDING THERE. HIS VOICE WAS GRAVE—
YOU'RE RIGHT, MISS. I COULDN'T HELP OVERHEARING. COURAGE AND FAITH CAN DO WONDERS, BUT THERE MUST BE A DESIRE TO LIVE!
WHAT—WHAT DO YOU MEAN, DOCTOR?
THERE'S A CHANCE AN OPERATION CAN HELP EARL LESTER'S CRUSHED FINGERS—JUST A CHANCE! BUT IT COULD NEVER SUCCEED WITHOUT A BURNING WILL TO LIVE ON THE PART OF THE PATIENT!
YOU—YOU THINK THERE'S A CHANCE HE CAN PLAY AGAIN, DOCTOR?
THAT DEPENDS. FIRST, EARL LESTER MUST BE GIVEN THE WILL—THE DESIRE TO LIVE. BUT HOW? HE FEELS HIS LIFE—HIS CAREER, IS OVER!
MAYBE—MAYBE I CAN GIVE HIM THAT WILL TO LIVE.
IF YOU COULD, AN OPERATION WOULD HAVE A FIGHTING CHANCE TO SUCCEED!
IF ONLY YOU COULD, TORCHY. BUT IT MAY MEAN ACTING—MASQUERADING—MAKING BELIEVE!
I KNOW, KING, BUT I—I WANT TO TRY, FOR ALL ITS SUCCESS WOULD MEAN TO HIM—TO YOU—TO THE WORLD!
3-3-51
BUT EVEN NOW AS SHE SPOKE, TORCHY'S HEART TOLD HER THAT WHAT SHE WAS ABOUT TO BEGIN, WOULD BE NO MASQUERADE!
TO BE CONT'D!

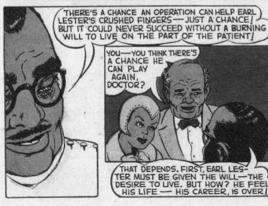

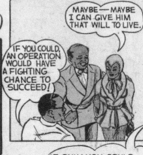

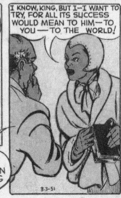

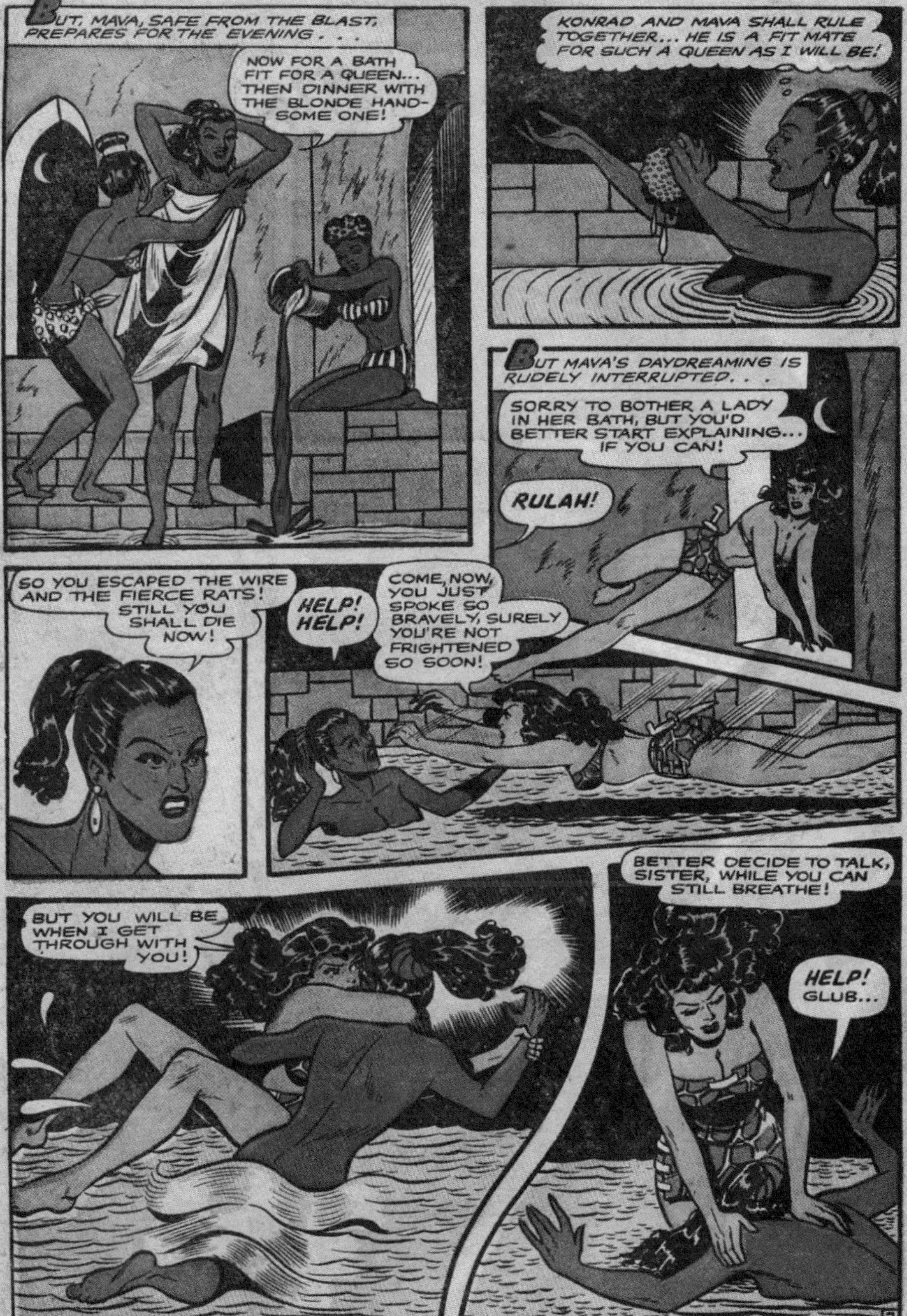
BUT, MAVA, SAFE FROM THE BLAST, PREPARES FOR THE EVENING . . .
NOW FOR A BATH FIT FOR A QUEEN... THEN DINNER WITH THE BLONDE HAND-SOME ONE!
KONRAD AND MAVA SHALL RULE TOGETHER... HE IS A FIT MATE FOR SUCH A QUEEN AS I WILL BE!
BUT MAVA'S DAYDREAMING IS RUDELY INTERRUPTED . . .
SORRY TO BOTHER A LADY IN HER BATH, BUT YOU'D BETTER START EXPLAINING... IF YOU CAN!
RULAH!
SO YOU ESCAPED THE WIRE AND THE FIERCE RATS! STILL YOU SHALL DIE NOW!
HELP! HELP!
COME, NOW, YOU JUST SPOKE SO BRAVELY, SURELY YOU'RE NOT FRIGHTENED SO SOON!
BUT YOU WILL BE WHEN I GET THROUGH WITH YOU!
BETTER DECIDE TO TALK, SISTER, WHILE YOU CAN STILL BREATHE!
HELP! GLUB...

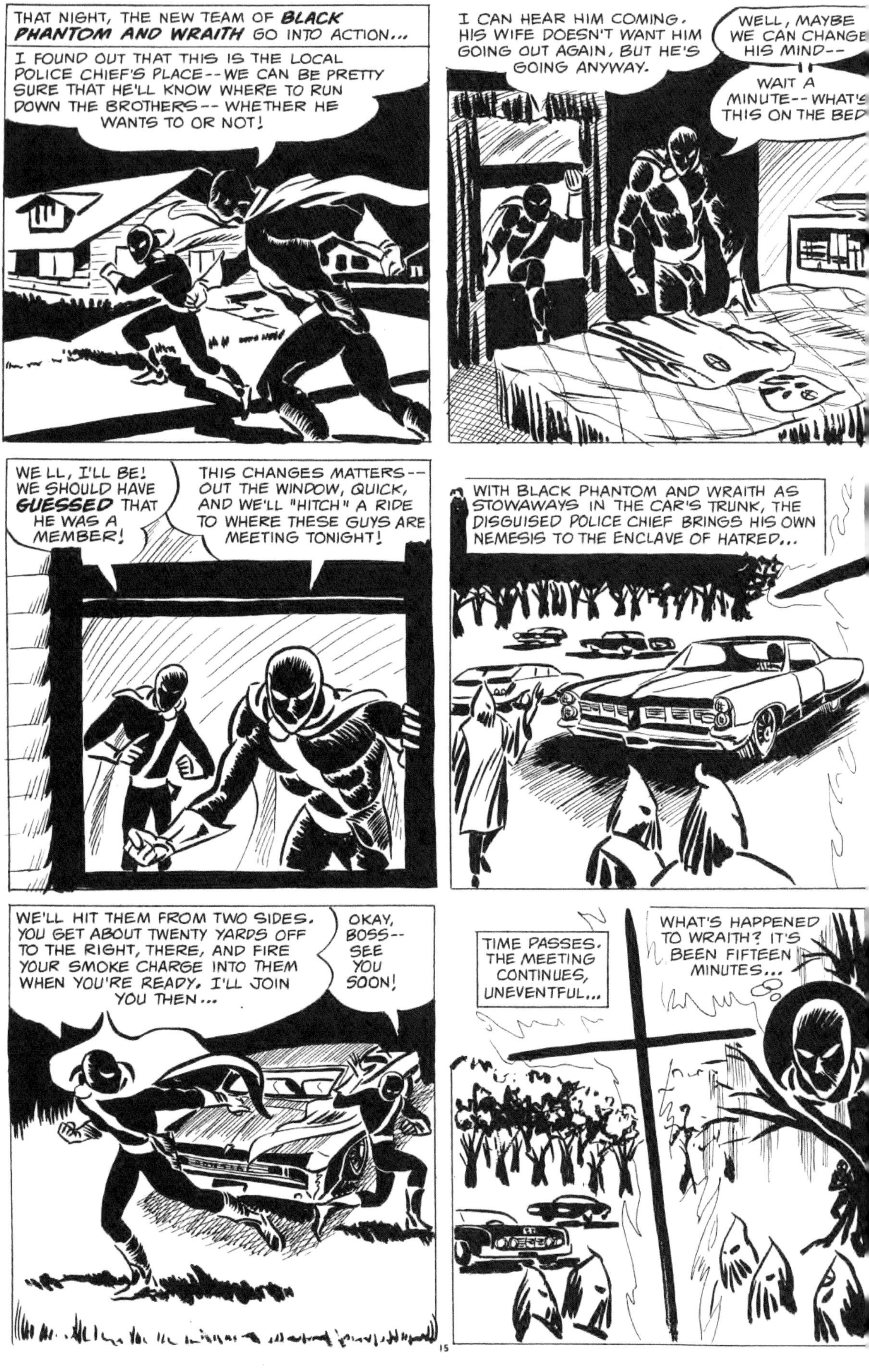
THAT NIGHT, THE NEW TEAM OF BLACK PHANTOM AND WRAITH GO INTO ACTION...
I FOUND OUT THAT THIS IS THE LOCAL POLICE CHIEF'S PLACE--WE CAN BE PRETTY SURE THAT HE'LL KNOW WHERE TO RUN DOWN THE BROTHERS--WHETHER HE WANTS TO OR NOT!
I CAN HEAR HIM COMING. HIS WIFE DOESN'T WANT HIM GOING OUT AGAIN, BUT HE'S GOING ANYWAY.
WELL, MAYBE WE CAN CHANGE HIS MIND--
WAIT A MINUTE--WHAT'S THIS ON THE BED
WE LL, I'LL BE! WE SHOULD HAVE GUESSED THAT HE WAS A MEMBER!
THIS CHANGES MATTERS--OUT THE WINDOW, QUICK, AND WE'LL "HITCH" A RIDE TO WHERE THESE GUYS ARE MEETING TONIGHT!
WITH BLACK PHANTOM AND WRAITH AS STOWAWAYS IN THE CAR'S TRUNK, THE DISGUISED POLICE CHIEF BRINGS HIS OWN NEMESIS TO THE ENCLAVE OF HATRED...
WE'LL HIT THEM FROM TWO SIDES. YOU GET ABOUT TWENTY YARDS OFF TO THE RIGHT, THERE, AND FIRE YOUR SMOKE CHARGE INTO THEM WHEN YOU'RE READY. I'LL JOIN YOU THEN...
OKAY, BOSS--SEE YOU SOON!
TIME PASSES. THE MEETING CONTINUES, UNEVENTFUL...
WHAT'S HAPPENED TO WRAITH? IT'S BEEN FIFTEEN MINUTES...

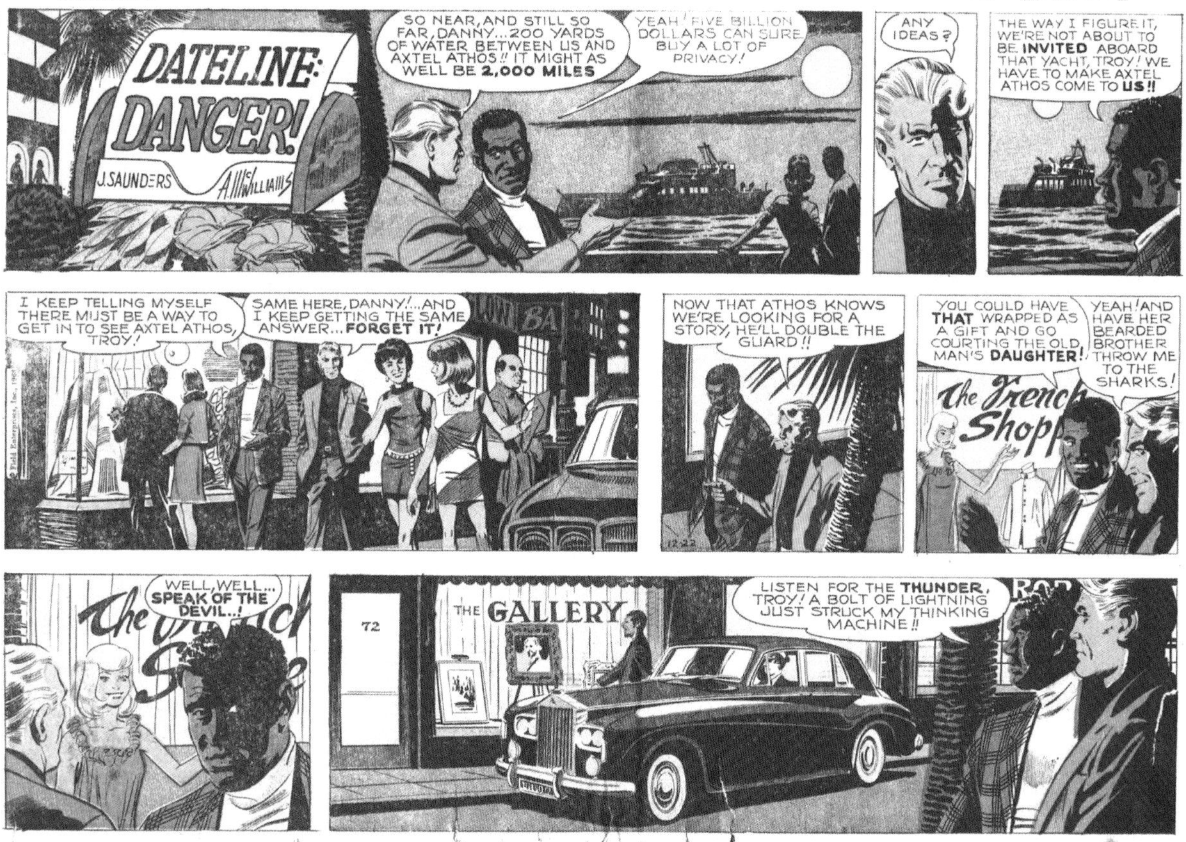
DATELINE: DANGER!
J. SAUNDERS
A. McWILLIAMS
SO NEAR, AND STILL SO FAR, DANNY... 200 YARDS OF WATER BETWEEN US AND AXTEL ATHOS!! IT MIGHT AS WELL BE 2,000 MILES
YEAH! FIVE BILLION DOLLARS CAN SURE BUY A LOT OF PRIVACY!
ANY IDEAS?
THE WAY I FIGURE IT, WE'RE NOT ABOUT TO BE INVITED ABOARD THAT YACHT, TROY! WE HAVE TO MAKE AXTEL ATHOS COME TO US!!
I KEEP TELLING MYSELF THERE MUST BE A WAY TO GET IN TO SEE AXTEL ATHOS, TROY!
SAME HERE, DANNY!...AND I KEEP GETTING THE SAME ANSWER... FORGET IT!
NOW THAT ATHOS KNOWS WE'RE LOOKING FOR A STORY, HE'LL DOUBLE THE GUARD!!
12-22
YOU COULD HAVE THAT WRAPPED AS A GIFT AND GO COURTING THE OLD MAN'S DAUGHTER!
YEAH! AND HAVE HER BEARDED BROTHER THROW ME TO THE SHARKS!
The French Shop
WELL, WELL... SPEAK OF THE DEVIL..!
THE GALLERY
72
LISTEN FOR THE THUNDER, TROY! A BOLT OF LIGHTNING JUST STRUCK MY THINKING MACHINE!!

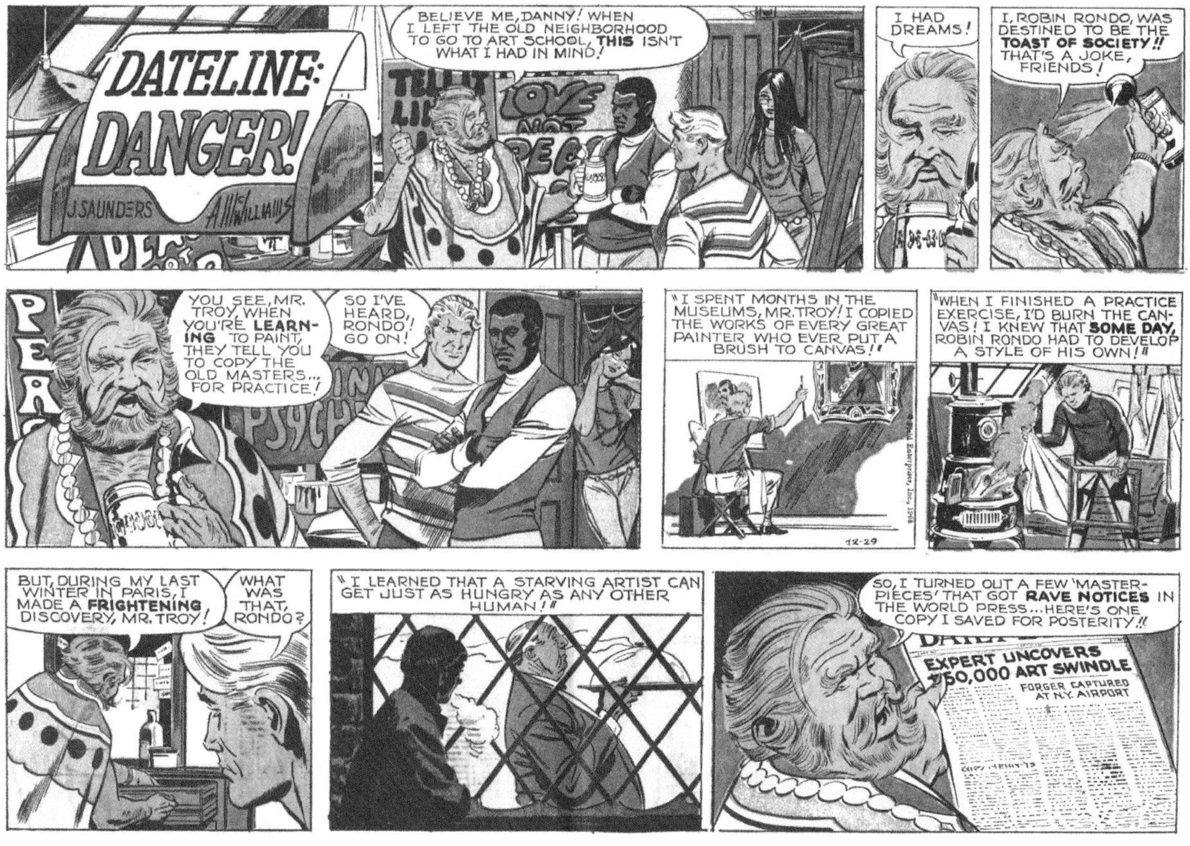
DATELINE: DANGER!
J. SAUNDERS
A. McWILLIAMS
BELIEVE ME, DANNY! WHEN I LEFT THE OLD NEIGHBORHOOD TO GO TO ART SCHOOL, THIS ISN'T WHAT I HAD IN MIND!
I HAD DREAMS!
I, ROBIN RONDO, WAS DESTINED TO BE THE TOAST OF SOCIETY!! THAT'S A JOKE, FRIENDS!
YOU SEE, MR. TROY, WHEN YOU'RE LEARNING TO PAINT, THEY TELL YOU TO COPY THE OLD MASTERS... FOR PRACTICE!
SO I'VE HEARD, RONDO! GO ON!
"I SPENT MONTHS IN THE MUSEUMS, MR. TROY! I COPIED THE WORKS OF EVERY GREAT PAINTER WHO EVER PUT A BRUSH TO CANVAS!"
12-29
"WHEN I FINISHED A PRACTICE EXERCISE, I'D BURN THE CANVAS! I KNEW THAT SOME DAY, ROBIN RONDO HAD TO DEVELOP A STYLE OF HIS OWN!"
BUT, DURING MY LAST WINTER IN PARIS, I MADE A FRIGHTENING DISCOVERY, MR. TROY!
WHAT WAS THAT, RONDO?
"I LEARNED THAT A STARVING ARTIST CAN GET JUST AS HUNGRY AS ANY OTHER HUMAN!"
SO, I TURNED OUT A FEW 'MASTERPIECES' THAT GOT RAVE NOTICES IN THE WORLD PRESS... HERE'S ONE COPY I SAVED FOR POSTERITY!!
EXPERT UNCOVERS $50,000 ART SWINDLE
FORGER CAPTURED AT N.Y. AIRPORT

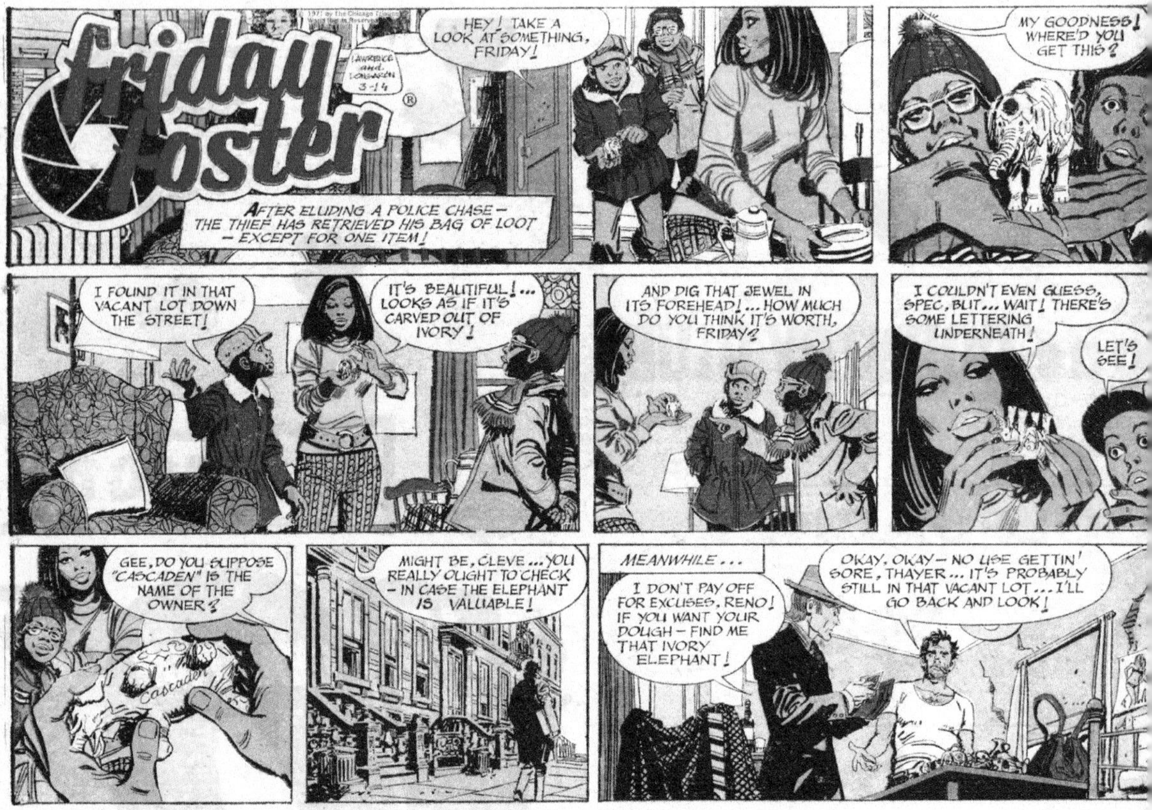
friday foster®
LAWRENCE and LONGARON 3-14
AFTER ELUDING A POLICE CHASE — THE THIEF HAS RETRIEVED HIS BAG OF LOOT — EXCEPT FOR ONE ITEM!
HEY! TAKE A LOOK AT SOMETHING, FRIDAY!
MY GOODNESS! WHERE'D YOU GET THIS?
I FOUND IT IN THAT VACANT LOT DOWN THE STREET!
IT'S BEAUTIFUL!... LOOKS AS IF IT'S CARVED OUT OF IVORY!
AND DIG THAT JEWEL IN ITS FOREHEAD!... HOW MUCH DO YOU THINK IT'S WORTH, FRIDAY?
I COULDN'T EVEN GUESS, SPEC, BUT... WAIT! THERE'S SOME LETTERING UNDERNEATH!
LET'S SEE!
GEE, DO YOU SUPPOSE "CASCADEN" IS THE NAME OF THE OWNER?
Cascaden
MIGHT BE, CLEVE ... YOU REALLY OUGHT TO CHECK — IN CASE THE ELEPHANT IS VALUABLE!
MEANWHILE ...
I DON'T PAY OFF FOR EXCUSES, RENO! IF YOU WANT YOUR DOUGH — FIND ME THAT IVORY ELEPHANT!
OKAY, OKAY — NO USE GETTIN' SORE, THAYER ... IT'S PROBABLY STILL IN THAT VACANT LOT ... I'LL GO BACK AND LOOK!

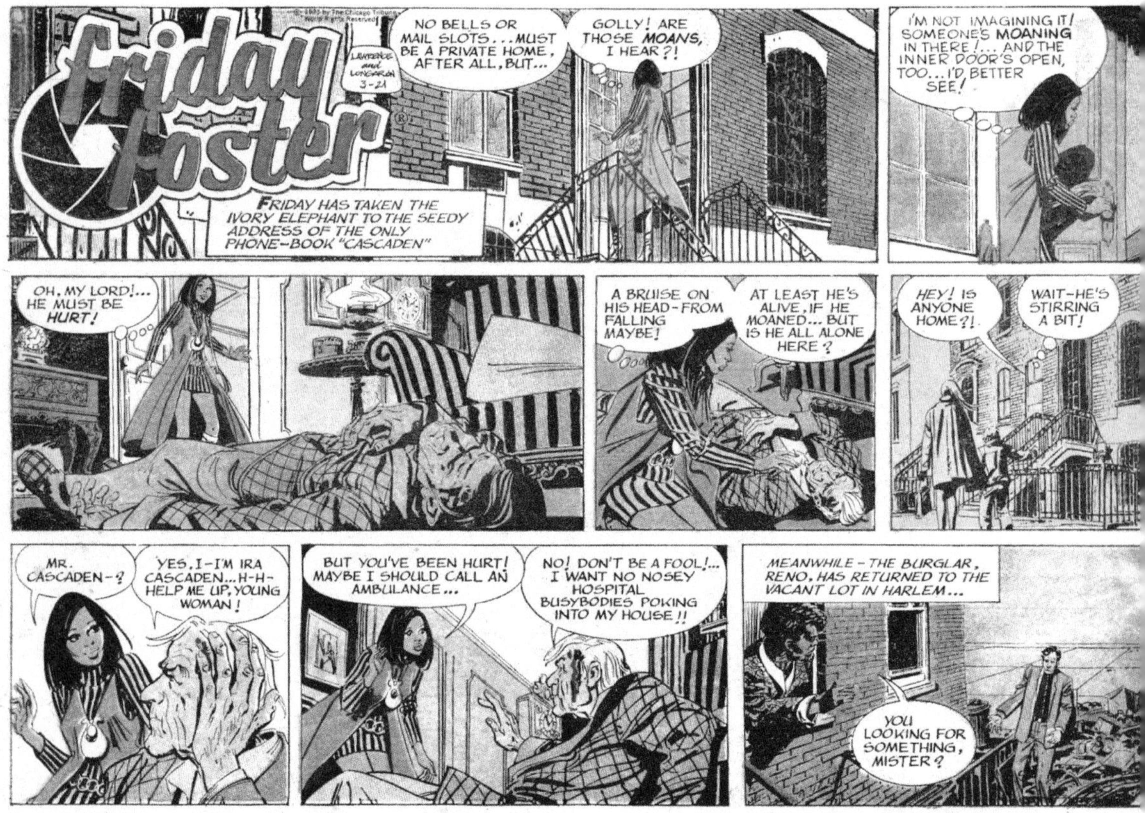
friday foster®
LAWRENCE and LONGARON 3-21
FRIDAY HAS TAKEN THE IVORY ELEPHANT TO THE SEEDY ADDRESS OF THE ONLY PHONE-BOOK "CASCADEN"
NO BELLS OR MAIL SLOTS ... MUST BE A PRIVATE HOME, AFTER ALL, BUT...
GOLLY! ARE THOSE MOANS, I HEAR?!
I'M NOT IMAGINING IT! SOMEONE'S MOANING IN THERE!... AND THE INNER DOOR'S OPEN, TOO... I'D BETTER SEE!
OH, MY LORD!... HE MUST BE HURT!
A BRUISE ON HIS HEAD — FROM FALLING MAYBE!
AT LEAST HE'S ALIVE, IF HE MOANED... BUT IS HE ALL ALONE HERE?
HEY! IS ANYONE HOME?!
WAIT — HE'S STIRRING A BIT!
MR. CASCADEN—?
YES. I—I'M IRA CASCADEN... H-H-HELP ME UP, YOUNG WOMAN!
BUT YOU'VE BEEN HURT! MAYBE I SHOULD CALL AN AMBULANCE...
NO! DON'T BE A FOOL!... I WANT NO NOSEY HOSPITAL BUSYBODIES POKING INTO MY HOUSE!!
MEANWHILE — THE BURGLAR, RENO, HAS RETURNED TO THE VACANT LOT IN HARLEM...
YOU LOOKING FOR SOMETHING, MISTER?

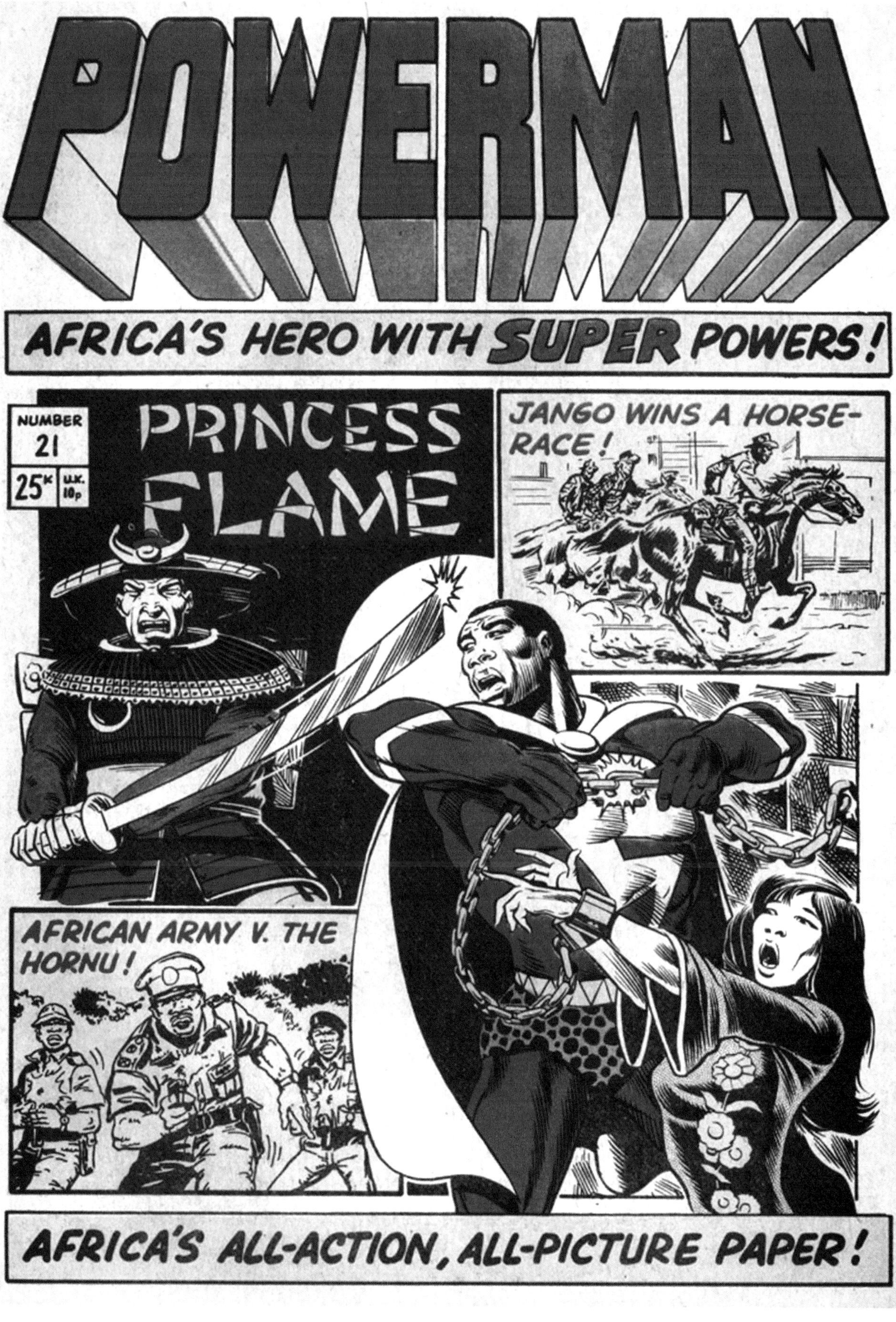

POWERMAN
AFRICA'S HERO WITH SUPER POWERS!
NUMBER 21
25K U.K. 10p
PRINCESS FLAME
JANGO WINS A HORSE-RACE!
AFRICAN ARMY V. THE HORNU!
AFRICA'S ALL-ACTION, ALL-PICTURE PAPER!

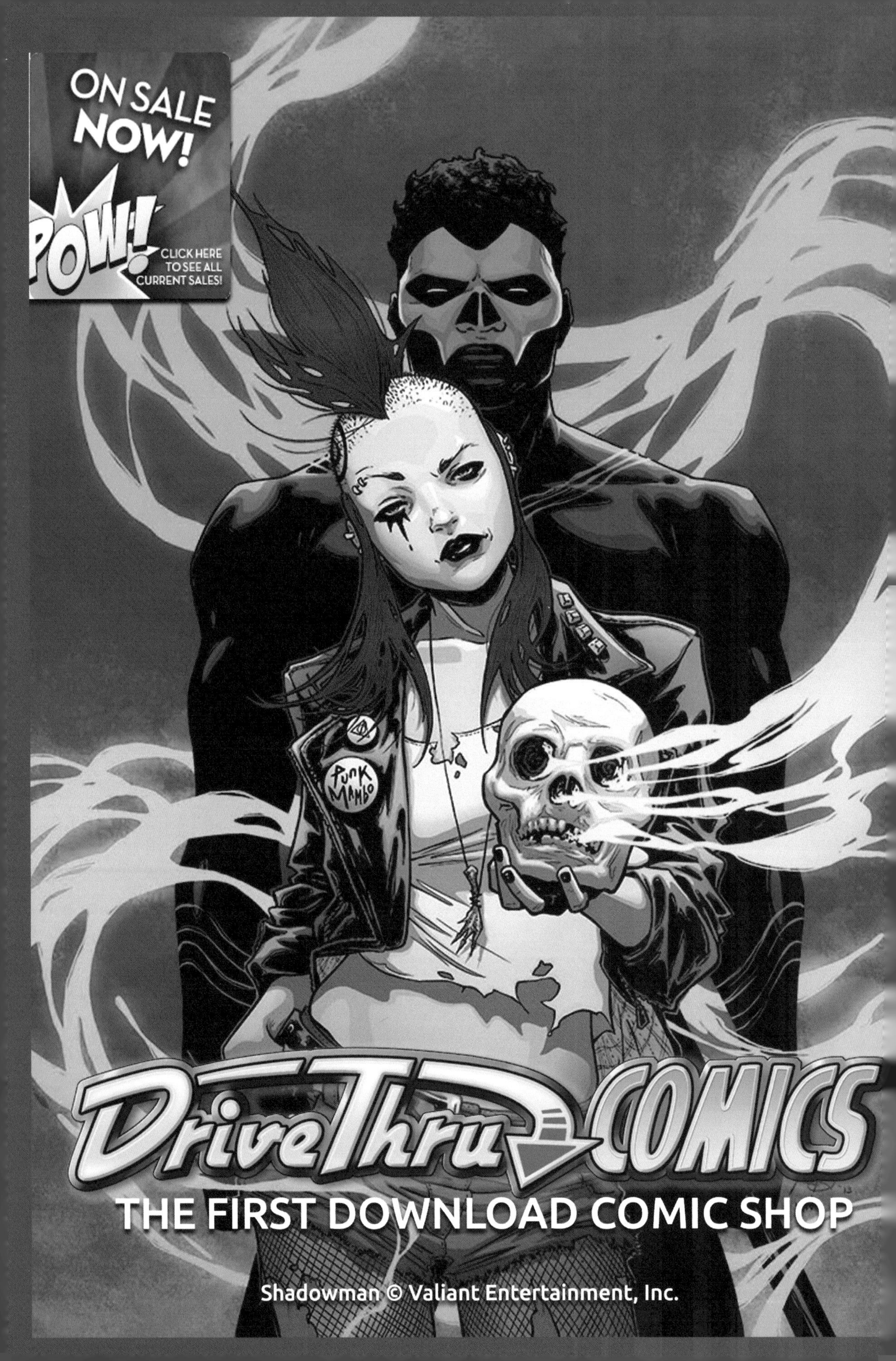

ON SALE NOW!
POW!
CLICK HERE TO SEE ALL CURRENT SALES!
PUNK MAMBO
DriveThru COMICS
THE FIRST DOWNLOAD COMIC SHOP
Shadowman © Valiant Entertainment, Inc.

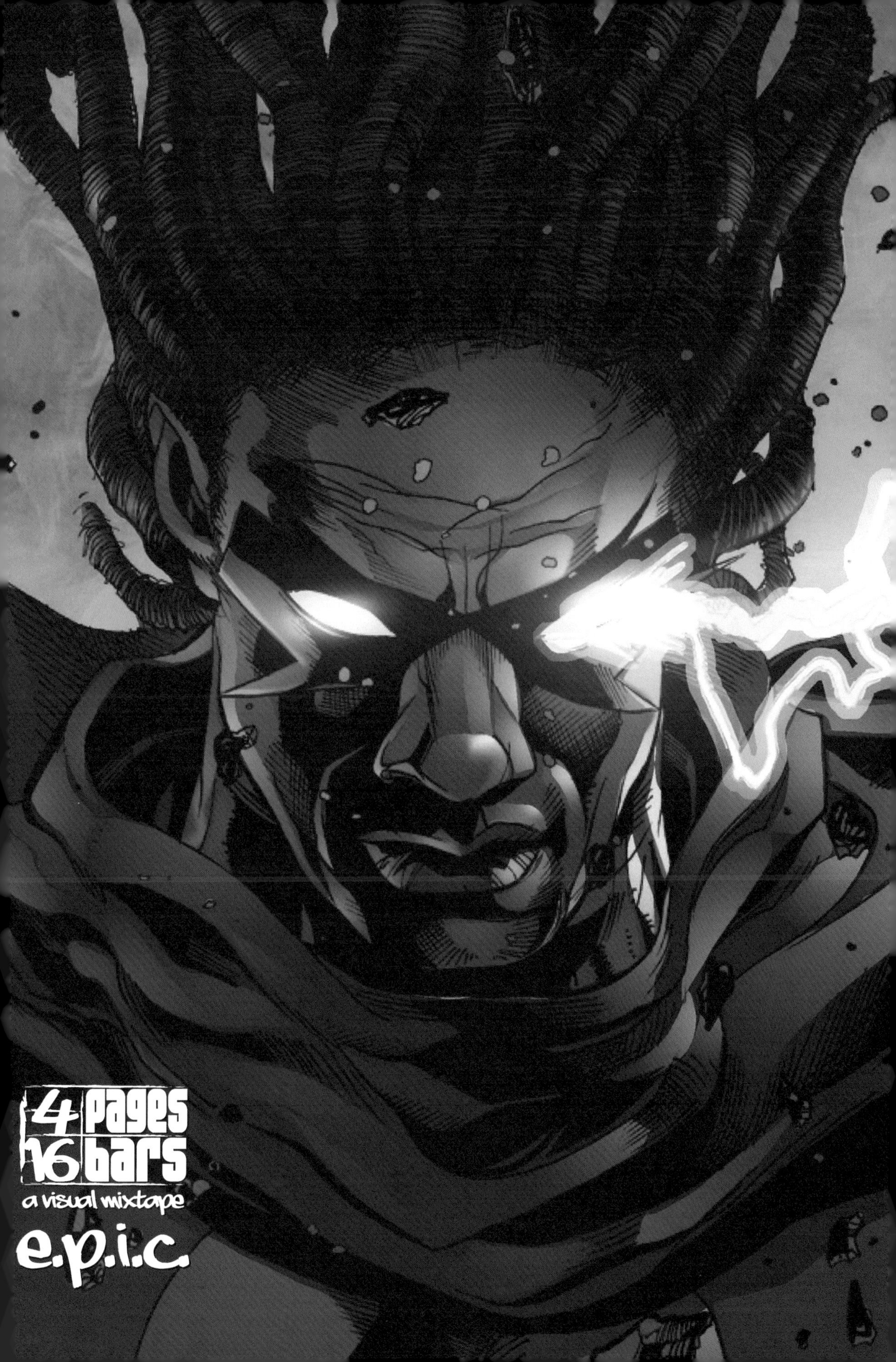
4 16 pages bars
a visual mixtape
e.p.i.c.

COVER ILLUSTRATION BY
CHRISCROSS

E.P.I.C: Earth's Protector in Crisis, is a comic series created and written by **Lonnie Lowe, Jr.** for his **Dark City Comics**. The story centers around college sophomore Christopher "Chris" Tayborne, a young and talented archeology major, that through a series of sudden twists and turns lands his hands on one of the most powerful weapons in the known Galaxy The Alpha Bands. In the same breath he also unleashes a power back into the world that it hasn't seen for thousands of years and has long since forgotten. Once these powers are release the planet goes from ordinary to extraordinary in a matter of minutes changing the scope of the entire globe and almost immediately creating our Alpha human population thus setting the events into place that give life to the Dark City comics Universe.

website: darkcitycomics.com

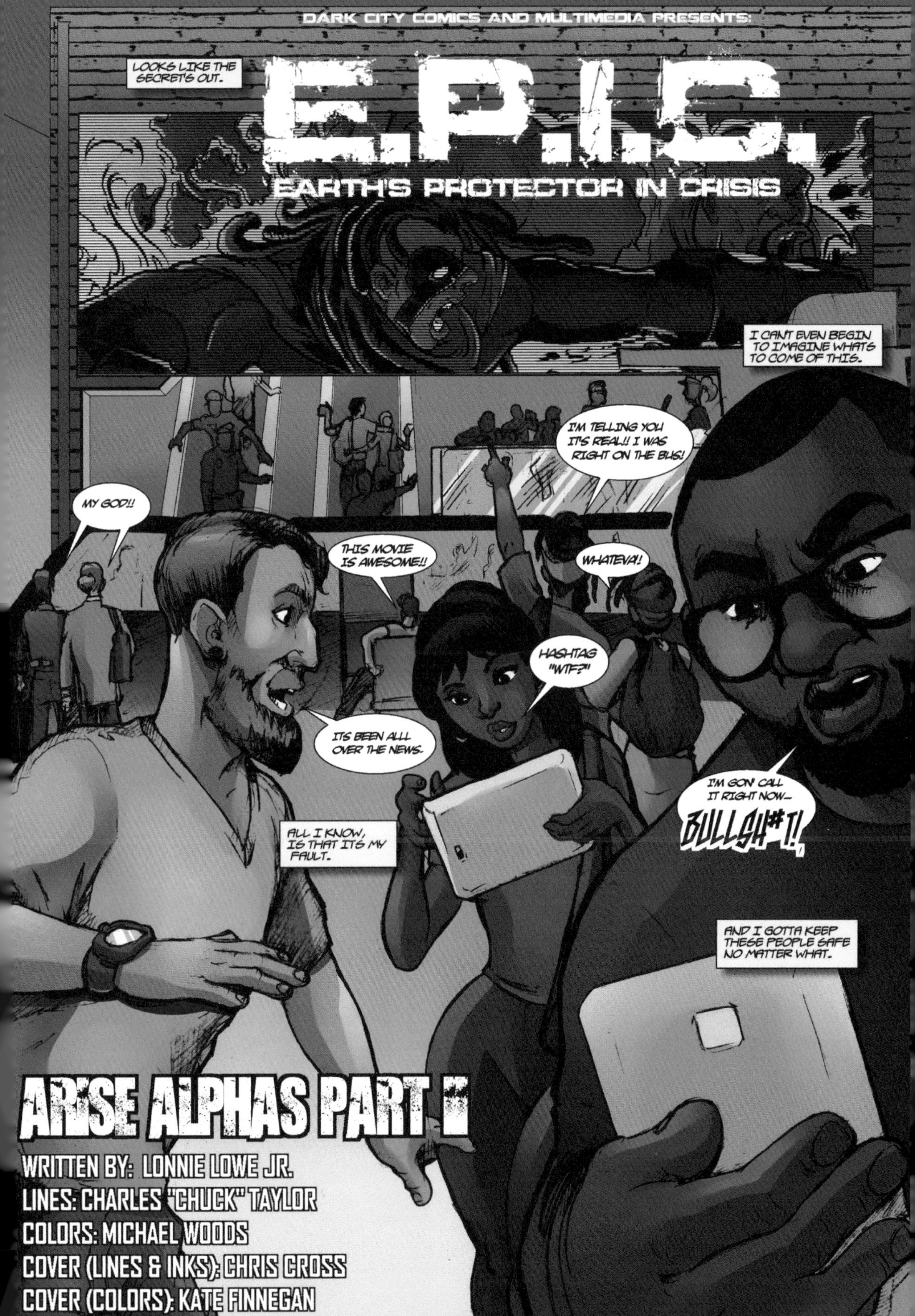

DARK CITY COMICS AND MULTIMEDIA PRESENTS:
E.P.I.C.
EARTH'S PROTECTOR IN CRISIS
LOOKS LIKE THE SECRET'S OUT.
I CANT EVEN BEGIN TO IMAGINE WHATS TO COME OF THIS.
I'M TELLING YOU! IT'S REAL!! I WAS RIGHT ON THE BUS!
MY GOD!!
THIS MOVIE IS AWESOME!!
WHATEVA!
HASHTAG "WTF?"
ITS BEEN ALLL OVER THE NEWS.
I'M GON' CALL IT RIGHT NOW... BULLSH#T!
ALL I KNOW, IS THAT ITS MY FAULT.
AND I GOTTA KEEP THESE PEOPLE SAFE NO MATTER WHAT.
ARISE ALPHAS PART I
WRITTEN BY: LONNIE LOWE JR.
LINES: CHARLES "CHUCK" TAYLOR
COLORS: MICHAEL WOODS
COVER (LINES & INKS): CHRIS CROSS
COVER (COLORS): KATE FINNEGAN

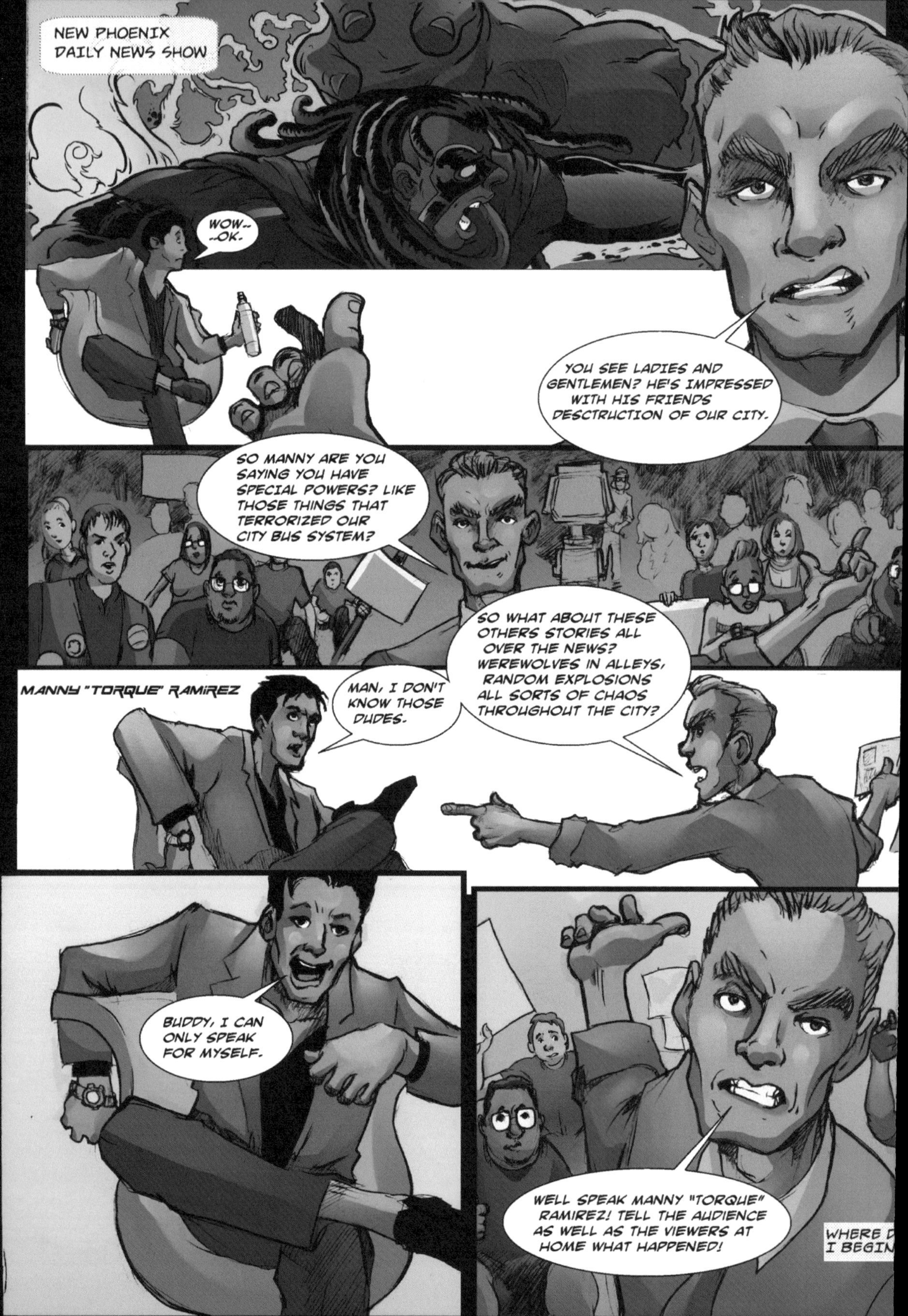
NEW PHOENIX DAILY NEWS SHOW
WOW-- --OK.
YOU SEE LADIES AND GENTLEMEN? HE'S IMPRESSED WITH HIS FRIENDS DESCTRUCTION OF OUR CITY.
SO MANNY ARE YOU SAYING YOU HAVE SPECIAL POWERS? LIKE THOSE THINGS THAT TERRORIZED OUR CITY BUS SYSTEM?
SO WHAT ABOUT THESE OTHERS STORIES ALL OVER THE NEWS? WEREWOLVES IN ALLEYS, RANDOM EXPLOSIONS ALL SORTS OF CHAOS THROUGHOUT THE CITY?
MANNY "TORQUE" RAMIREZ
MAN, I DON'T KNOW THOSE DUDES.
BUDDY, I CAN ONLY SPEAK FOR MYSELF.
WELL SPEAK MANNY "TORQUE" RAMIREZ! TELL THE AUDIENCE AS WELL AS THE VIEWERS AT HOME WHAT HAPPENED!

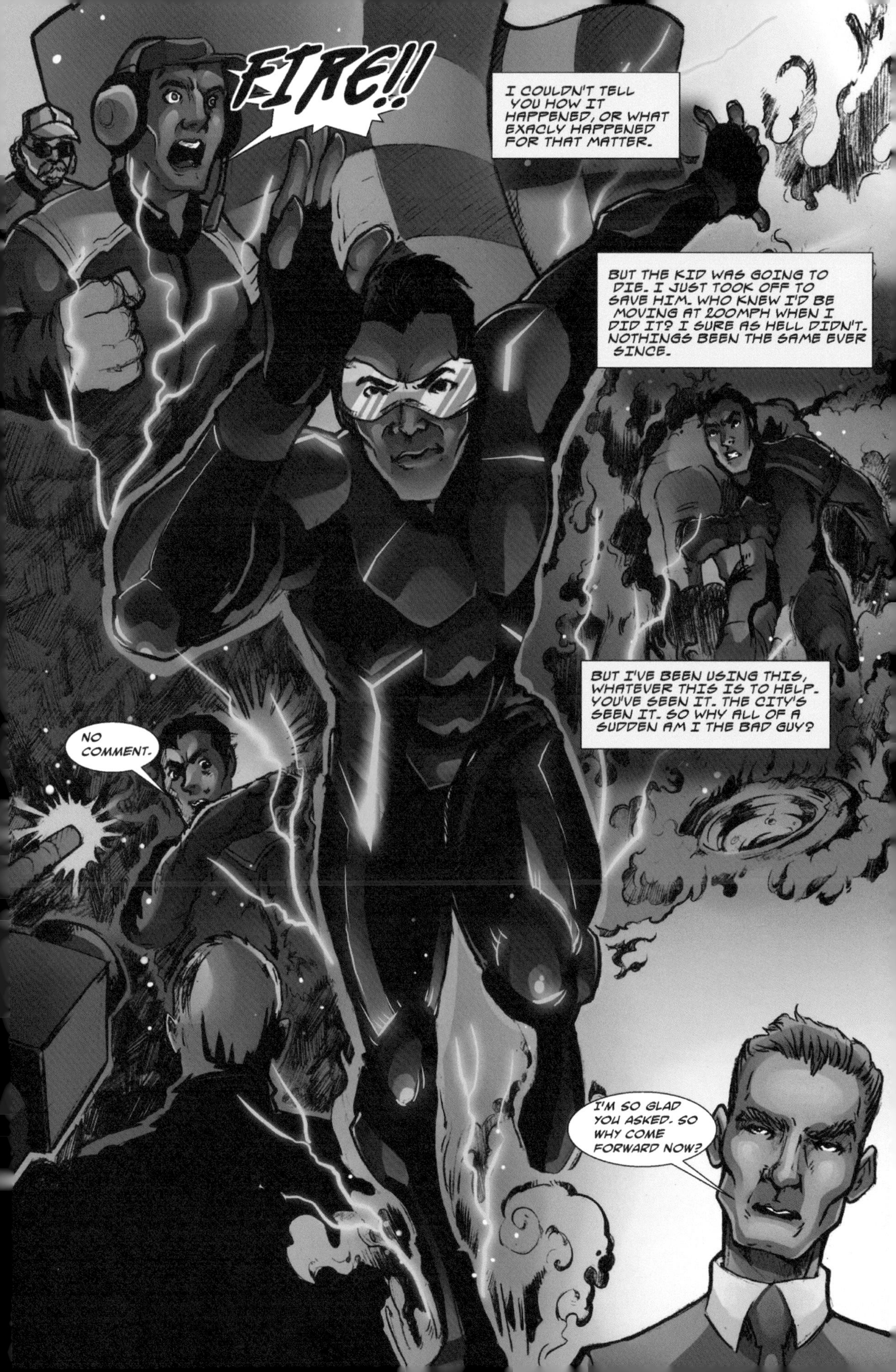
FIRE!!
I COULDN'T TELL YOU HOW IT HAPPENED, OR WHAT EXACLY HAPPENED FOR THAT MATTER.
BUT THE KID WAS GOING TO DIE. I JUST TOOK OFF TO SAVE HIM. WHO KNEW I'D BE MOVING AT 200MPH WHEN I DID IT? I SURE AS HELL DIDN'T. NOTHINGS BEEN THE SAME EVER SINCE.
BUT I'VE BEEN USING THIS, WHATEVER THIS IS TO HELP. YOU'VE SEEN IT. THE CITY'S SEEN IT. SO WHY ALL OF A SUDDEN AM I THE BAD GUY?
NO COMMENT.
I'M SO GLAD YOU ASKED. SO WHY COME FORWARD NOW?

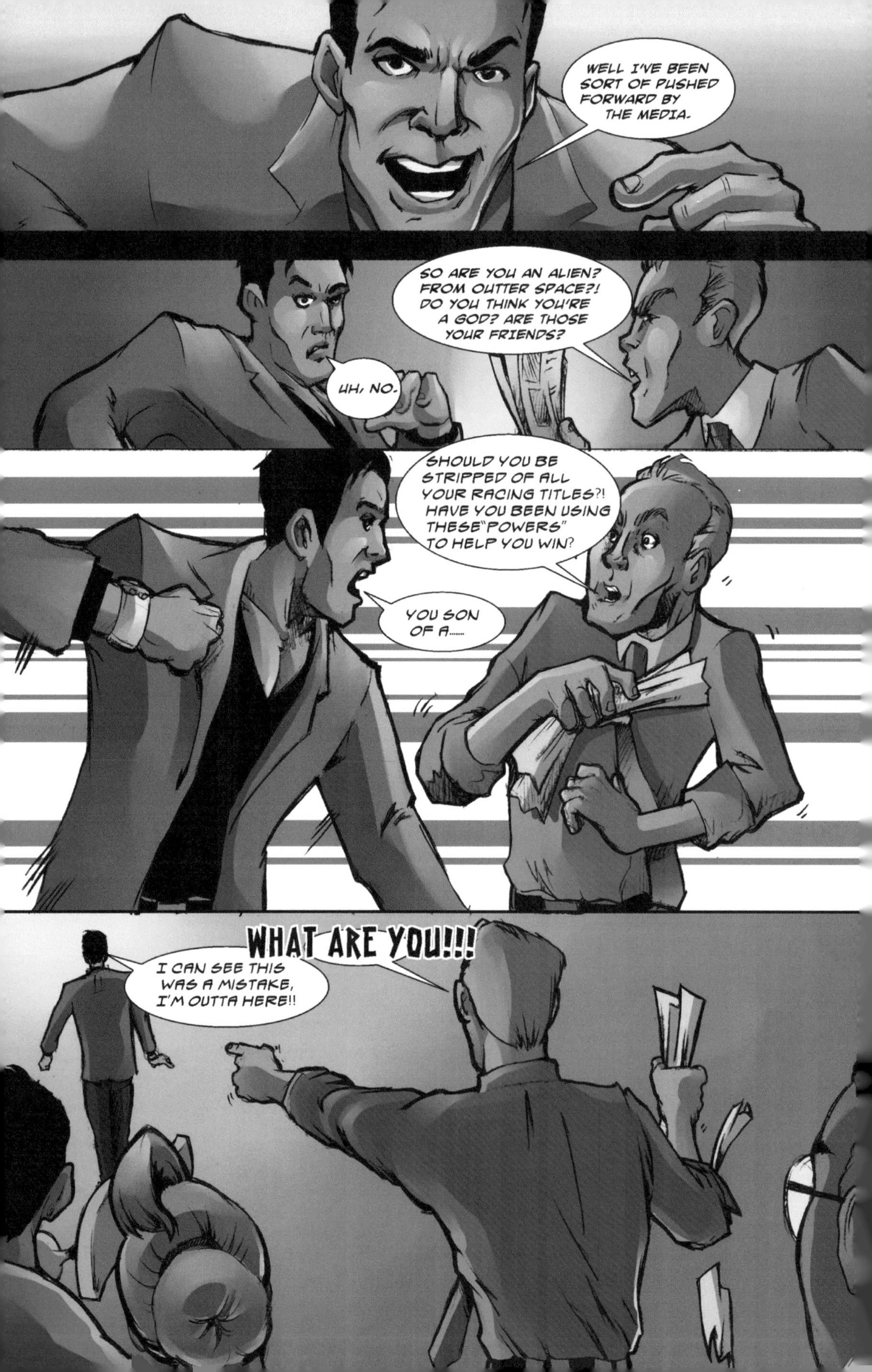
WELL I'VE BEEN SORT OF PUSHED FORWARD BY THE MEDIA.
SO ARE YOU AN ALIEN? FROM OUTTER SPACE?! DO YOU THINK YOU'RE A GOD? ARE THOSE YOUR FRIENDS?
UH, NO.
SHOULD YOU BE STRIPPED OF ALL YOUR RACING TITLES?! HAVE YOU BEEN USING THESE "POWERS" TO HELP YOU WIN?
YOU SON OF A......
WHAT ARE YOU!!!
I CAN SEE THIS WAS A MISTAKE, I'M OUTTA HERE!!

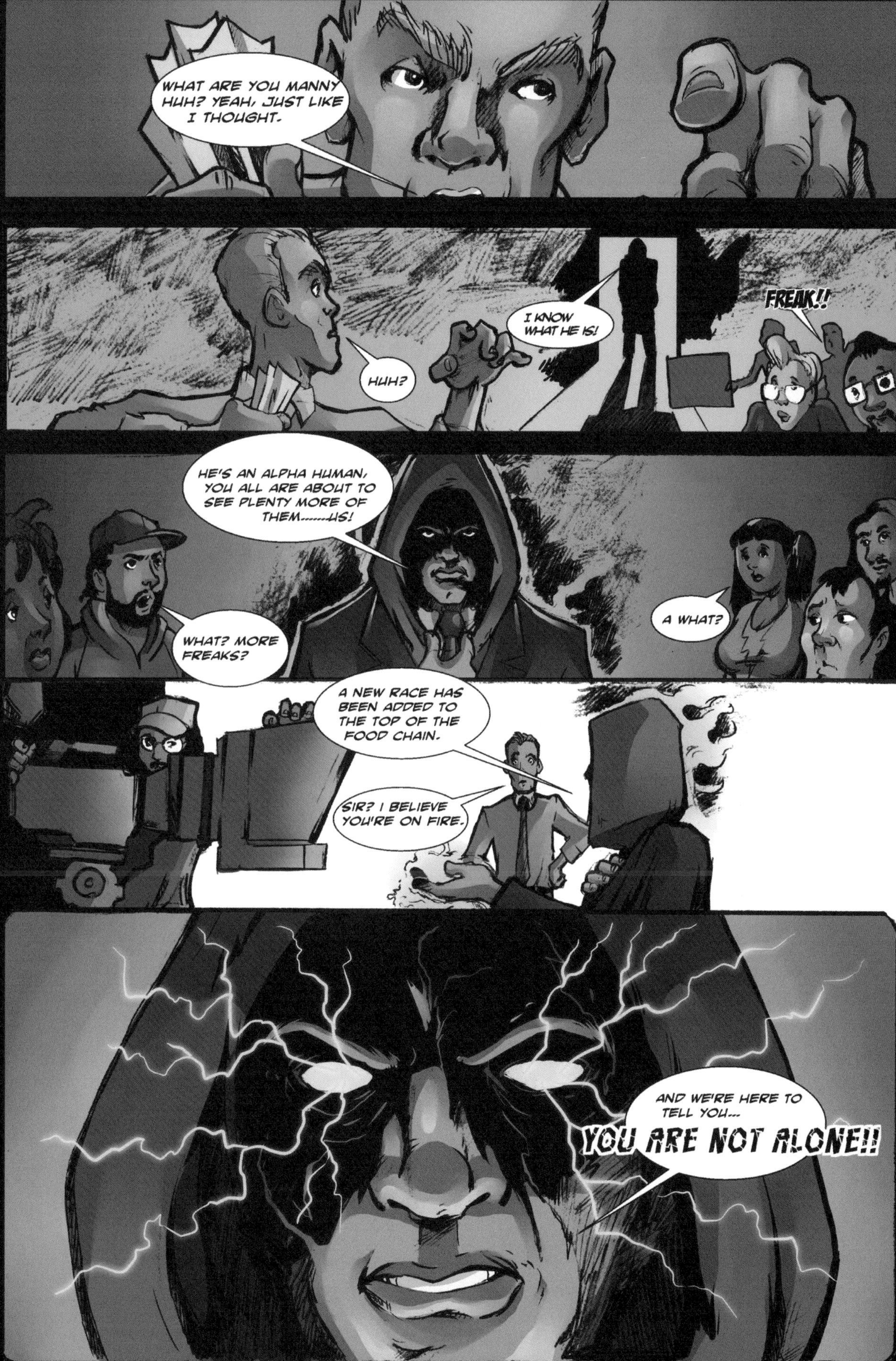
WHAT ARE YOU MANNY HUH? YEAH, JUST LIKE I THOUGHT.
HUH?
I KNOW WHAT HE IS!
FREAK!!
HE'S AN ALPHA HUMAN, YOU ALL ARE ABOUT TO SEE PLENTY MORE OF THEM.......US!
WHAT? MORE FREAKS?
A WHAT?
A NEW RACE HAS BEEN ADDED TO THE TOP OF THE FOOD CHAIN.
SIR? I BELIEVE YOU'RE ON FIRE.
AND WE'RE HERE TO TELL YOU...
YOU ARE NOT ALONE!!

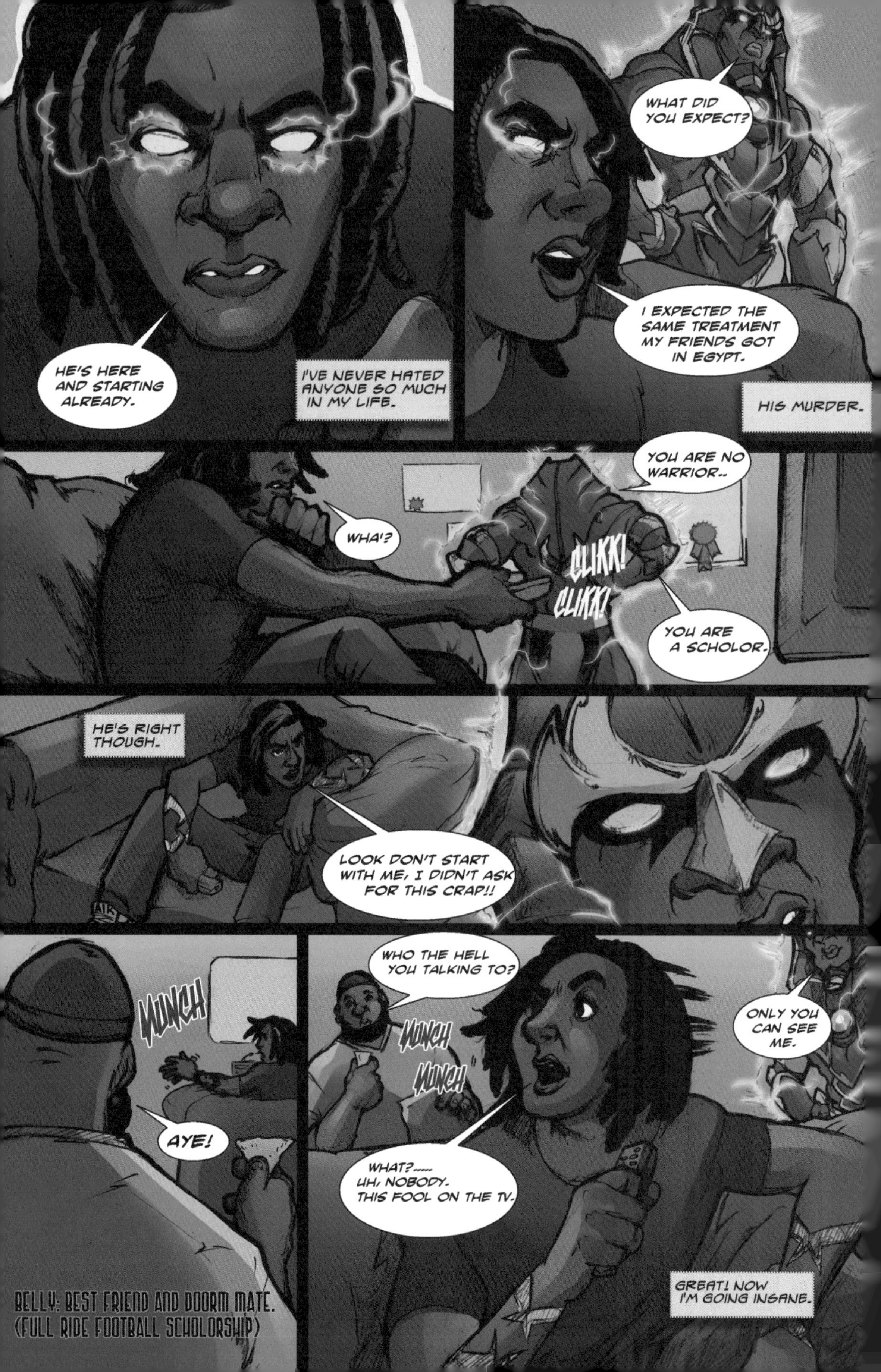
HE'S HERE AND STARTING ALREADY.
I'VE NEVER HATED ANYONE SO MUCH IN MY LIFE.
WHAT DID YOU EXPECT?
I EXPECTED THE SAME TREATMENT MY FRIENDS GOT IN EGYPT.
HIS MURDER.
WHA'?
YOU ARE NO WARRIOR..
CLIKK!
CLIKK!
YOU ARE A SCHOLOR.
HE'S RIGHT THOUGH.
LOOK DON'T START WITH ME, I DIDN'T ASK FOR THIS CRAP!!
MUNCH
AYE!
BELLY: BEST FRIEND AND DOORM MATE.
(FULL RIDE FOOTBALL SCHOLORSHIP)
WHO THE HELL YOU TALKING TO?
MUNCH
MUNCH
ONLY YOU CAN SEE ME.
WHAT?..... UH, NOBODY. THIS FOOL ON THE TV.
GREAT! NOW I'M GOING INSANE.

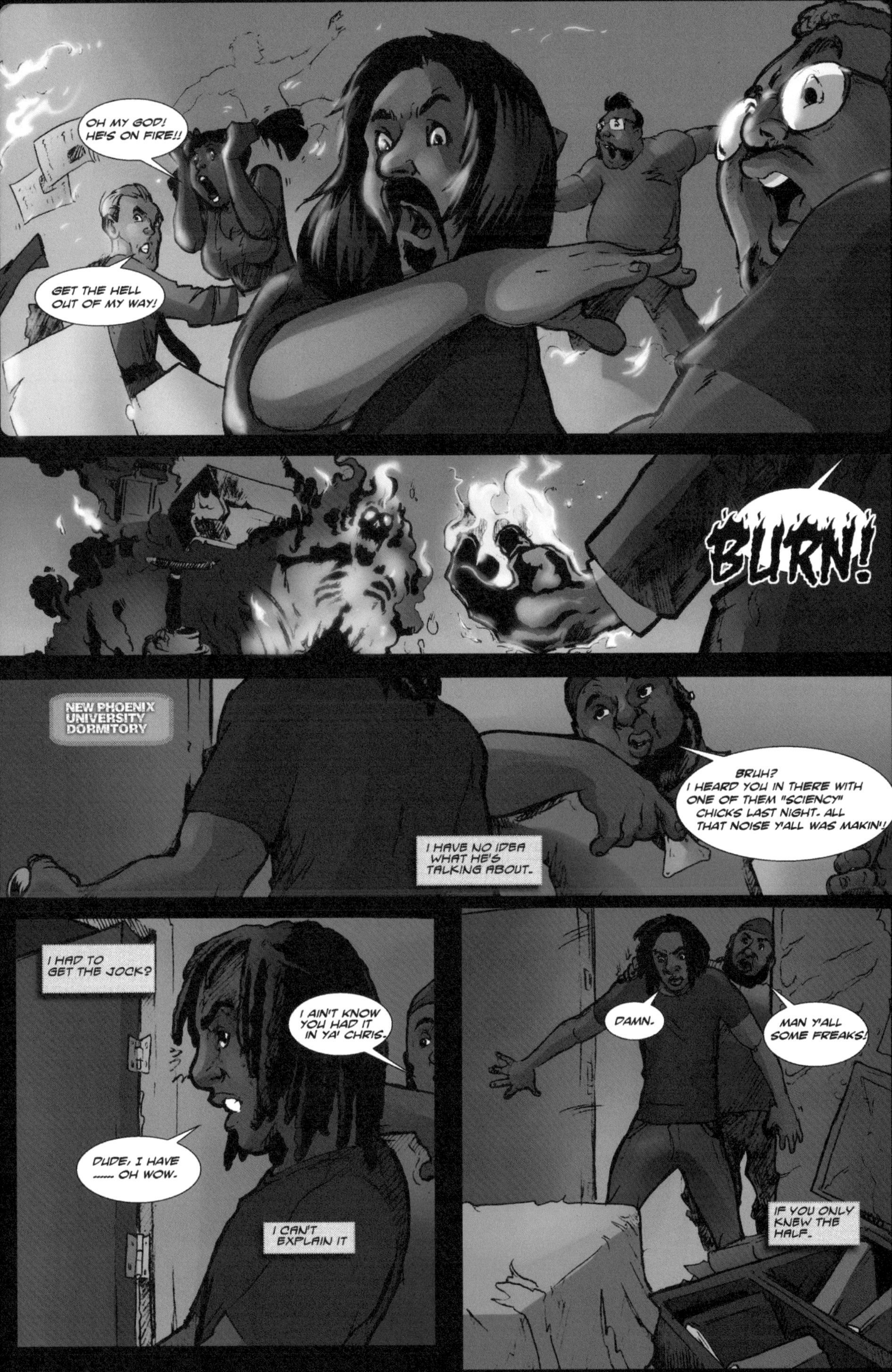
OH MY GOD! HE'S ON FIRE!!
GET THE HELL OUT OF MY WAY!
BURN!
NEW PHOENIX UNIVERSITY DORMITORY
BRUH? I HEARD YOU IN THERE WITH ONE OF THEM "SCIENCY" CHICKS LAST NIGHT. ALL THAT NOISE Y'ALL WAS MAKIN'!
I HAVE NO IDEA WHAT HE'S TALKING ABOUT.
I HAD TO GET THE JOCK?
I AIN'T KNOW YOU HAD IT IN YA' CHRIS.
DUDE, I HAVE ----- OH WOW.
I CAN'T EXPLAIN IT
DAMN.
MAN Y'ALL SOME FREAKS!
IF YOU ONLY KNEW THE HALF.

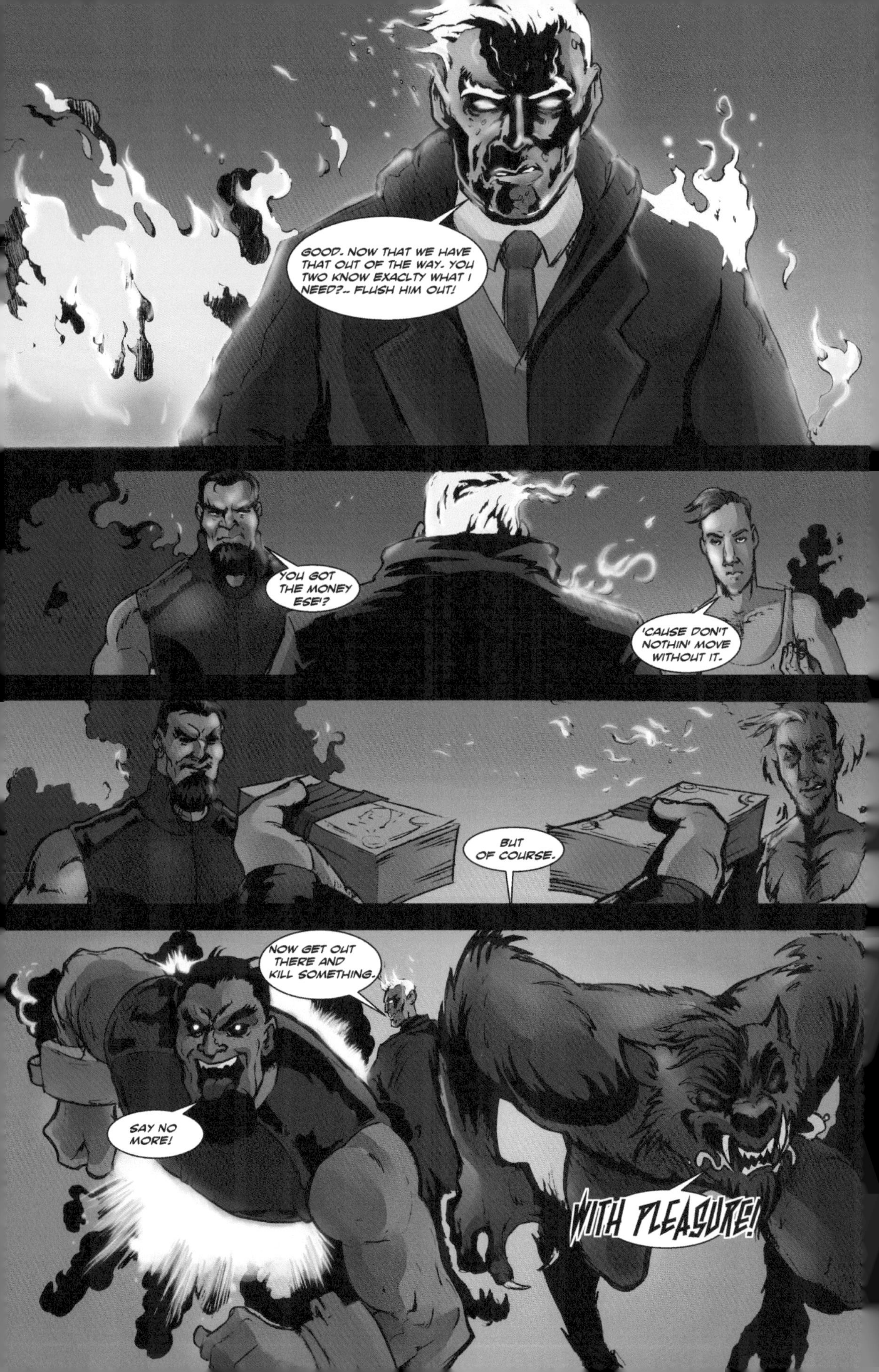
GOOD. NOW THAT WE HAVE THAT OUT OF THE WAY. YOU TWO KNOW EXACLTY WHAT I NEED?.. FLUSH HIM OUT!
YOU GOT THE MONEY ESE!?
'CAUSE DON'T NOTHIN' MOVE WITHOUT IT.
BUT OF COURSE.
NOW GET OUT THERE AND KILL SOMETHING.
SAY NO MORE!
WITH PLEASURE!

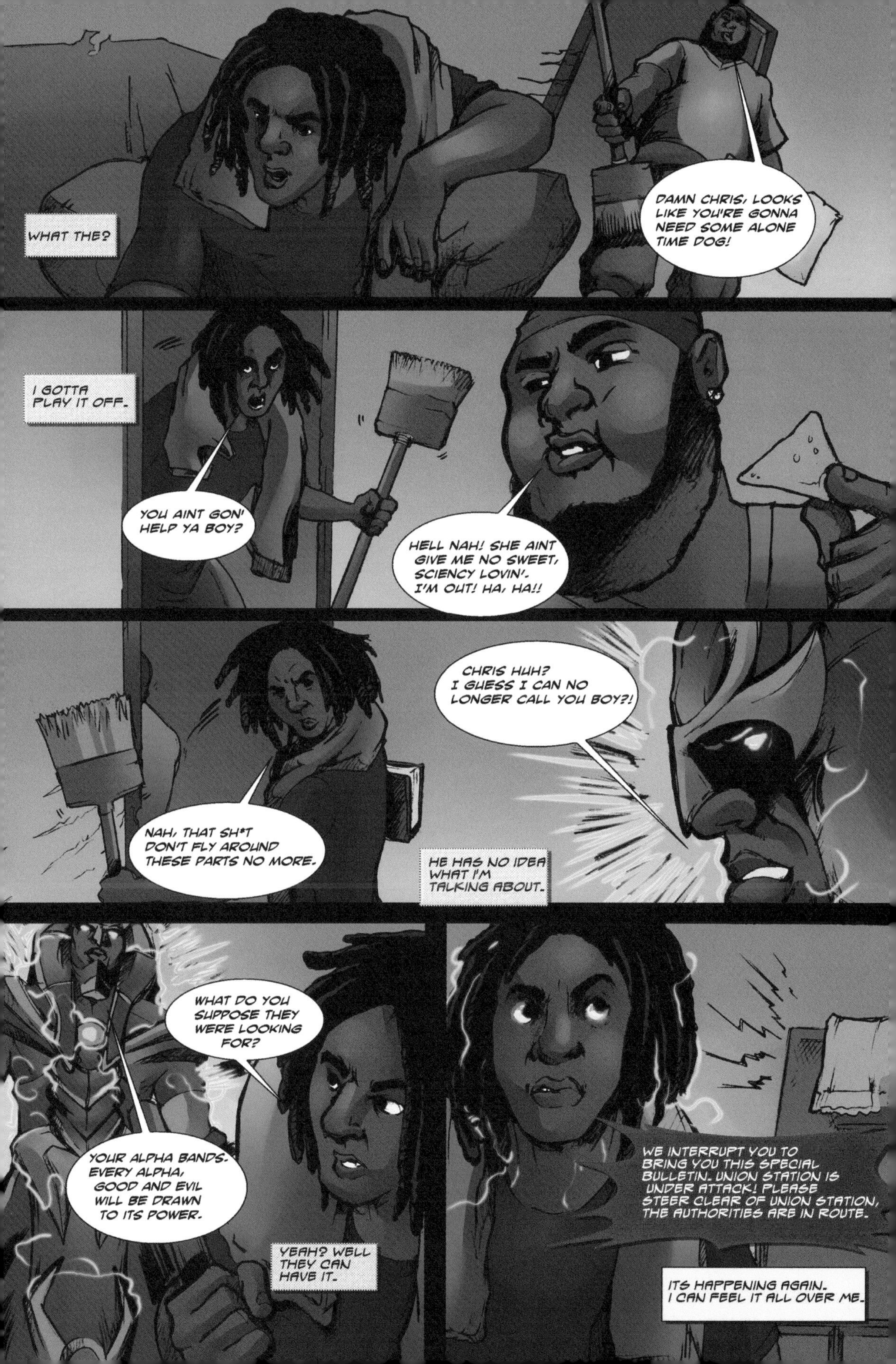
WHAT THE?
DAMN CHRIS, LOOKS LIKE YOU'RE GONNA NEED SOME ALONE TIME DOG!
I GOTTA PLAY IT OFF.
YOU AINT GON' HELP YA BOY?
HELL NAH! SHE AINT GIVE ME NO SWEET, SCIENCY LOVIN'. I'M OUT! HA, HA!!
CHRIS HUH? I GUESS I CAN NO LONGER CALL YOU BOY?!
NAH, THAT SH*T DON'T FLY AROUND THESE PARTS NO MORE.
HE HAS NO IDEA WHAT I'M TALKING ABOUT.
WHAT DO YOU SUPPOSE THEY WERE LOOKING FOR?
YOUR ALPHA BANDS. EVERY ALPHA, GOOD AND EVIL WILL BE DRAWN TO ITS POWER.
YEAH? WELL THEY CAN HAVE IT.
WE INTERRUPT YOU TO BRING YOU THIS SPECIAL BULLETIN. UNION STATION IS UNDER ATTACK! PLEASE STEER CLEAR OF UNION STATION, THE AUTHORITIES ARE IN ROUTE.
ITS HAPPENING AGAIN. I CAN FEEL IT ALL OVER ME.

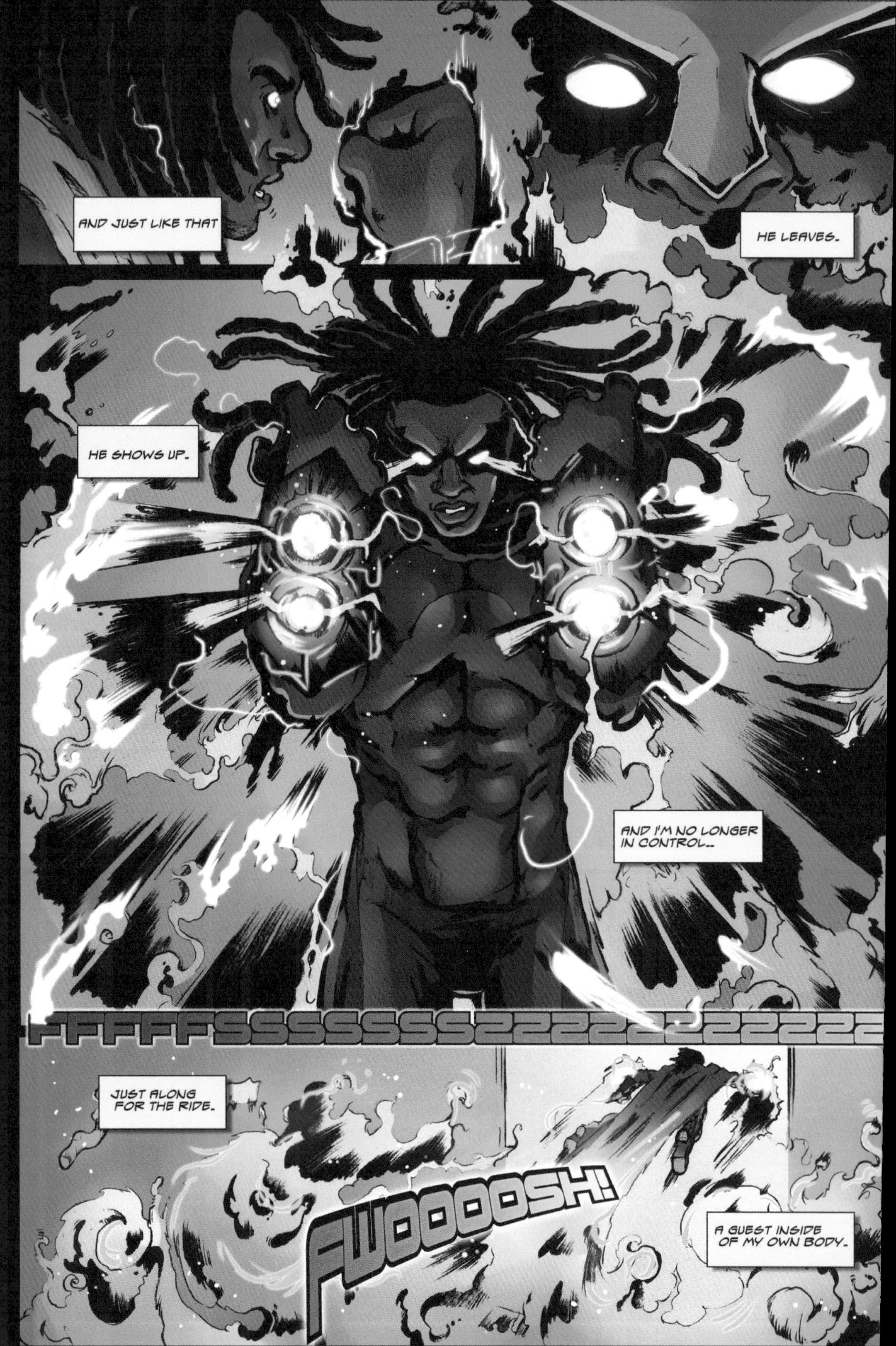
AND JUST LIKE THAT
HE LEAVES.
HE SHOWS UP.
AND I'M NO LONGER IN CONTROL..
FFFFFSSSSSSSSSZZZZZZZZZZZZZZ
JUST ALONG FOR THE RIDE.
FWOOOOSH!
A GUEST INSIDE OF MY OWN BODY.

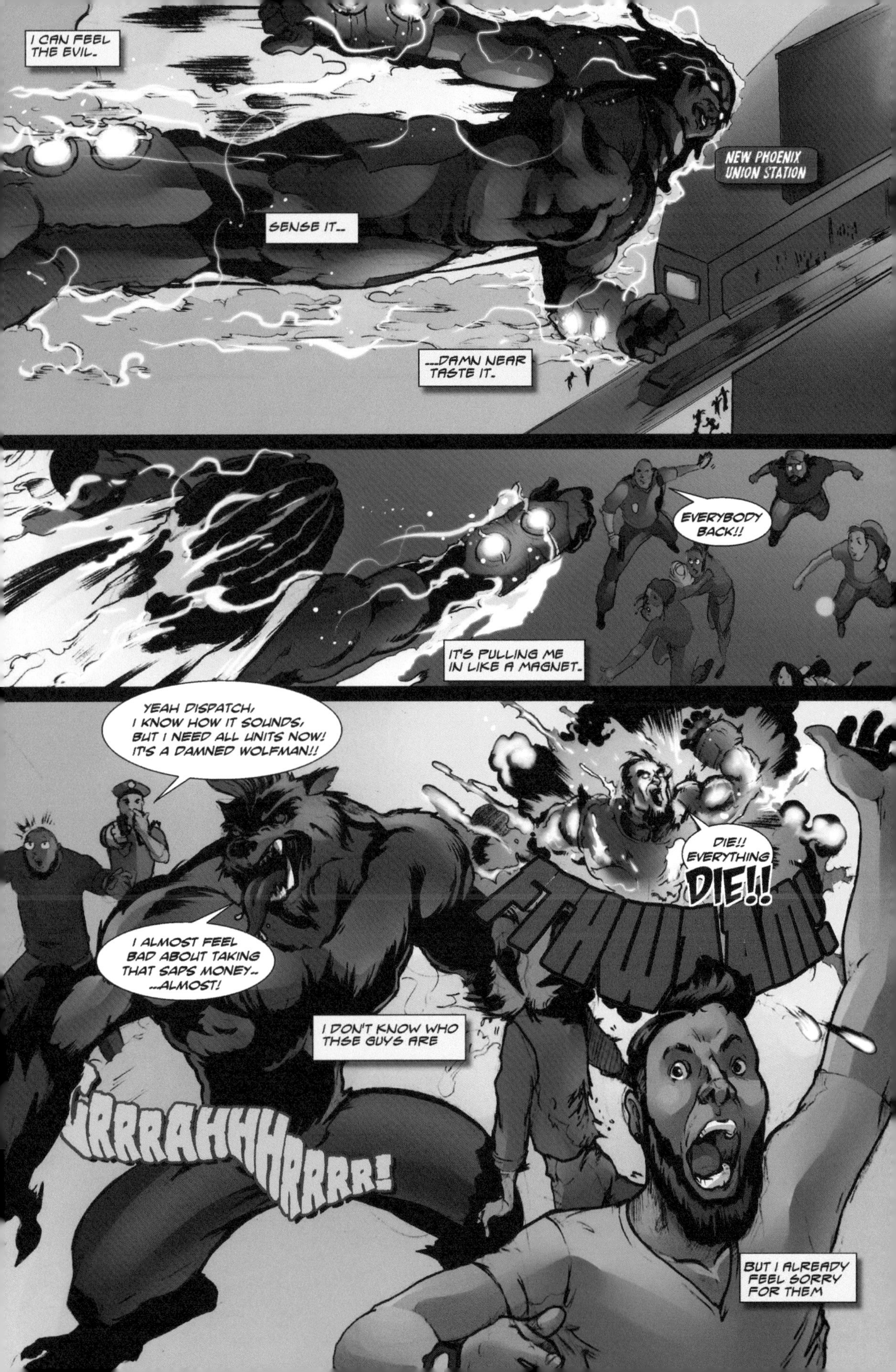
I CAN FEEL THE EVIL...
NEW PHOENIX UNION STATION
SENSE IT...
...DAMN NEAR TASTE IT...
EVERYBODY BACK!!
IT'S PULLING ME IN LIKE A MAGNET...
YEAH DISPATCH, I KNOW HOW IT SOUNDS, BUT I NEED ALL UNITS NOW! IT'S A DAMNED WOLFMAN!!
DIE!! EVERYTHING DIE!!
THWUMM!
I ALMOST FEEL BAD ABOUT TAKING THAT SAPS MONEY... ...ALMOST!
I DON'T KNOW WHO THSE GUYS ARE
RRRAHHHRRRR!
BUT I ALREADY FEEL SORRY FOR THEM

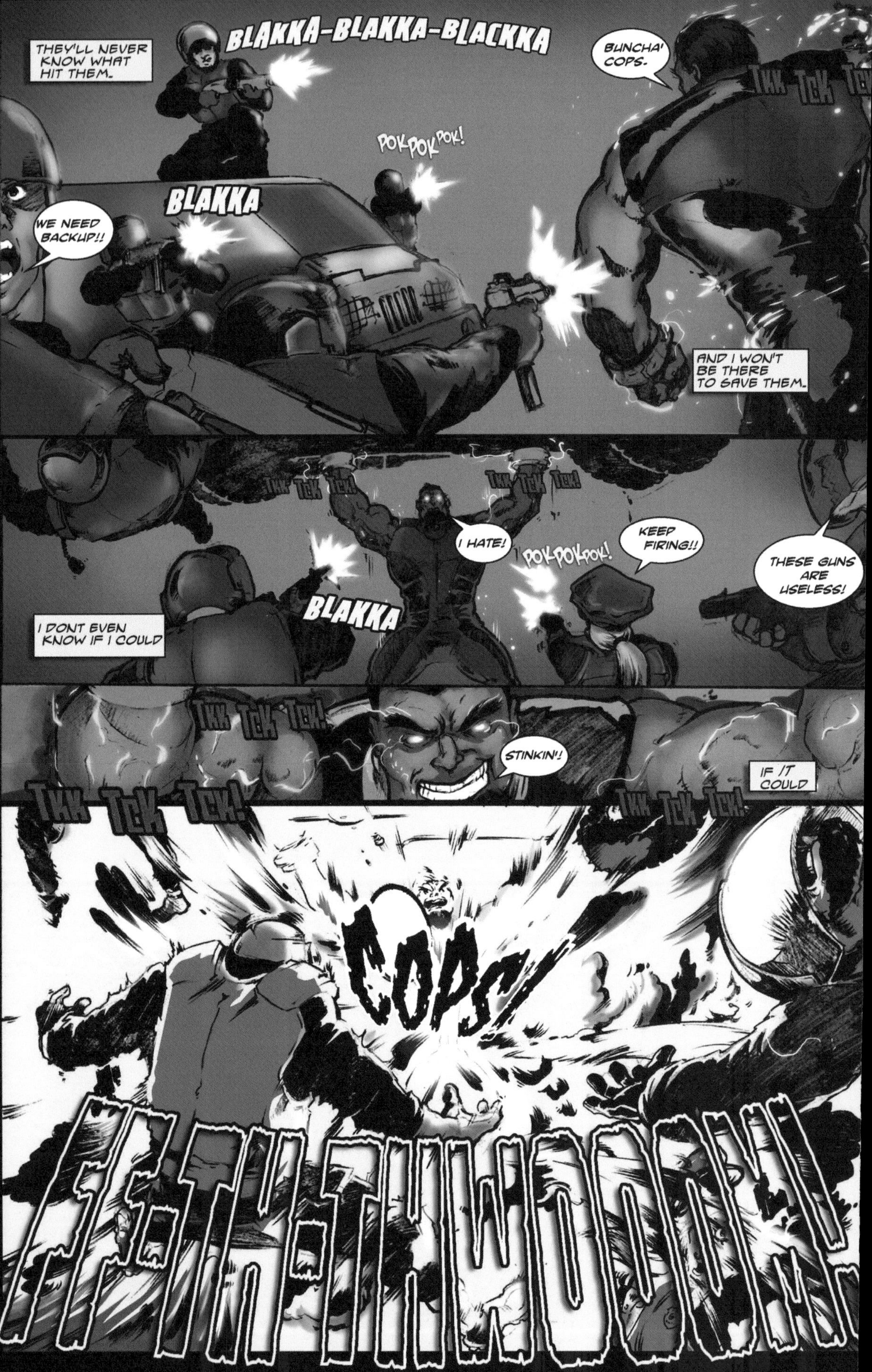
THEY'LL NEVER KNOW WHAT HIT THEM.
BLAKKA-BLAKKA-BLACKKA
BUNCHA' COPS.
TKK TCK TCK
POKPOKPOK!
BLAKKA
WE NEED BACKUP!!
AND I WON'T BE THERE TO SAVE THEM.
TKK TCK TCK!
TKK TCK TCK!
I HATE!
KEEP FIRING!!
POKPOKPOK!
THESE GUNS ARE USELESS!
BLAKKA
I DONT EVEN KNOW IF I COULD
TKK TCK TCK!
STINKIN'!
IF IT COULD
TKK TCK TCK!
TKK TCK TCK!
COPS!

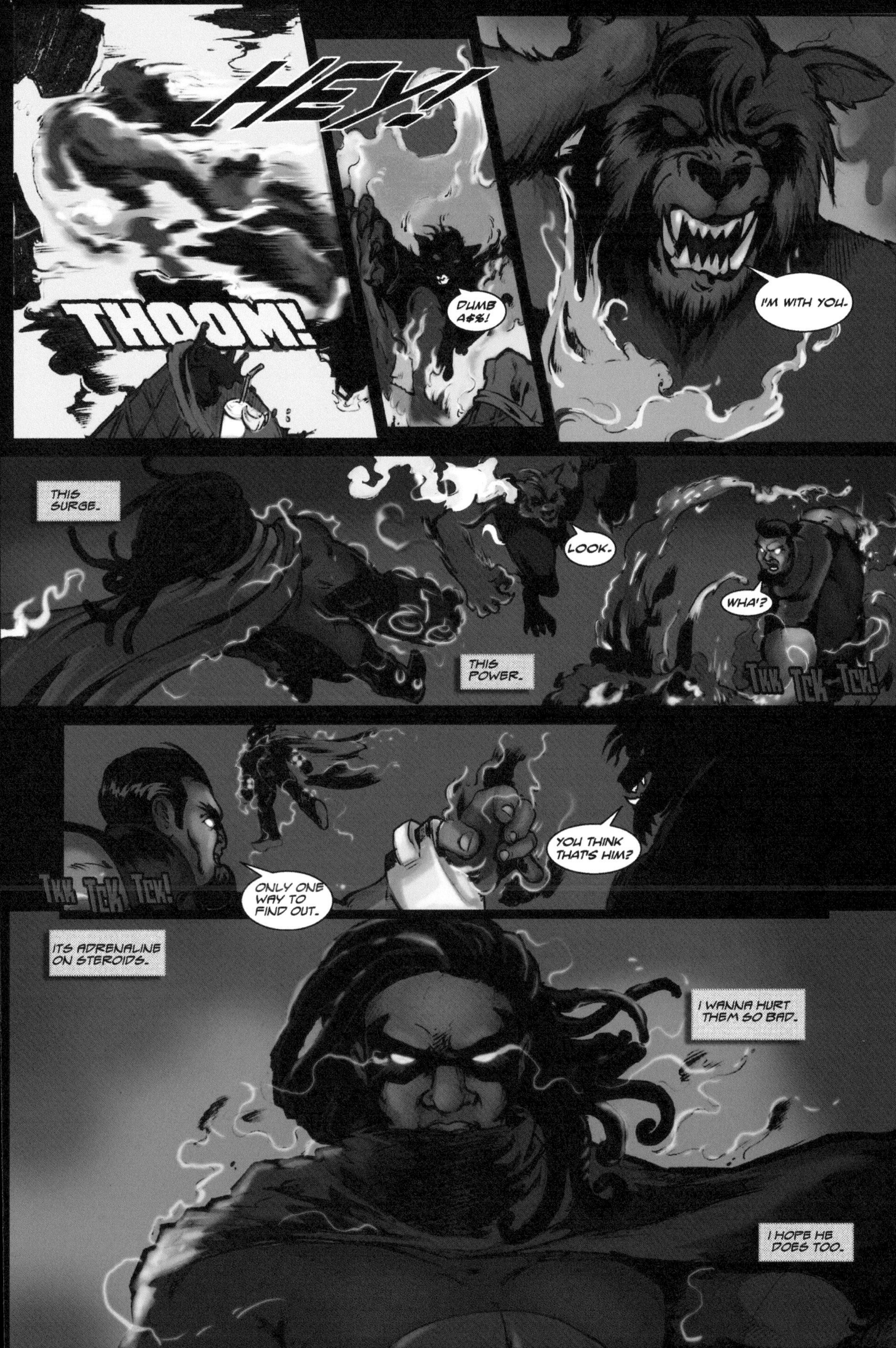
HEY!
THOOM!
DUMB A$%!
I'M WITH YOU.
THIS SURGE.
LOOK.
WHA'?
THIS POWER.
TKK TCK-TCK!
TKK TCK TCK!
YOU THINK THAT'S HIM?
ONLY ONE WAY TO FIND OUT.
ITS ADRENALINE ON STEROIDS.
I WANNA HURT THEM SO BAD.
I HOPE HE DOES TOO.

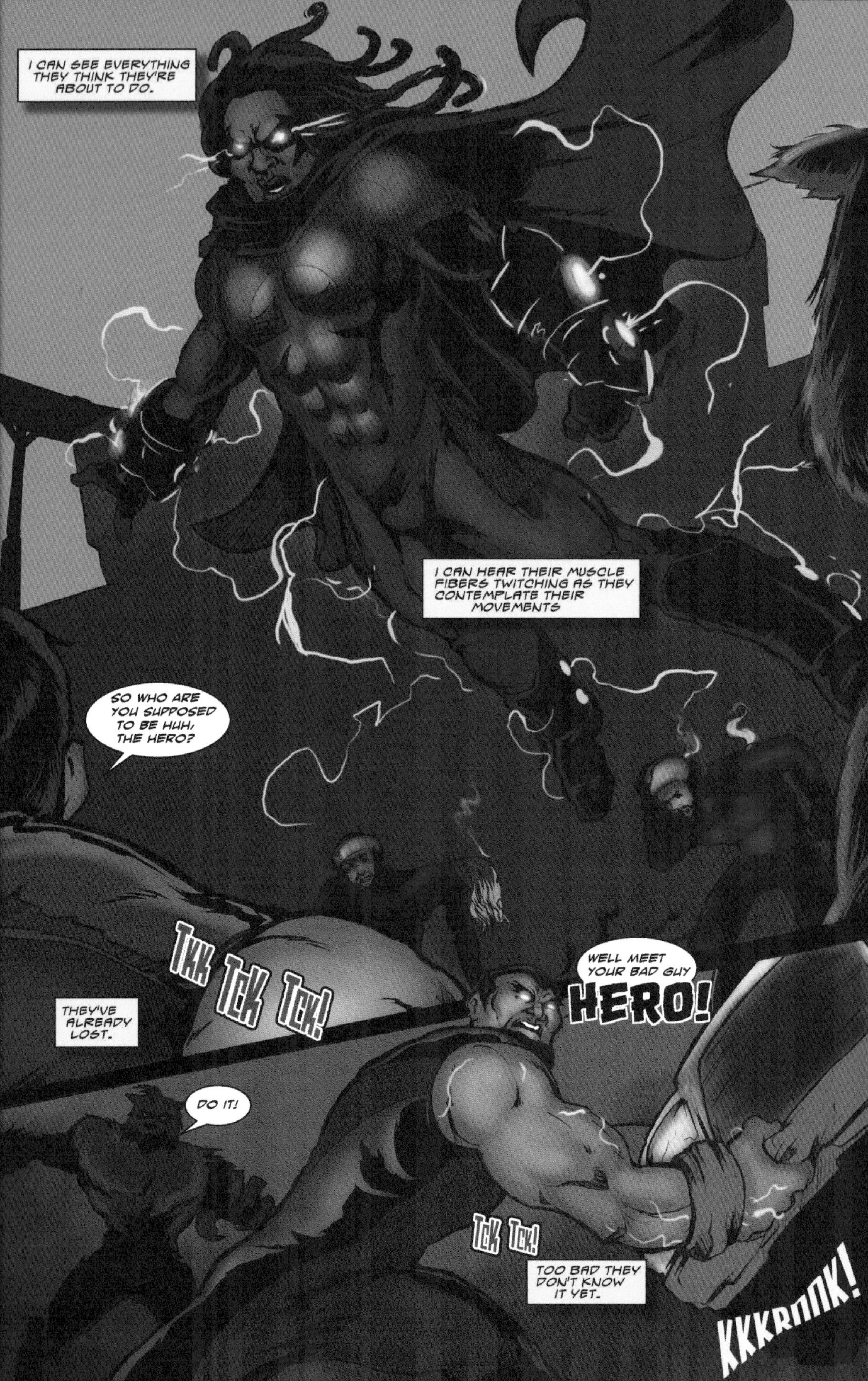
I CAN SEE EVERYTHING THEY THINK THEY'RE ABOUT TO DO.
I CAN HEAR THEIR MUSCLE FIBERS TWITCHING AS THEY CONTEMPLATE THEIR MOVEMENTS
SO WHO ARE YOU SUPPOSED TO BE HUH, THE HERO?
TKK TCK TCK!
THEY'VE ALREADY LOST.
WELL MEET YOUR BAD GUY
HERO!
DO IT!
TCK TCK!
TOO BAD THEY DON'T KNOW IT YET.
KKKRNNK!

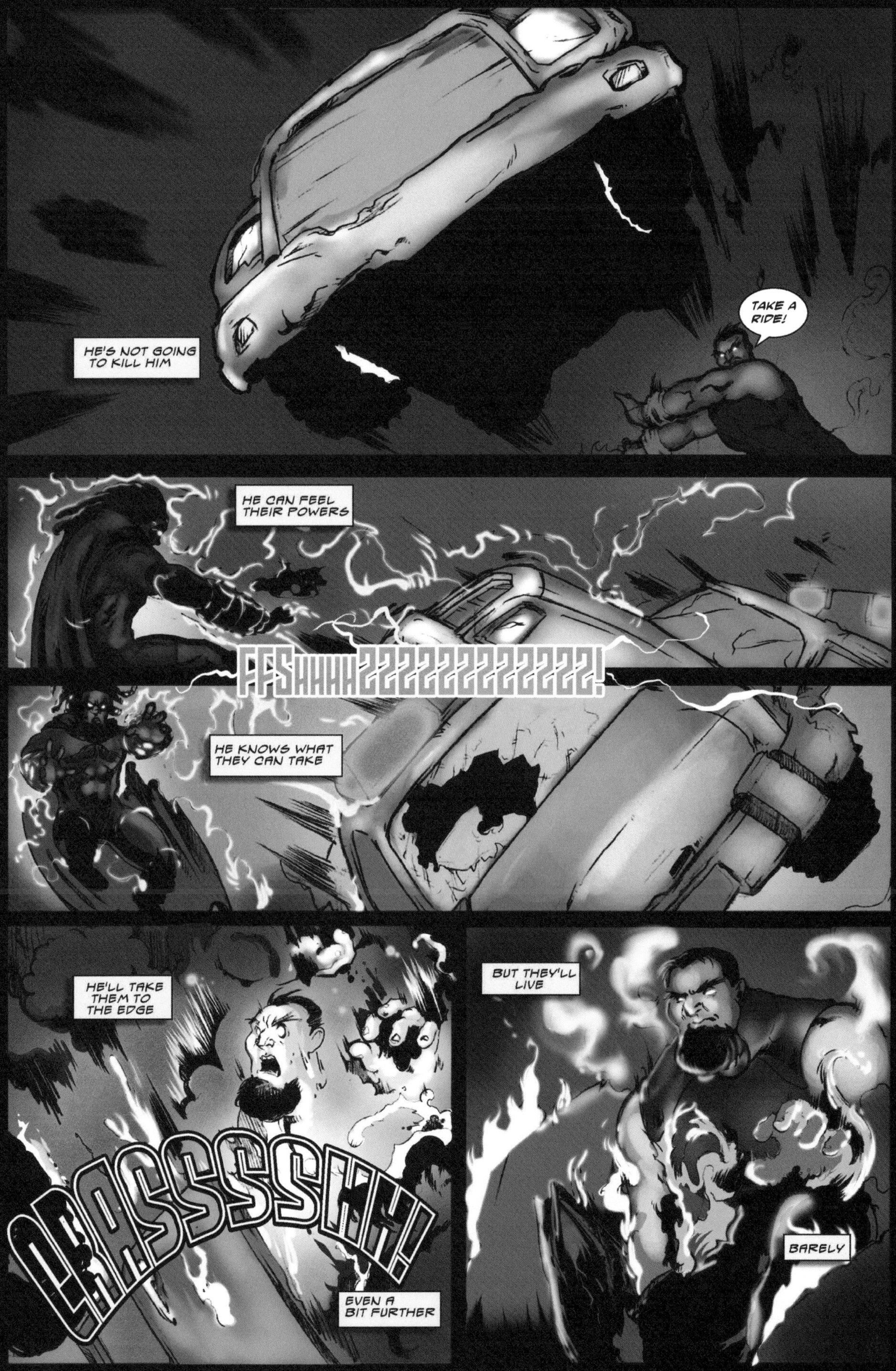
HE'S NOT GOING TO KILL HIM
TAKE A RIDE!
HE CAN FEEL THEIR POWERS
FFSHHHHZZZZZZZZZZZZ!
HE KNOWS WHAT THEY CAN TAKE
HE'LL TAKE THEM TO THE EDGE
CRASSSSSHH!
EVEN A BIT FURTHER
BUT THEY'LL LIVE
BARELY

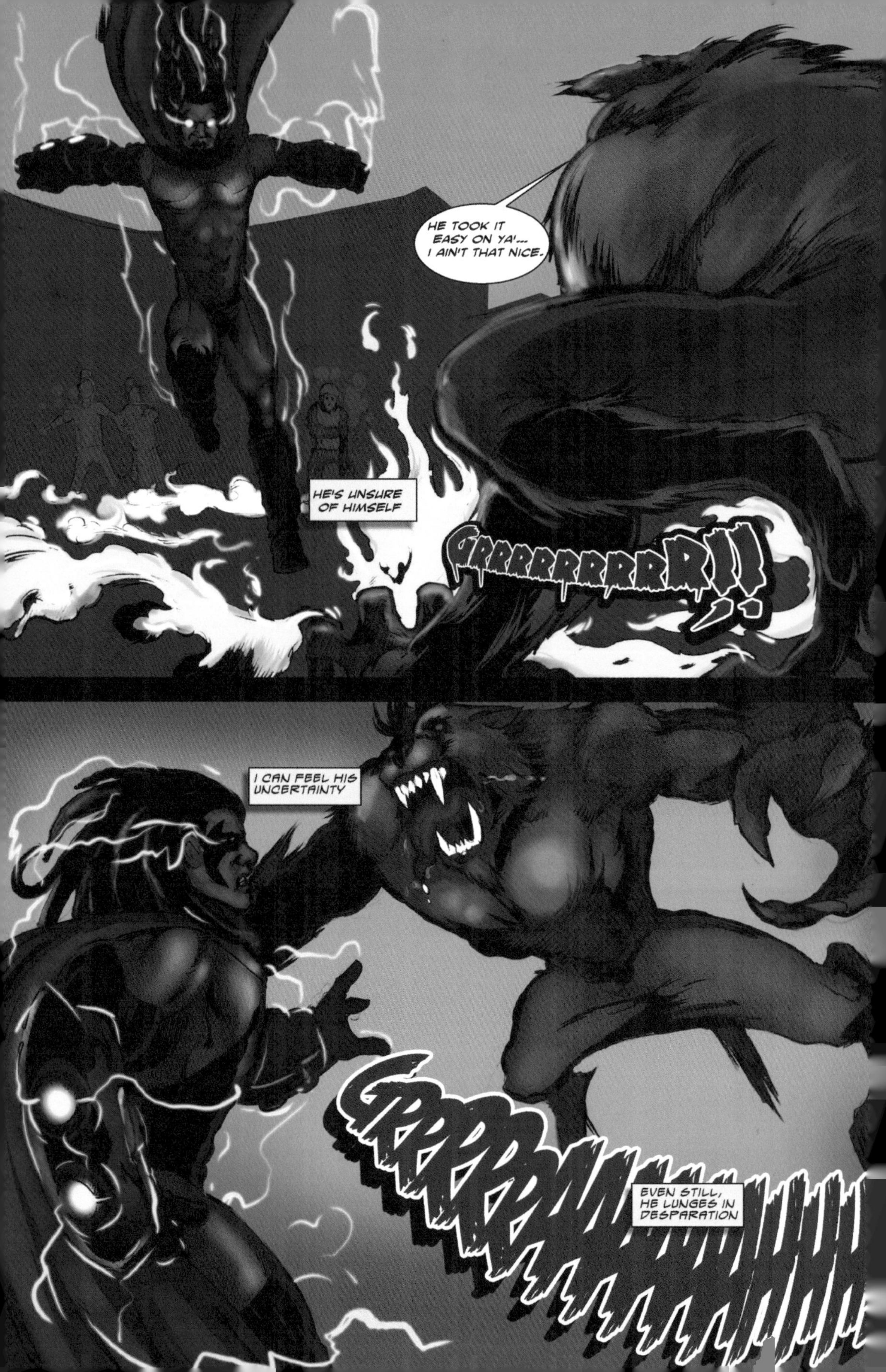
HE TOOK IT
EASY ON YA'...
I AIN'T THAT NICE.
HE'S UNSURE
OF HIMSELF
GRRRRRRRRRRR!!
I CAN FEEL HIS
UNCERTAINTY
EVEN STILL,
HE LUNGES IN
DESPARATION

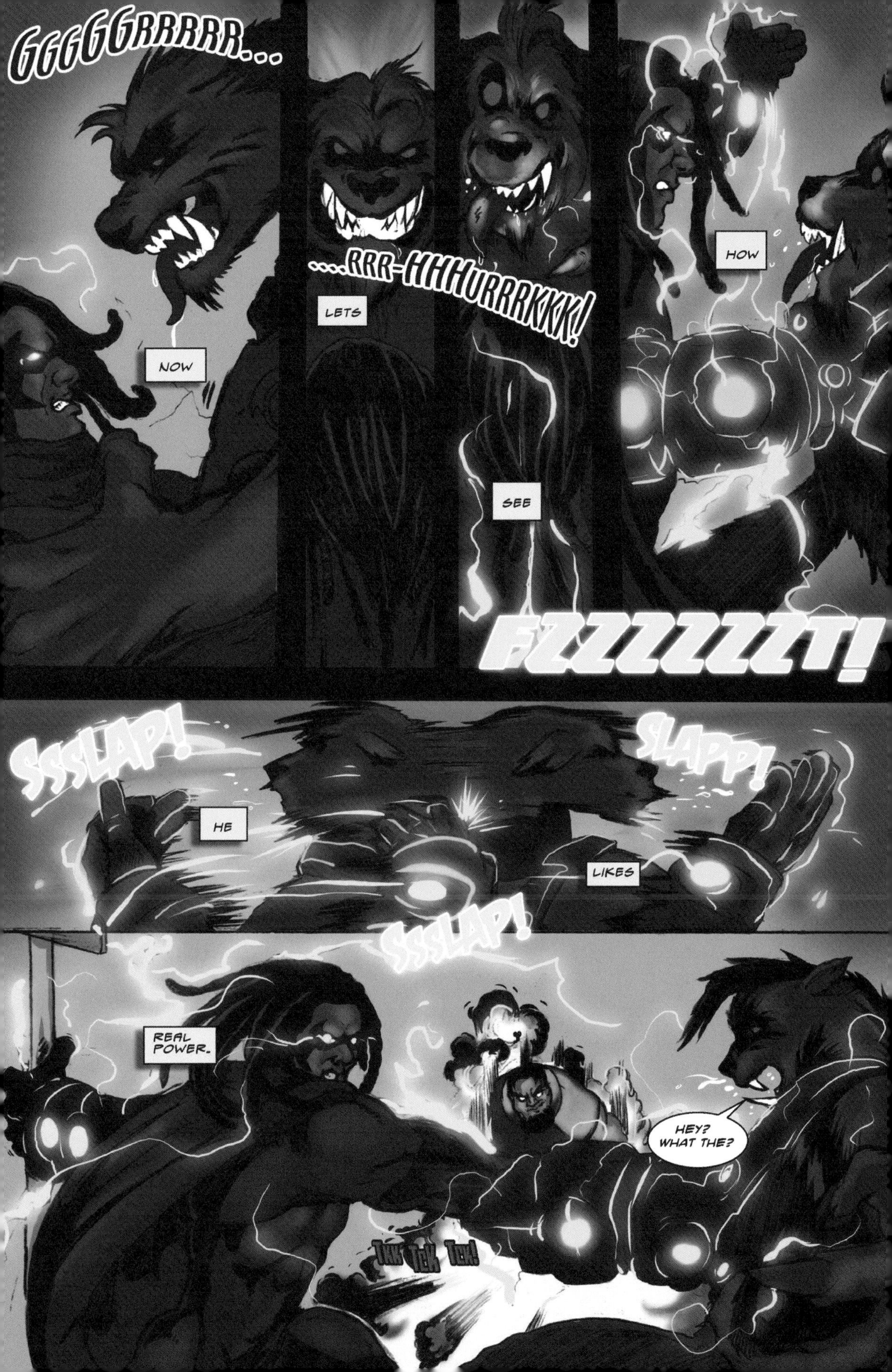
GGGGGRRRRRR...
NOW
....RRR-HHHURRRKKK!
LETS
SEE
HOW
FZZZZZZZT!
SSSLAP!
HE
SLAPP!
LIKES
SSSLAP!
REAL POWER.
HEY? WHAT THE?
TKK TEK TKK!

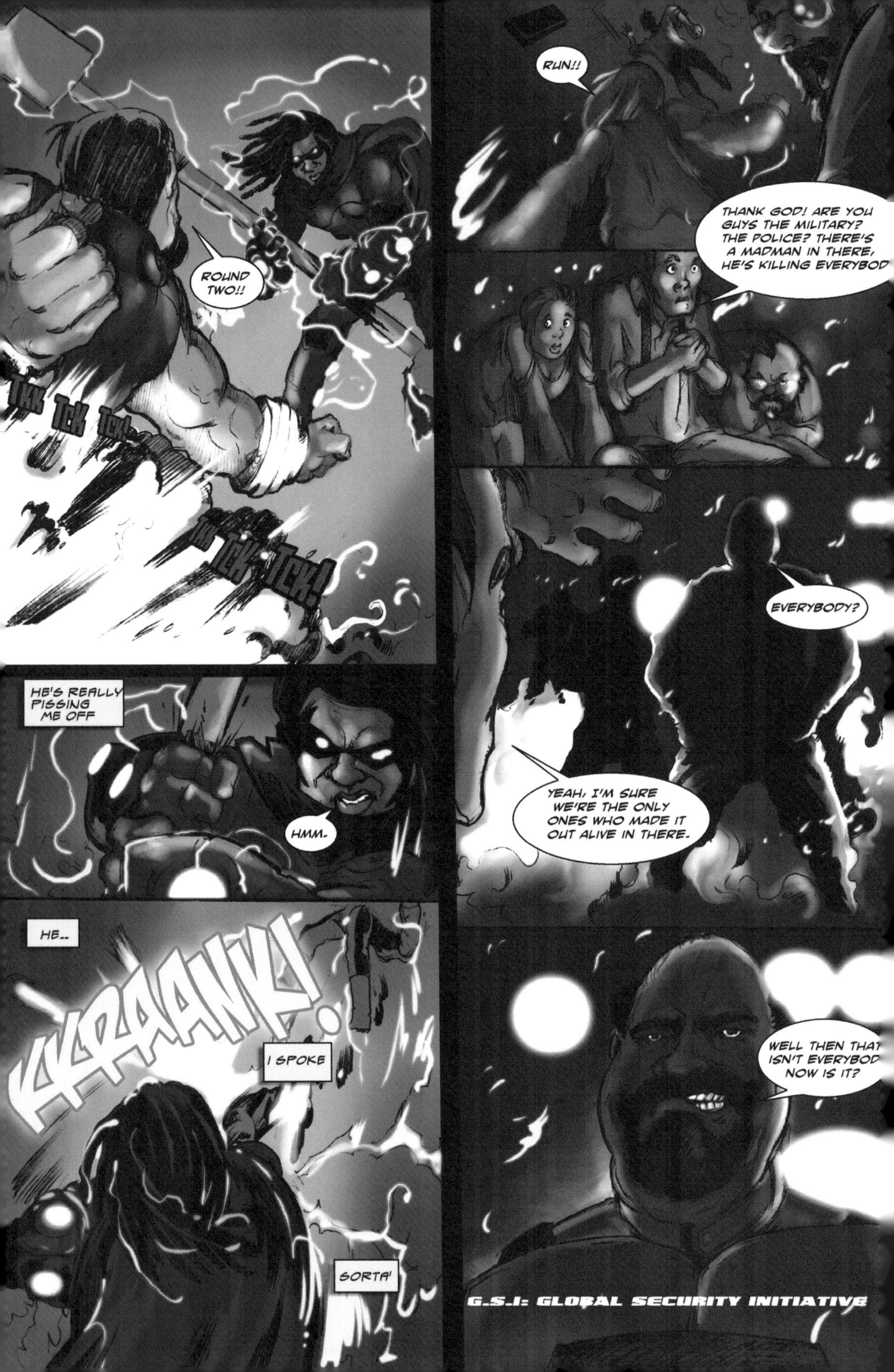
ROUND TWO!!
TKK TCK TCK!
TKK TCK TCK!
HE'S REALLY PISSING ME OFF
HMM.
HE..
KKRAANK!
I SPOKE
SORTA'
RUN!!
THANK GOD! ARE YOU GUYS THE MILITARY? THE POLICE? THERE'S A MADMAN IN THERE, HE'S KILLING EVERYBOD
EVERYBODY?
YEAH, I'M SURE WE'RE THE ONLY ONES WHO MADE IT OUT ALIVE IN THERE.
WELL THEN THAT ISN'T EVERYBOD NOW IS IT?
G.S.I: GLOBAL SECURITY INITIATIVE

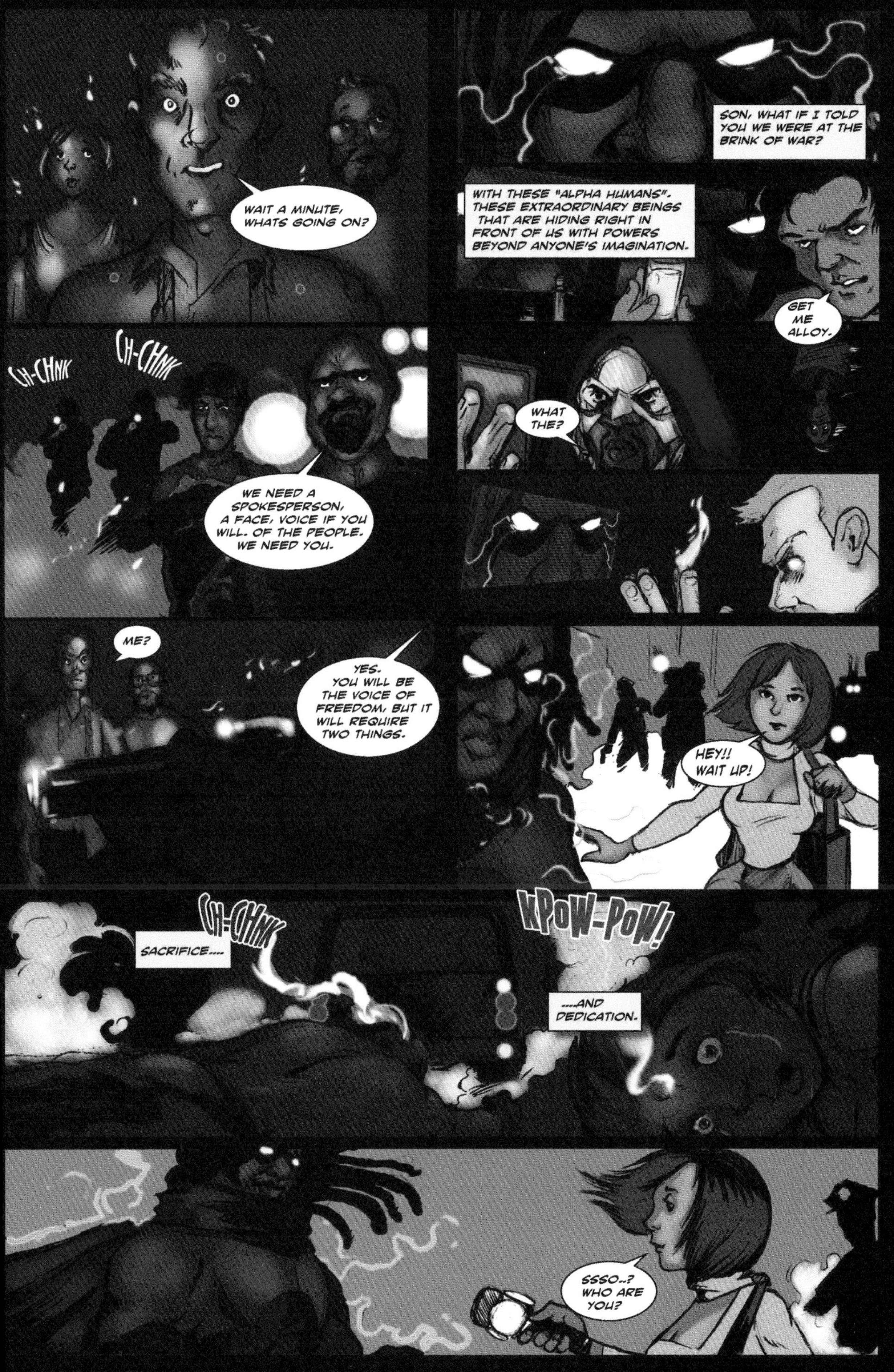
WAIT A MINUTE, WHATS GOING ON?
SON, WHAT IF I TOLD YOU WE WERE AT THE BRINK OF WAR?
WITH THESE "ALPHA HUMANS". THESE EXTRAORDINARY BEINGS THAT ARE HIDING RIGHT IN FRONT OF US WITH POWERS BEYOND ANYONE'S IMAGINATION.
GET ME ALLOY.
CH-CHNK
CH-CHNK
WE NEED A SPOKESPERSON, A FACE, VOICE IF YOU WILL. OF THE PEOPLE. WE NEED YOU.
WHAT THE?
ME?
YES. YOU WILL BE THE VOICE OF FREEDOM, BUT IT WILL REQUIRE TWO THINGS.
HEY!! WAIT UP!
SACRIFICE....
CH-CHNK
KPOW-POW!
....AND DEDICATION.
SSSO..? WHO ARE YOU?

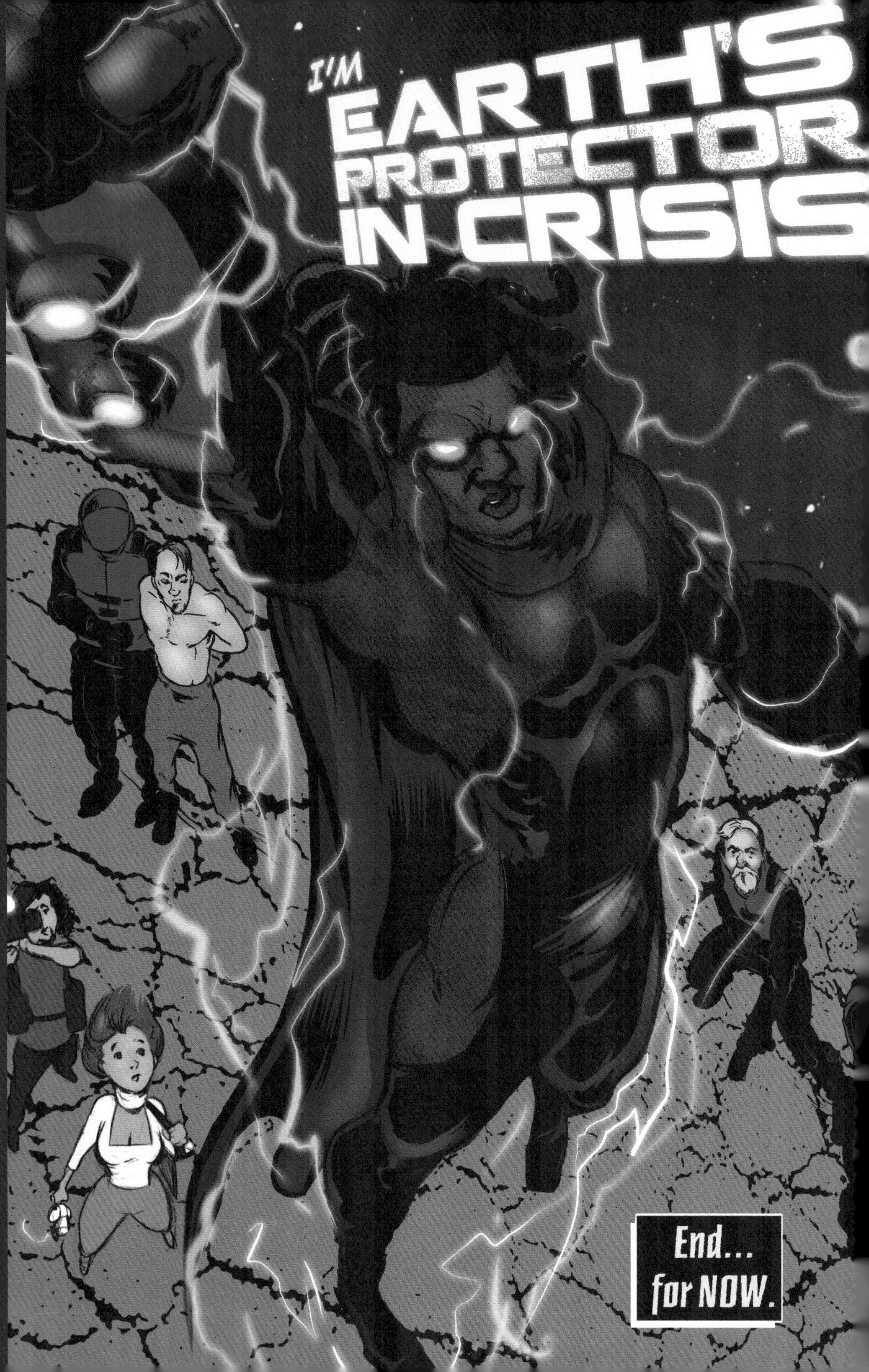
I'M
EARTH'S
PROTECTOR
IN CRISIS
End...
for NOW.

NUMBER 13

ROBERT LOVE WITH DAVID WALKER

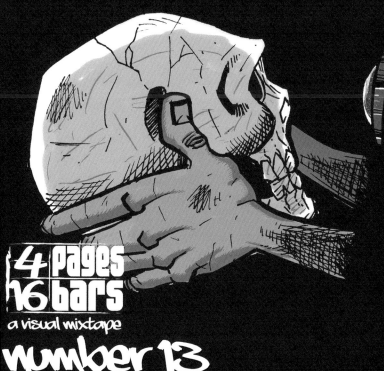

4 pages 16 bars
a visual mixtape
number 13

David F. Walker is an award-winning comic book writer, author, filmmaker, journalist, and educator. His work in comic books includes **Shaft** (Dynamite Entertainment**),** winner of the **2015 Glyph Award** for Story of the Year, **Power Man and Iron Fist**, **Nighthawk**, **Fury**, **Secret Wars: Battleworld** (Marvel Comics), **Cyborg** (DC Comics) and **The Army of Dr. Moreau** (IDW/ Monkeybrain Comics). In 2015, he wrote the novel **Shaft's Revenge**, the first new novel starring private detective John Shaft in nearly 40 years. He is also the creator of the critically-acclaimed YA series **The Adventures of Darius Logan**.

Robert Love exploded onto the comic book scene in the beginning of the new millenium **Gettosake Entertainment**, an independent comic company co-founded with his brother **Jeremy Love**. Featuring such diverse concepts as **Venus Kincaid** and the underground hit **Chocolate Thunder**, Love quickly garnered the attention of larger companies, particualrly Dark Horse Comics. Love's work include Image Comics' **Alpha Girl**, Dark Horse's **Fierce** (with Jeremy Love) and others.

4 Pages 16 Bars is extremely blessed to have these talented brothers join the cypher with the post-apocalyptic **Number 13**.

website: thedavidwalkersite.com
website: robertlovesart.blogspot.com

NUMBER 13
CHAPTER ONE

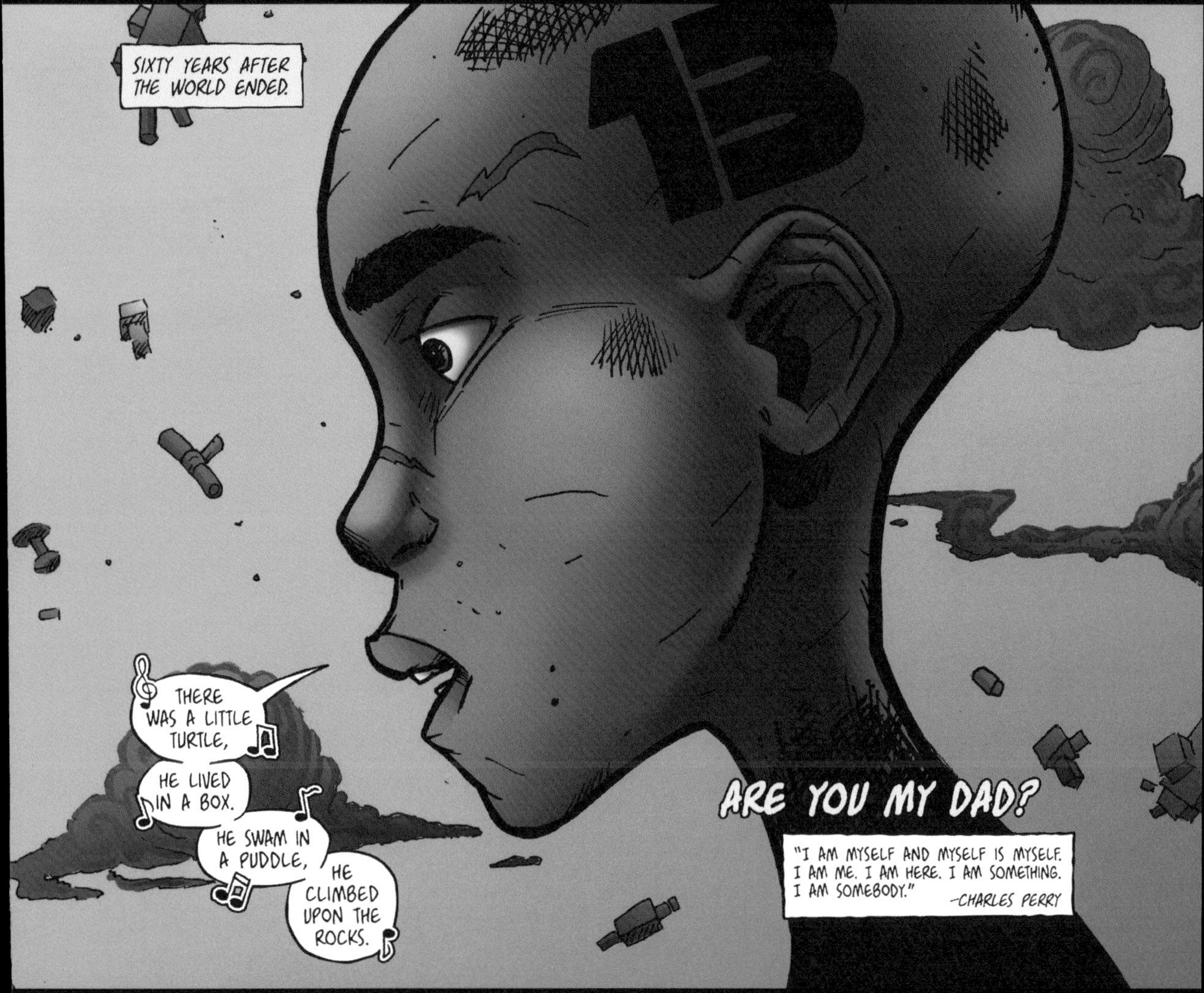
SIXTY YEARS AFTER THE WORLD ENDED.
THERE WAS A LITTLE TURTLE,
HE LIVED IN A BOX.
HE SWAM IN A PUDDLE,
HE CLIMBED UPON THE ROCKS.
ARE YOU MY DAD?
"I AM MYSELF AND MYSELF IS MYSELF. I AM ME. I AM HERE. I AM SOMETHING. I AM SOMEBODY." —CHARLES PERRY

ROBERT LOVE
CO-WRITER AND ARTIST

DAVID WALKER
CO-WRITER

MICHELLE DAVIES
COLORS

DIEGO SIMONE
COLORS

TOMAS MAUER
LETTERS

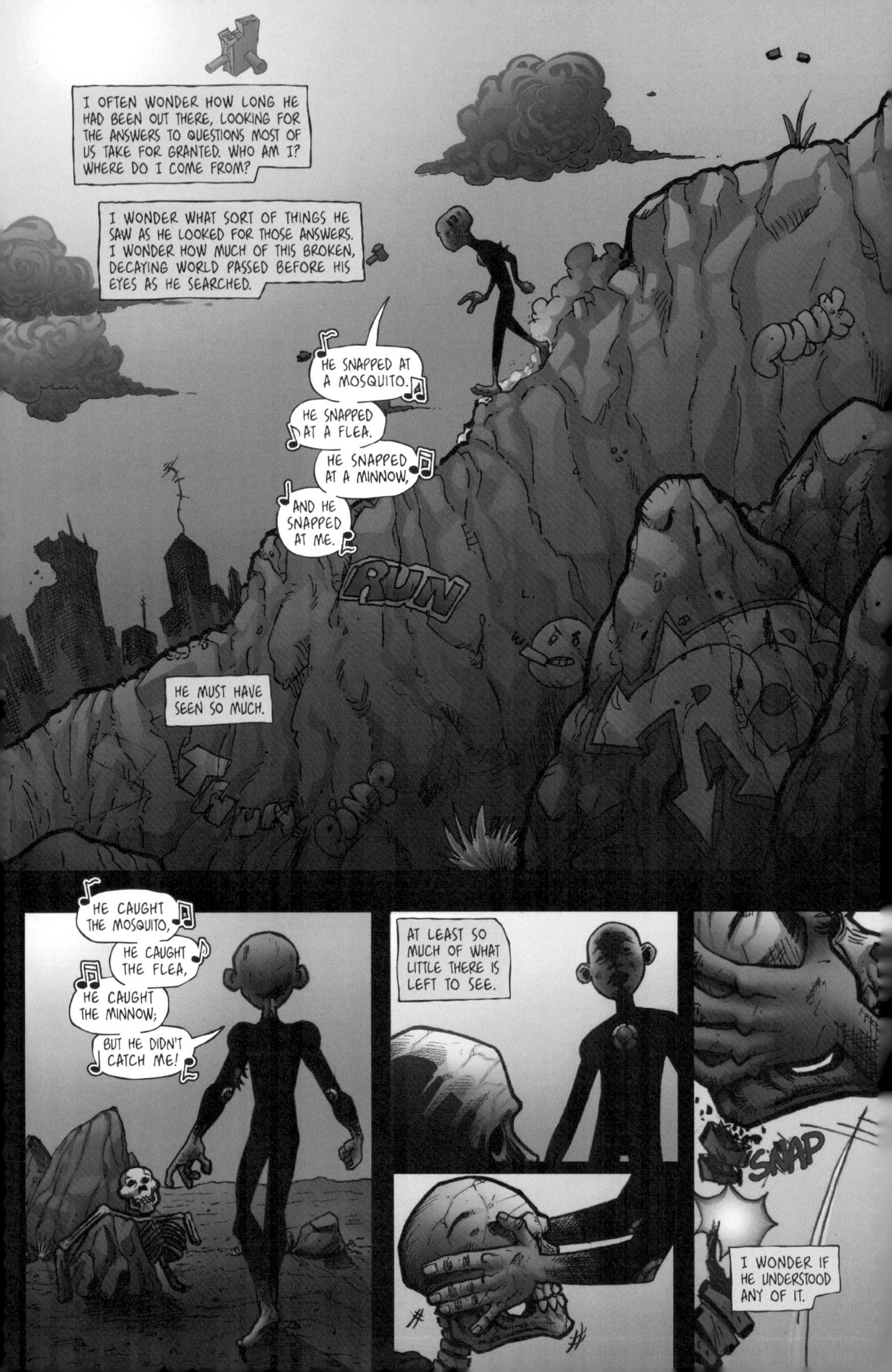
I OFTEN WONDER HOW LONG HE HAD BEEN OUT THERE, LOOKING FOR THE ANSWERS TO QUESTIONS MOST OF US TAKE FOR GRANTED. WHO AM I? WHERE DO I COME FROM?
I WONDER WHAT SORT OF THINGS HE SAW AS HE LOOKED FOR THOSE ANSWERS. I WONDER HOW MUCH OF THIS BROKEN, DECAYING WORLD PASSED BEFORE HIS EYES AS HE SEARCHED.
HE SNAPPED AT A MOSQUITO.
HE SNAPPED AT A FLEA.
HE SNAPPED AT A MINNOW,
AND HE SNAPPED AT ME.
RUN
HE MUST HAVE SEEN SO MUCH.
HE CAUGHT THE MOSQUITO,
HE CAUGHT THE FLEA,
HE CAUGHT THE MINNOW;
BUT HE DIDN'T CATCH ME!
AT LEAST SO MUCH OF WHAT LITTLE THERE IS LEFT TO SEE.
SNAP
I WONDER IF HE UNDERSTOOD ANY OF IT.

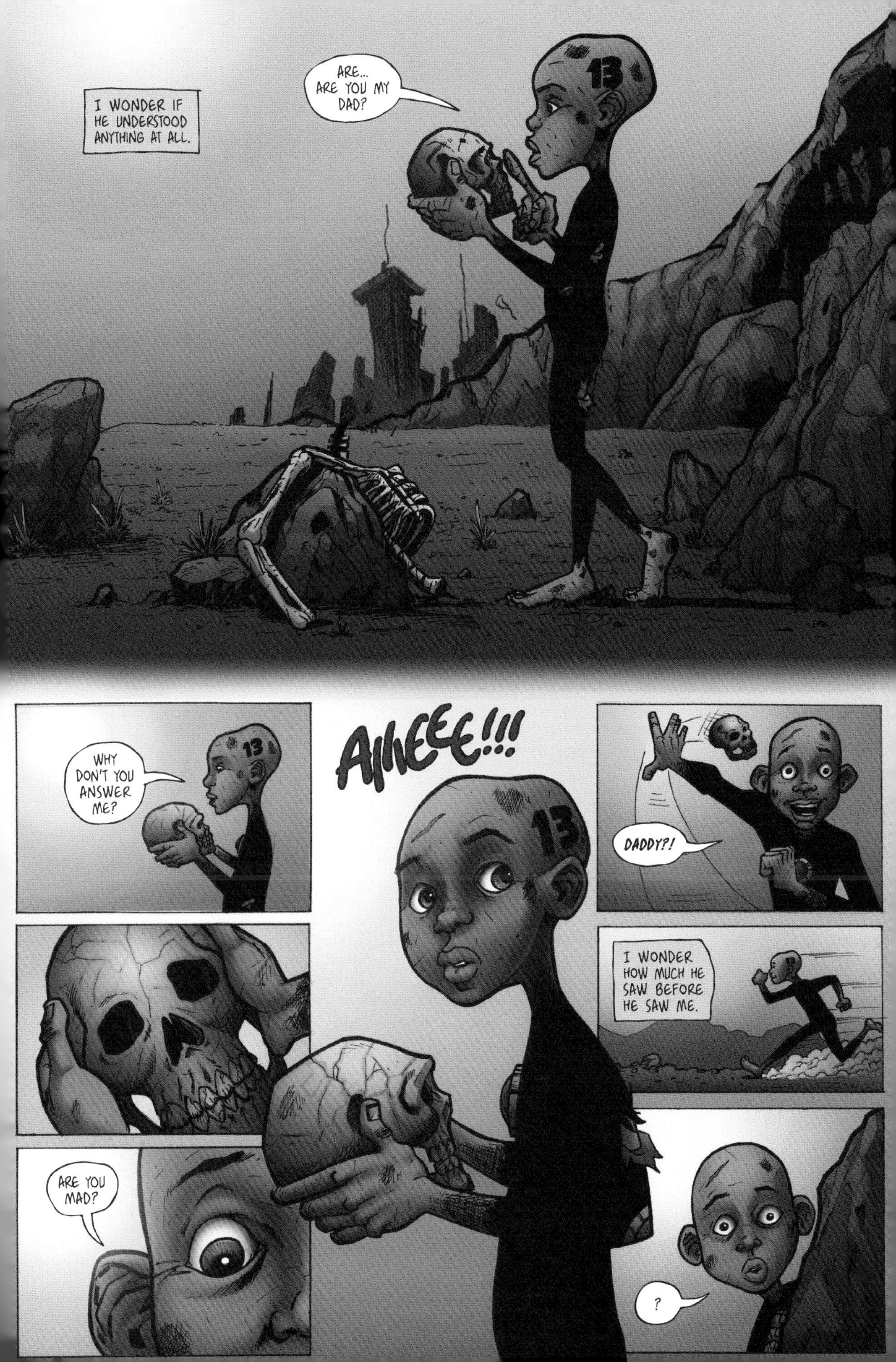
I WONDER IF HE UNDERSTOOD ANYTHING AT ALL.
ARE... ARE YOU MY DAD?
WHY DON'T YOU ANSWER ME?
AIIEEE!!!
DADDY?!
I WONDER HOW MUCH HE SAW BEFORE HE SAW ME.
ARE YOU MAD?
?

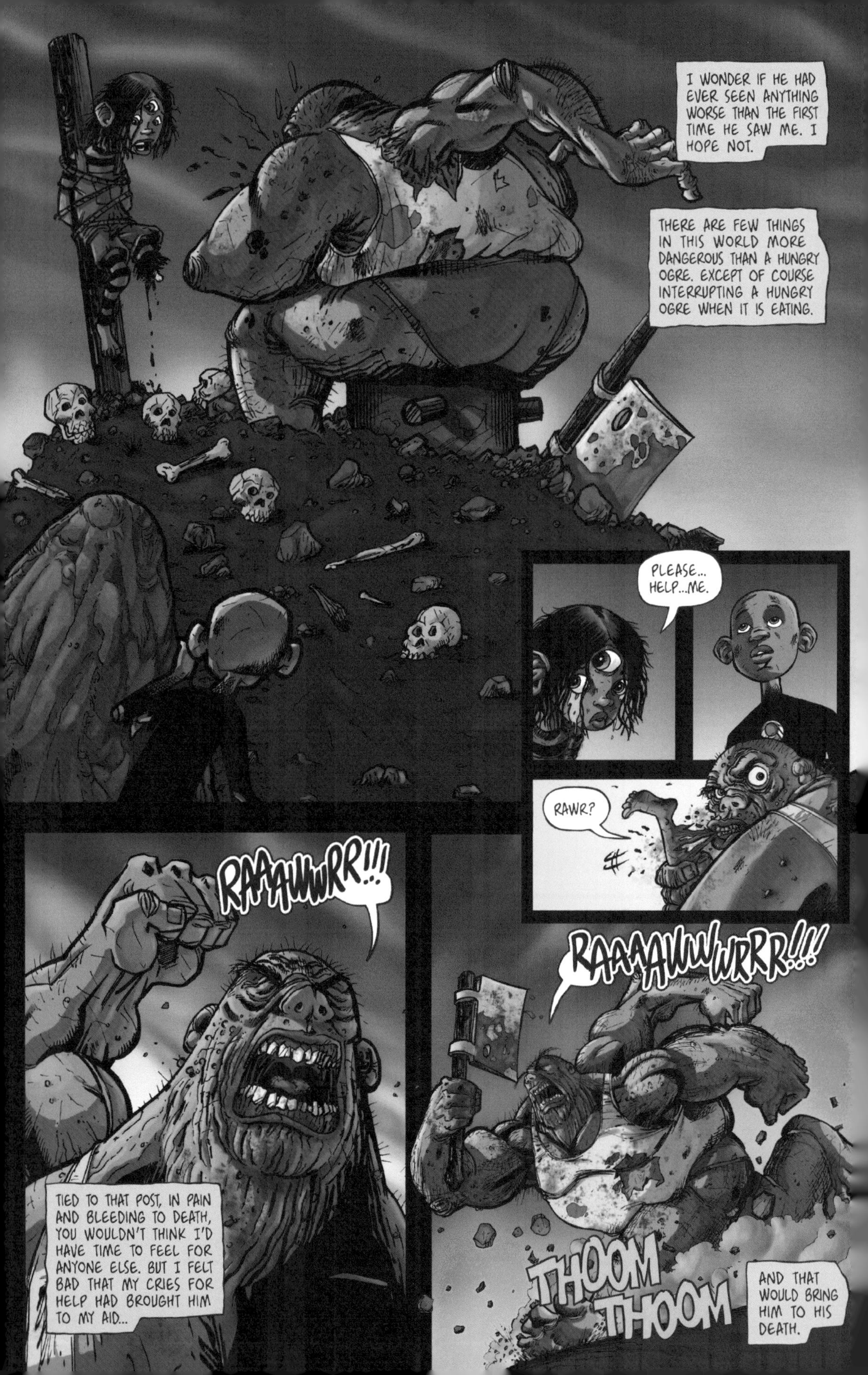
I WONDER IF HE HAD EVER SEEN ANYTHING WORSE THAN THE FIRST TIME HE SAW ME. I HOPE NOT.
THERE ARE FEW THINGS IN THIS WORLD MORE DANGEROUS THAN A HUNGRY OGRE. EXCEPT OF COURSE INTERRUPTING A HUNGRY OGRE WHEN IT IS EATING.
PLEASE... HELP...ME.
RAWR?
RAAAUWWRR!!!
TIED TO THAT POST, IN PAIN AND BLEEDING TO DEATH, YOU WOULDN'T THINK I'D HAVE TIME TO FEEL FOR ANYONE ELSE. BUT I FELT BAD THAT MY CRIES FOR HELP HAD BROUGHT HIM TO MY AID...
RAAAAUWWRRR!!!
THOOM
THOOM
AND THAT WOULD BRING HIM TO HIS DEATH.

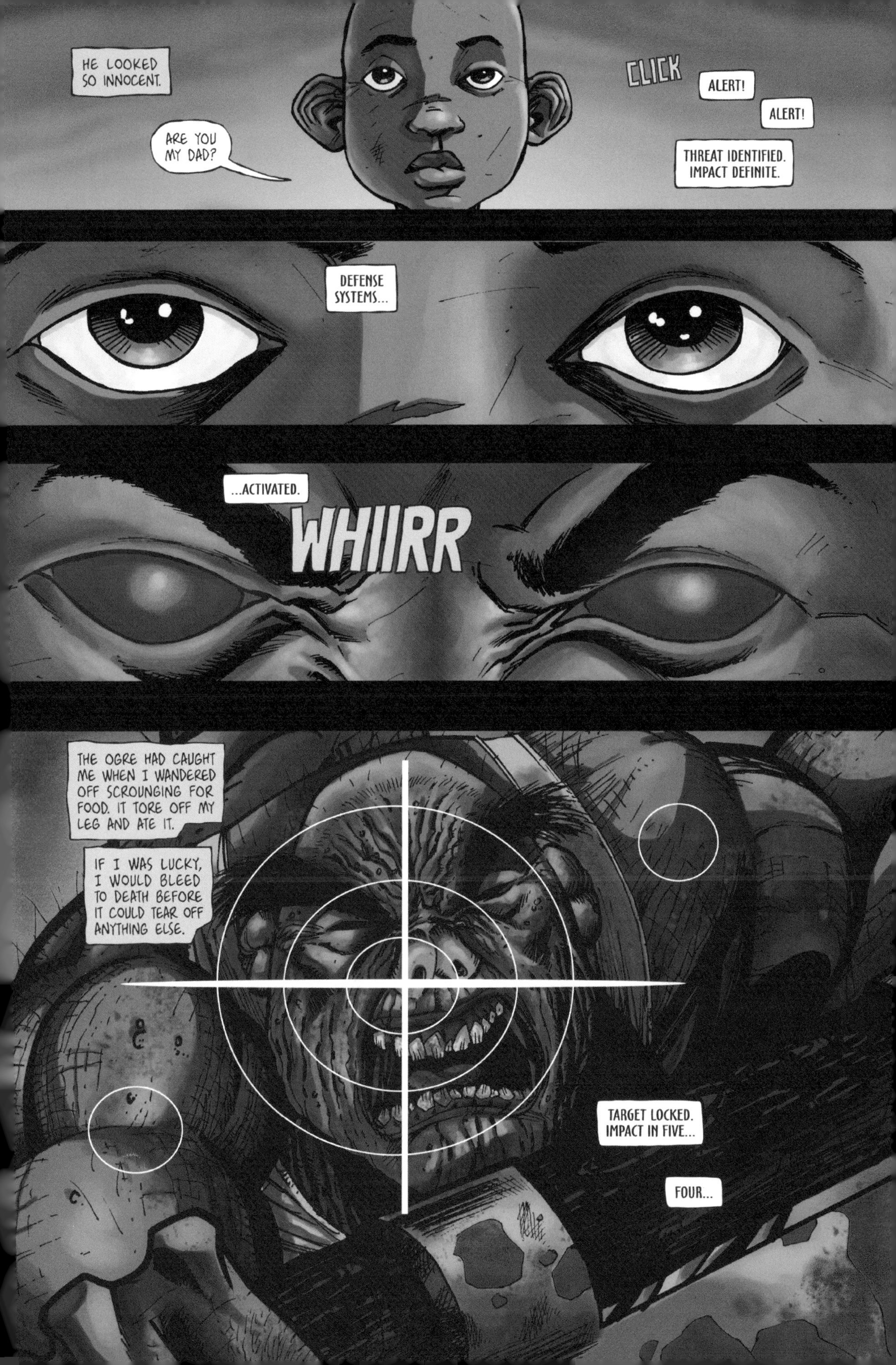
HE LOOKED SO INNOCENT.
ARE YOU MY DAD?
CLICK
ALERT!
ALERT!
THREAT IDENTIFIED. IMPACT DEFINITE.
DEFENSE SYSTEMS...
...ACTIVATED.
WHIIRR
THE OGRE HAD CAUGHT ME WHEN I WANDERED OFF SCROUNGING FOR FOOD. IT TORE OFF MY LEG AND ATE IT.
IF I WAS LUCKY, I WOULD BLEED TO DEATH BEFORE IT COULD TEAR OFF ANYTHING ELSE.
TARGET LOCKED. IMPACT IN FIVE...
FOUR...

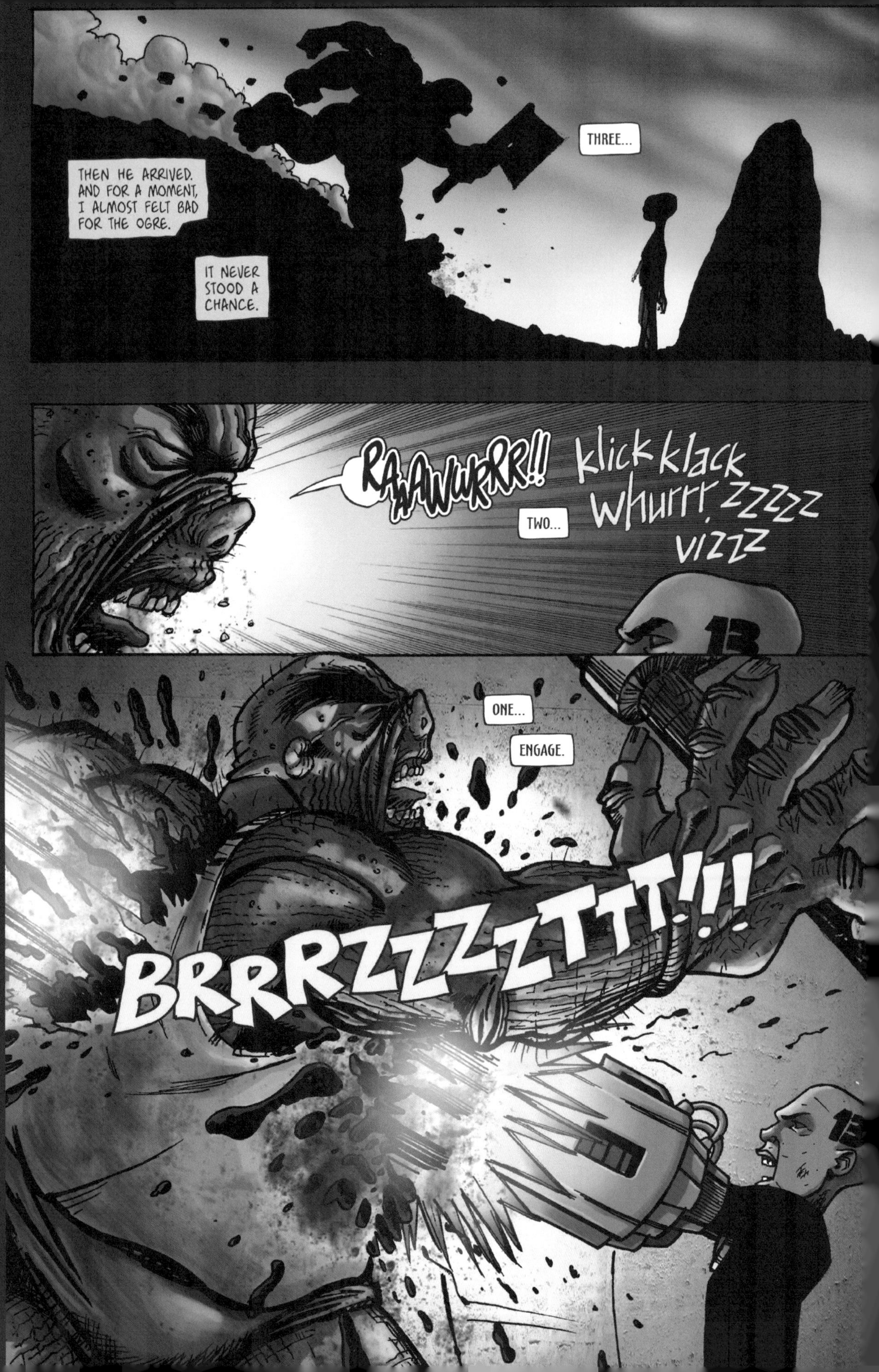
THEN HE ARRIVED. AND FOR A MOMENT, I ALMOST FELT BAD FOR THE OGRE.
IT NEVER STOOD A CHANCE.
THREE...
RAAAWURRR!!
klick klack whurrr zzzzz vizzz
TWO...
ONE...
ENGAGE.
BRRRZZZZTTT!!!

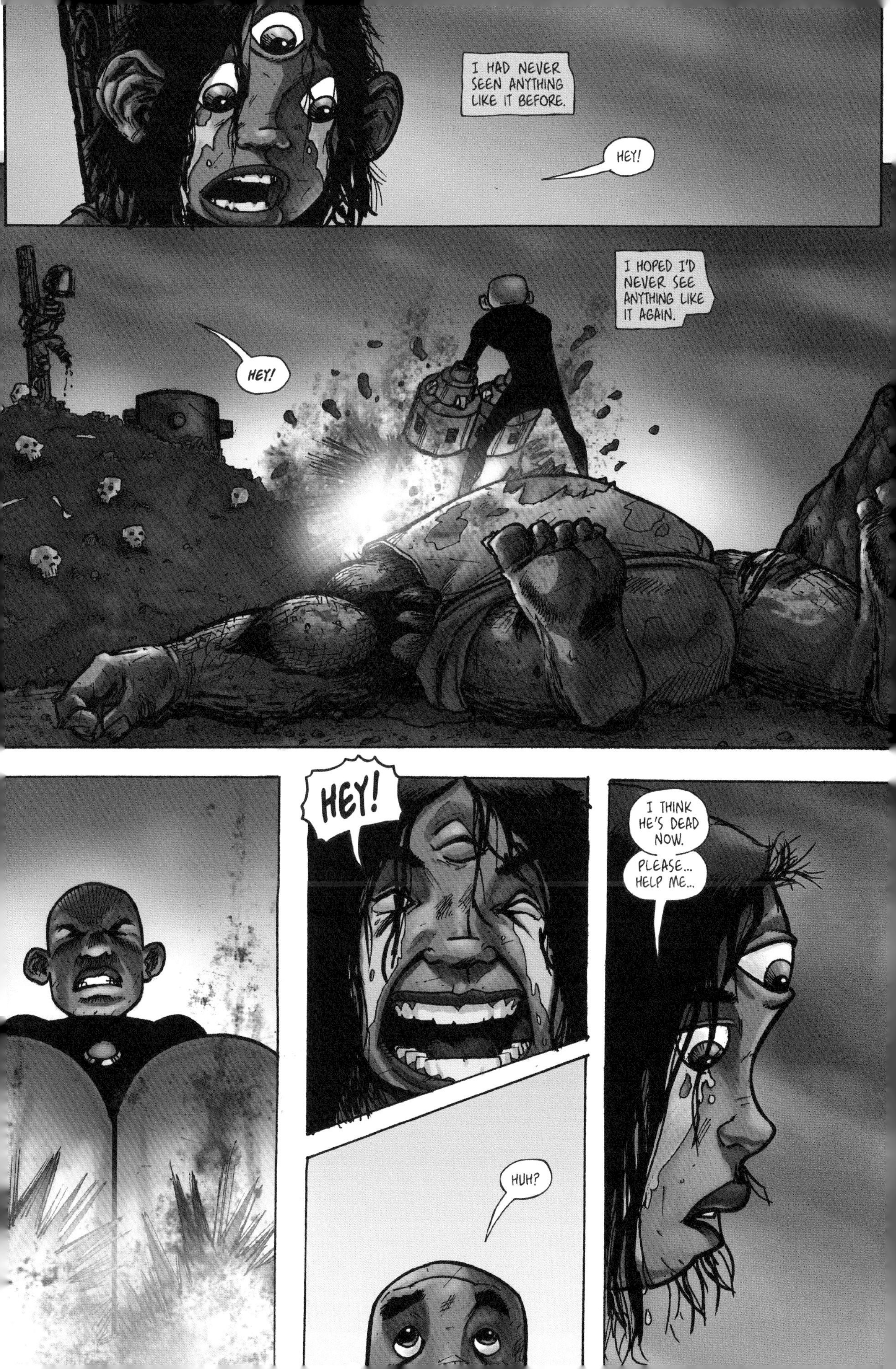
I HAD NEVER SEEN ANYTHING LIKE IT BEFORE.
HEY!
I HOPED I'D NEVER SEE ANYTHING LIKE IT AGAIN.
HEY!
HEY!
HUH?
I THINK HE'S DEAD NOW.
PLEASE... HELP ME...

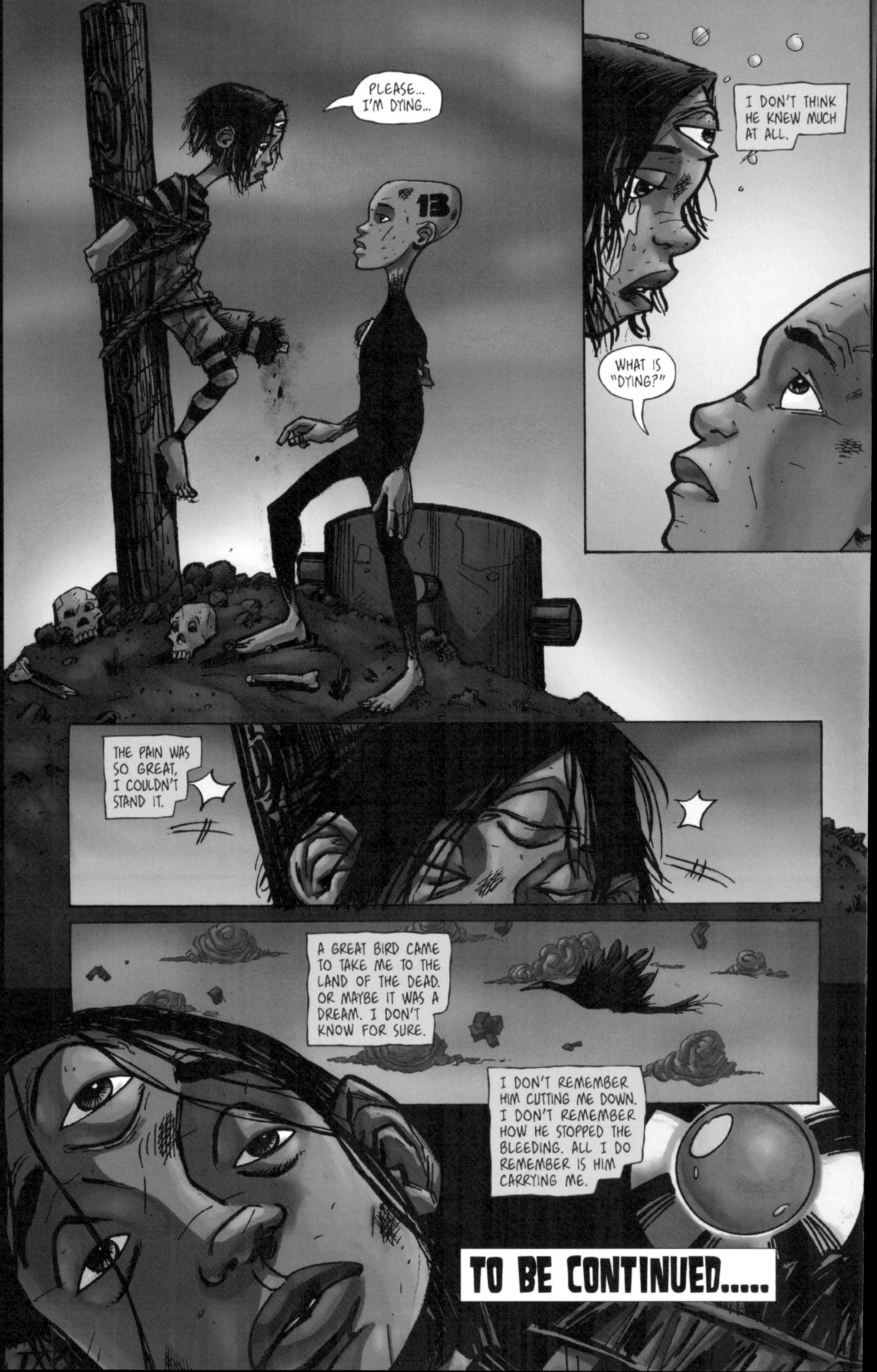
PLEASE... I'M DYING...
I DON'T THINK HE KNEW MUCH AT ALL.
WHAT IS "DYING?"
THE PAIN WAS SO GREAT, I COULDN'T STAND IT.
A GREAT BIRD CAME TO TAKE ME TO THE LAND OF THE DEAD. OR MAYBE IT WAS A DREAM. I DON'T KNOW FOR SURE.
I DON'T REMEMBER HIM CUTTING ME DOWN. I DON'T REMEMBER HOW HE STOPPED THE BLEEDING. ALL I DO REMEMBER IS HIM CARRYING ME.
TO BE CONTINUED.....

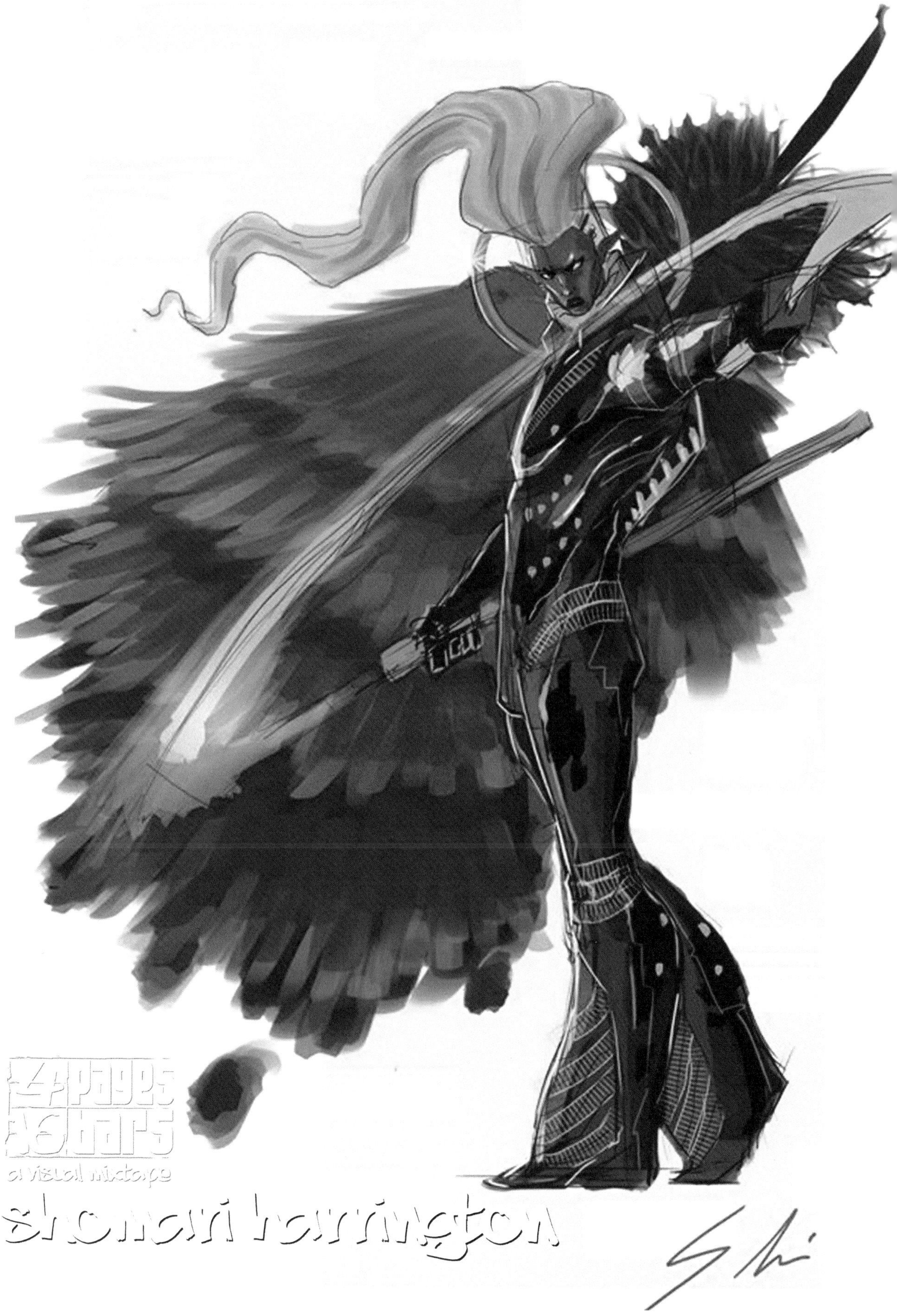
24 pages 16 bars
a visual mixtape
shomari harrington

Shomari Harrington is a Visual Artist born and raised in Chicago. From an early age, he has always been fascinated by the wonders of what a pencil and a sheet of paper could create. The desire and passion to create has helped him to become the artist that he is today.

Shomari graduated with a Bachelors degree in Film majoring in Animation from Columbia College Chicago, where he learned from some of the best and brightest in the field. Shomari has also worked closely with professional comic book artist as an intern at **Four Star Studios**, located in Chicago, Illinois.

In early 2014, his desire to become a better artist lead him to study abroad at Tongji University in Shanghai, China. Upon his return to the U.S., Shomari has vigorously pursued numerous projects within animation and illustration, which includes the completion of the children's book, **Q Saves the Sun**. Shomari's Art work has also appeared at the **Milestones: African American in Comics, Pop Culture and Beyond** gallery hosted at the **Geppi Museum of Entertainment** in Baltimore, MD.

Shomari is an artist who enjoys working with others on a team, being productive, and creating thought provoking works of art. Currently Shomari works as an Illustrator/Animator at **Hi5 Design Studio** in Chicago, IL.

website: shomariharrington.com

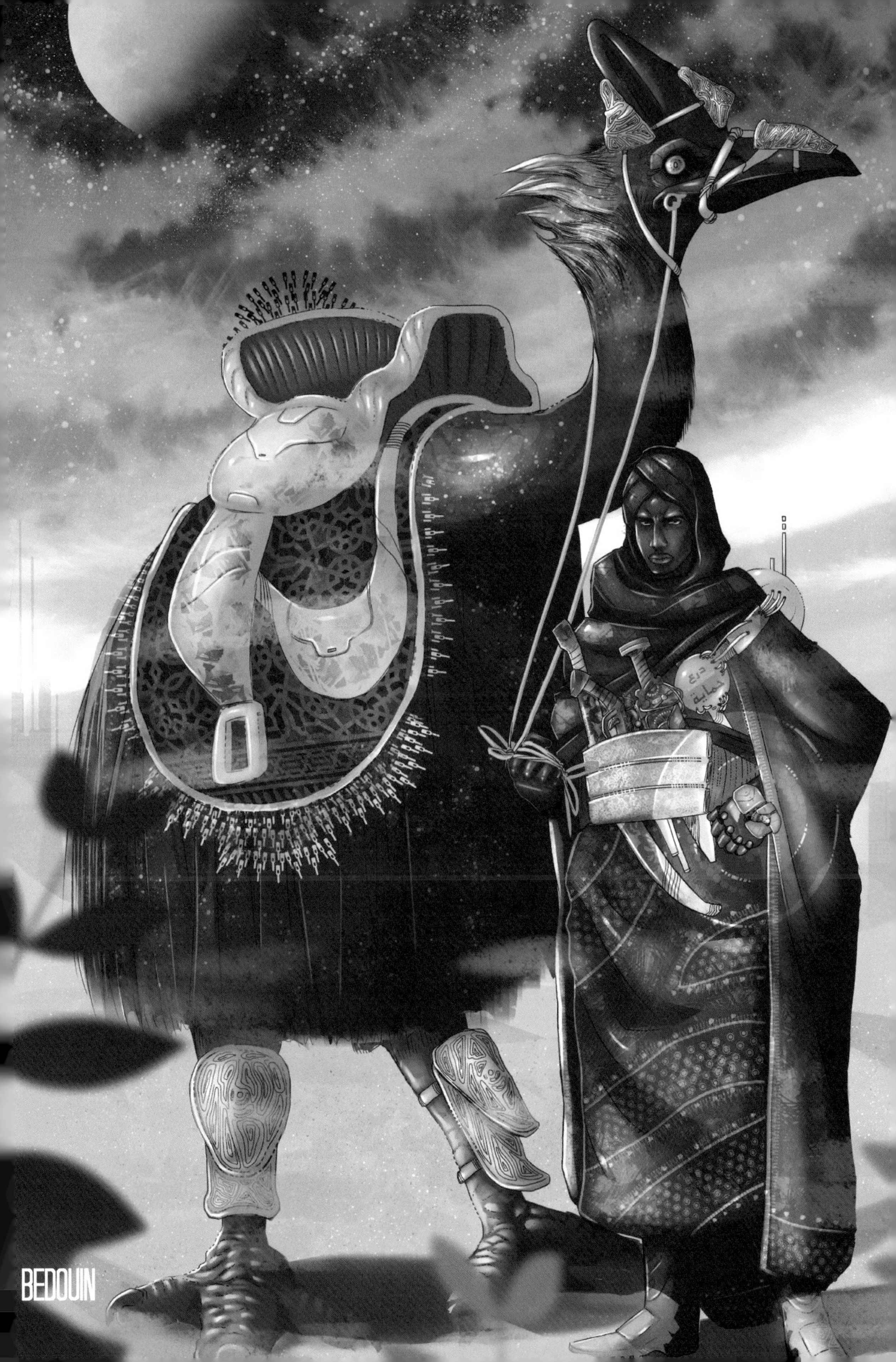
BEDOUIN

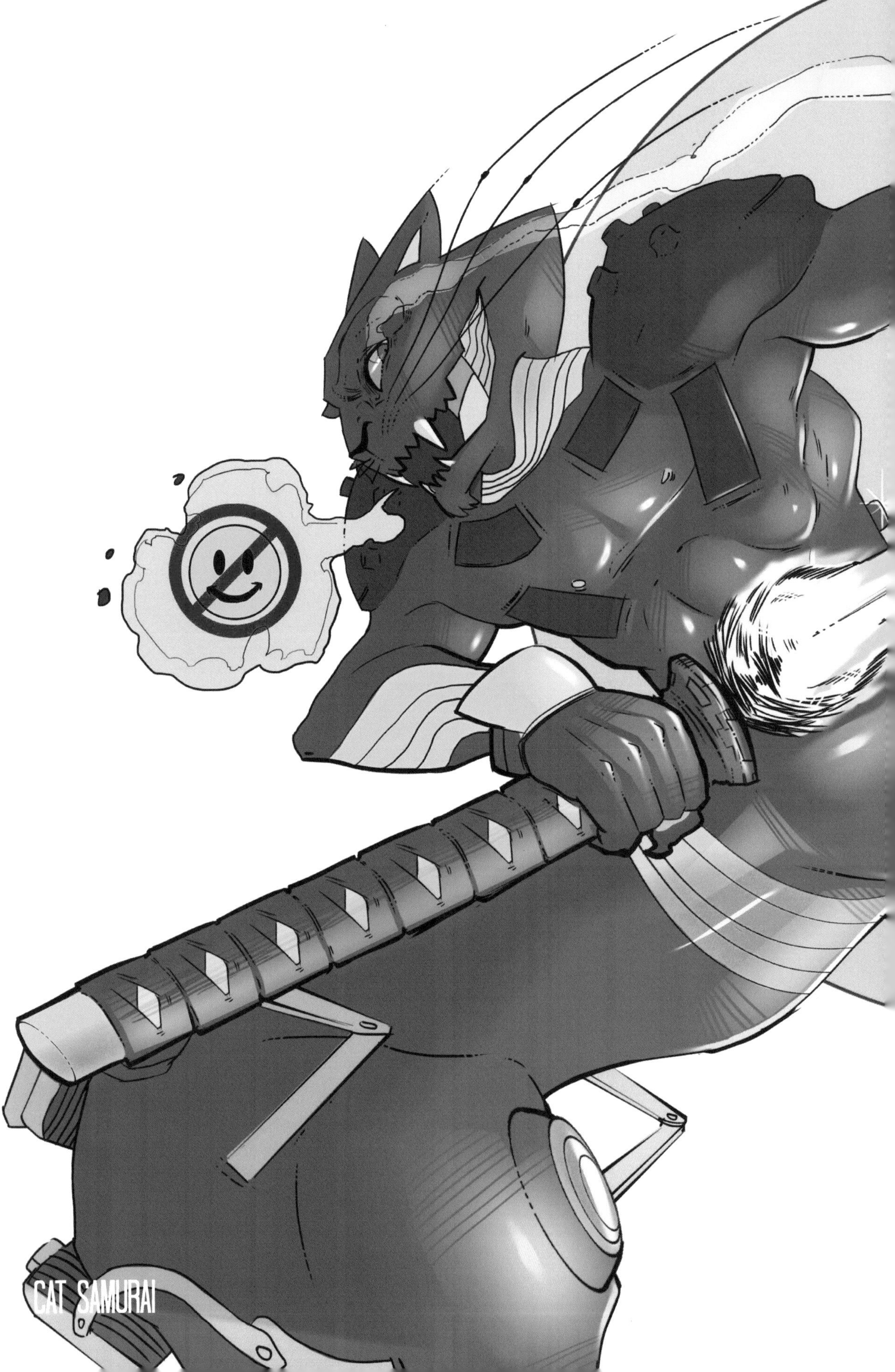

CAT SAMURAI

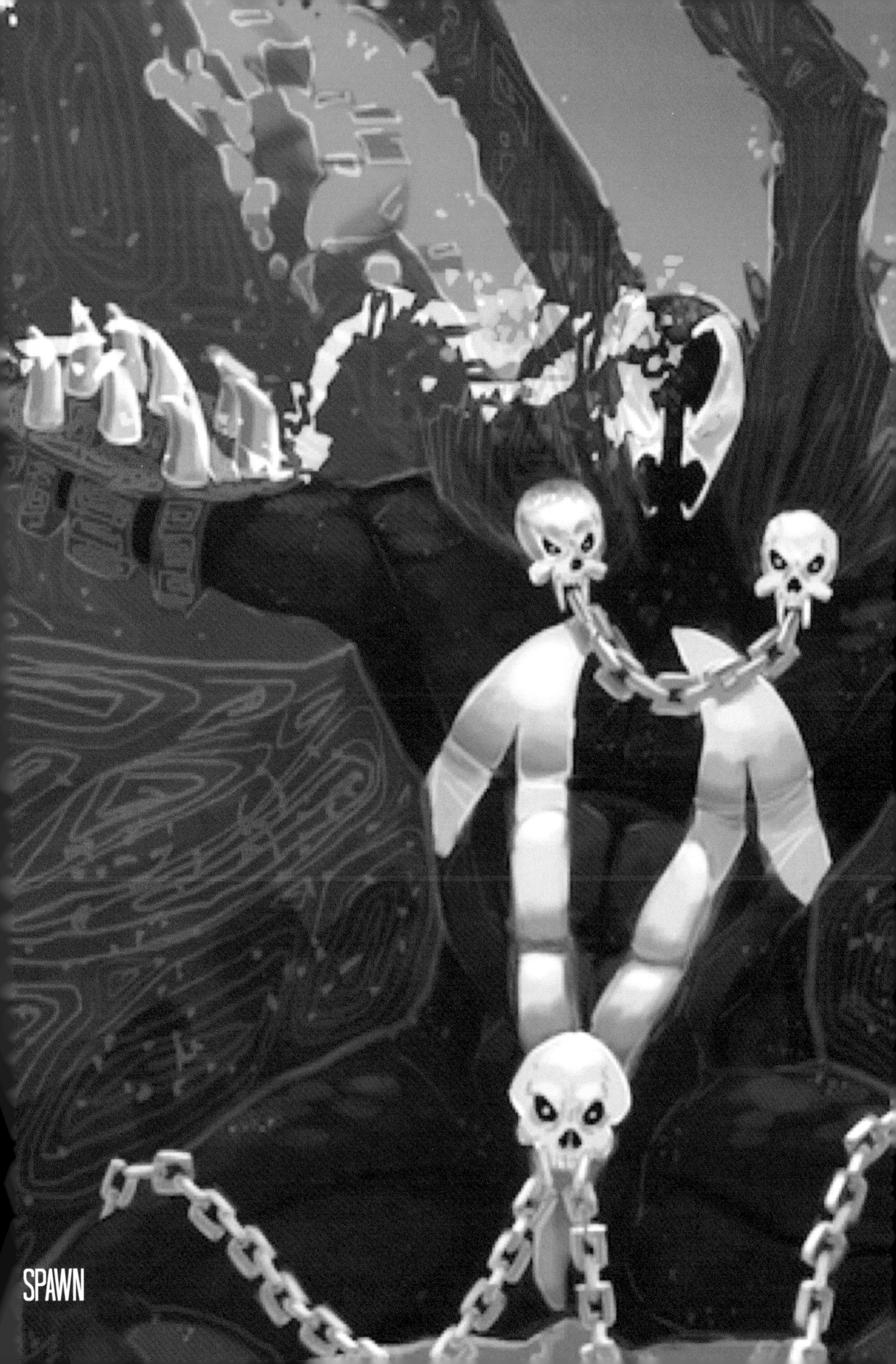
SPAWN

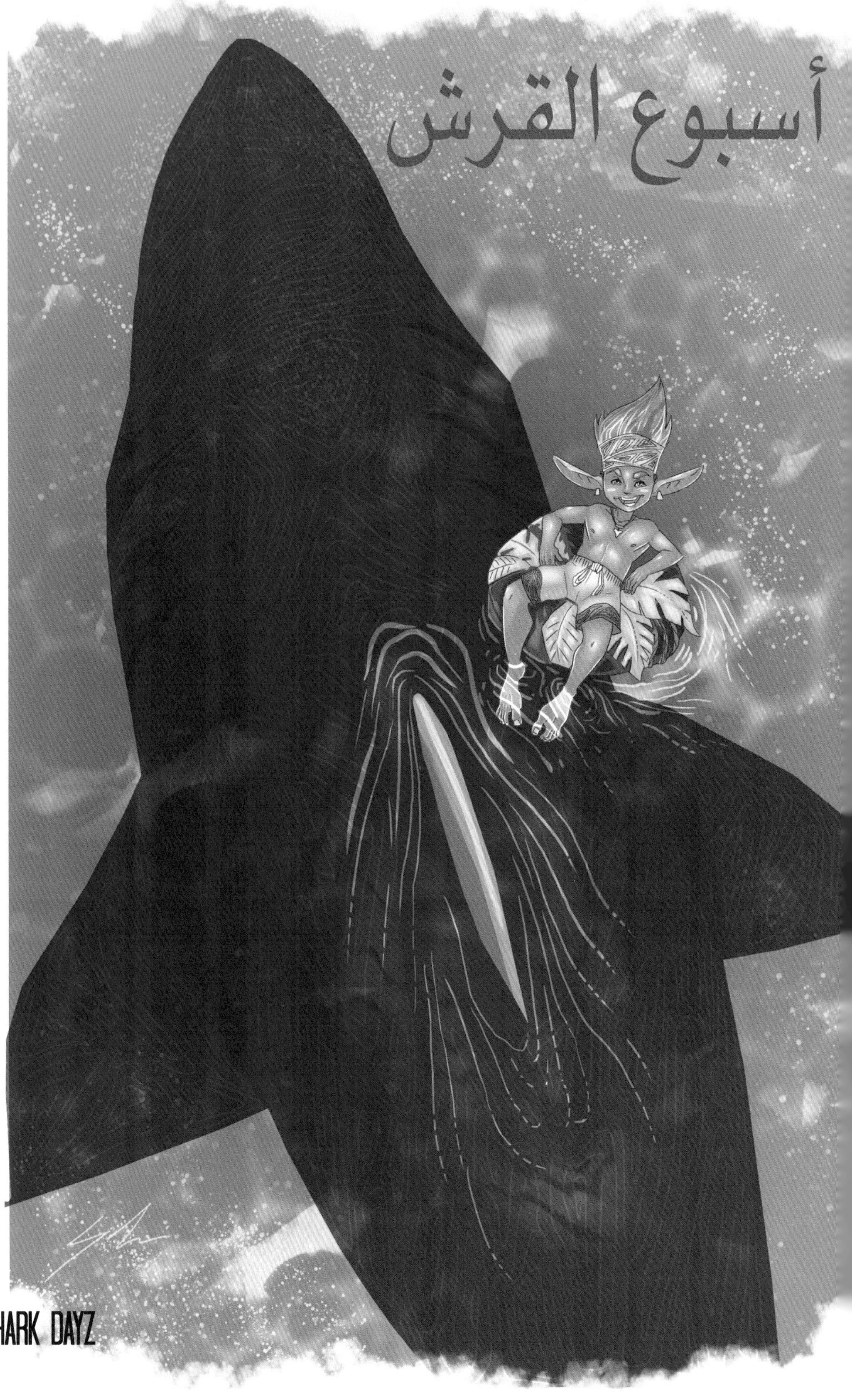
أسبوع القرش
SHARK DAYZ

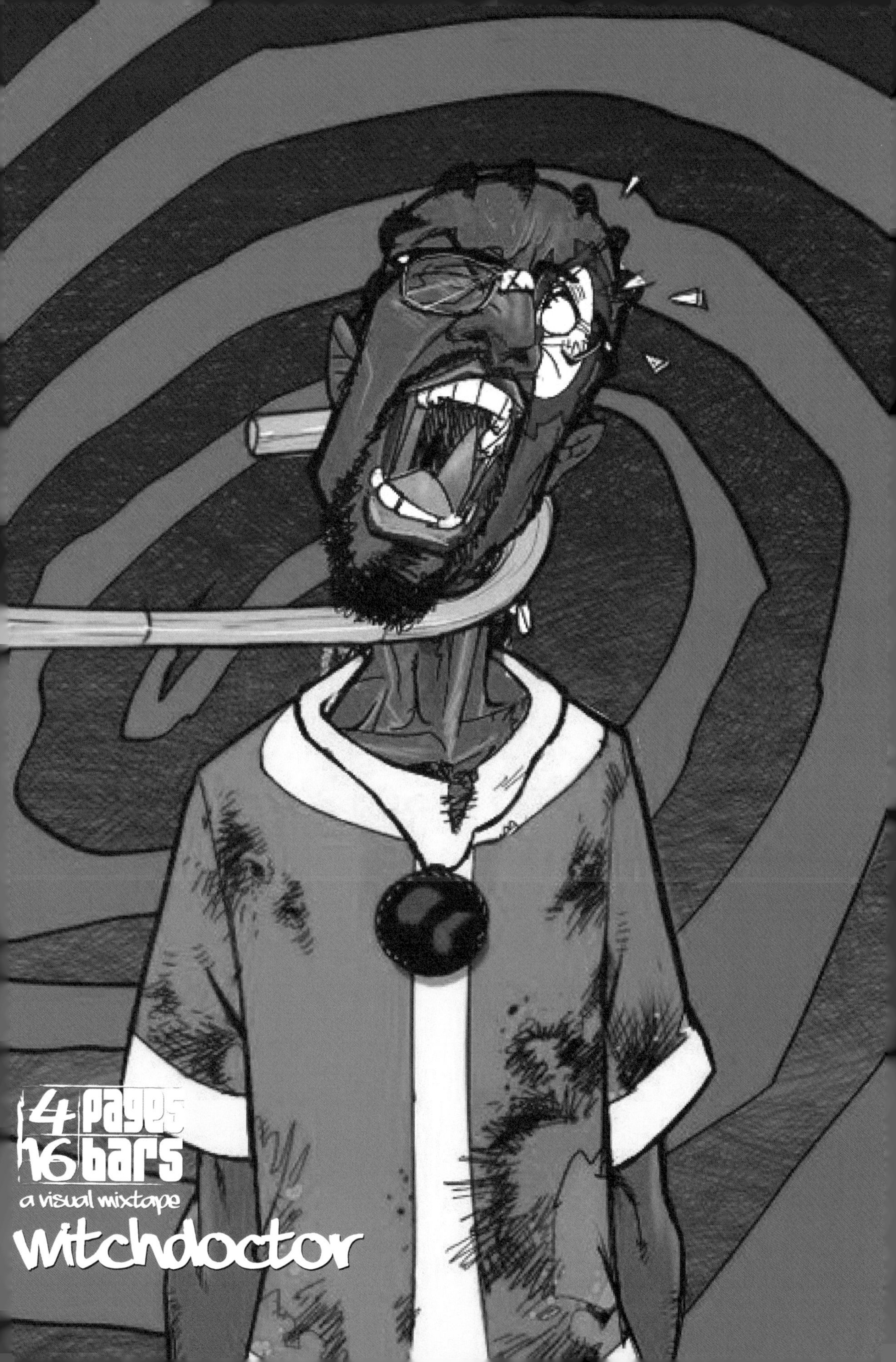
4 pages
16 bars
a visual mixtape
witchdoctor

Kenjji Jumanne-Marshall is a freelance illustrator and comic artist whose work has appeared worldwide. A Detroit native, Kenjji includes 80's television, Hip Hop and the Motor City among his influences. Kenjji continues to work on new episodes of his true Voodoo action series *WitchDoctor* for **Griot Enterprises** and has recently published children's books like *Money Smart Kids* and *Read Roared the Lion* as well as producing artwork for **MTV's** *Teen Wolf*. Recently, Kenjji has made the foray into film and television as the creative director for the independent Grindhouse series *Frankie*.

website: kenjji.com

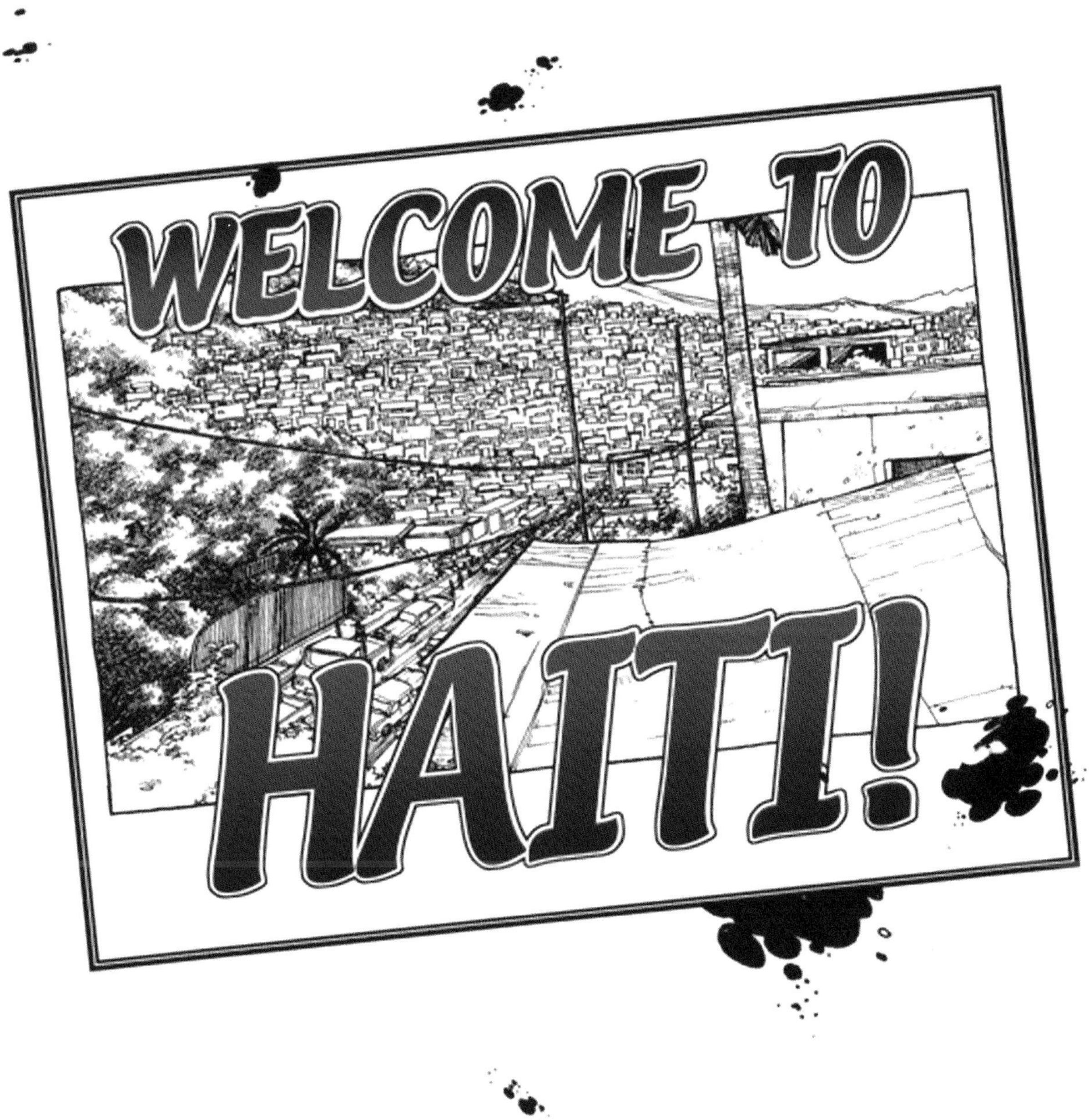
WELCOME TO
HAITI!

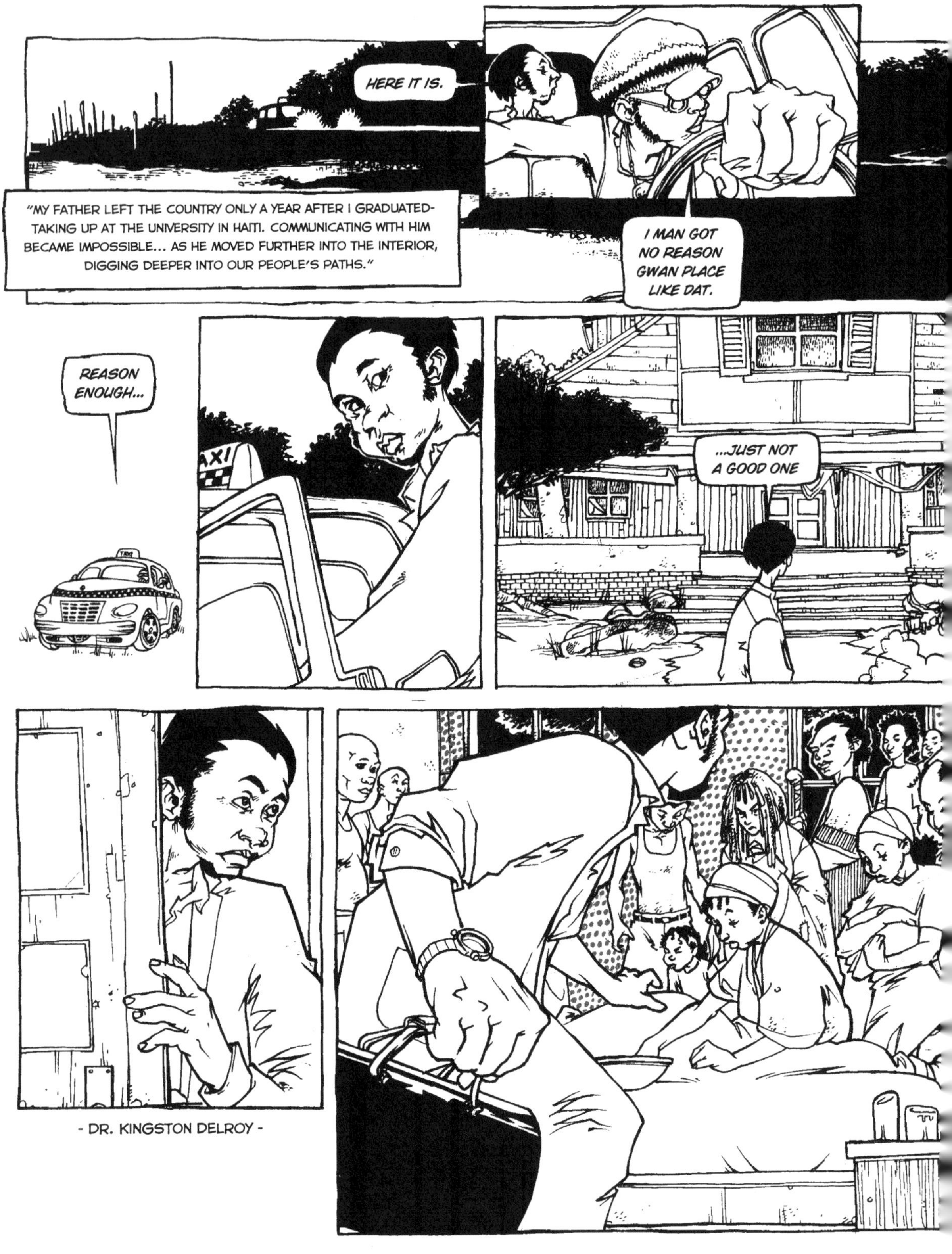
HERE IT IS.
"MY FATHER LEFT THE COUNTRY ONLY A YEAR AFTER I GRADUATED- TAKING UP AT THE UNIVERSITY IN HAITI. COMMUNICATING WITH HIM BECAME IMPOSSIBLE... AS HE MOVED FURTHER INTO THE INTERIOR, DIGGING DEEPER INTO OUR PEOPLE'S PATHS."
I MAN GOT NO REASON GWAN PLACE LIKE DAT.
REASON ENOUGH...
TAXI
...JUST NOT A GOOD ONE
- DR. KINGSTON DELROY -

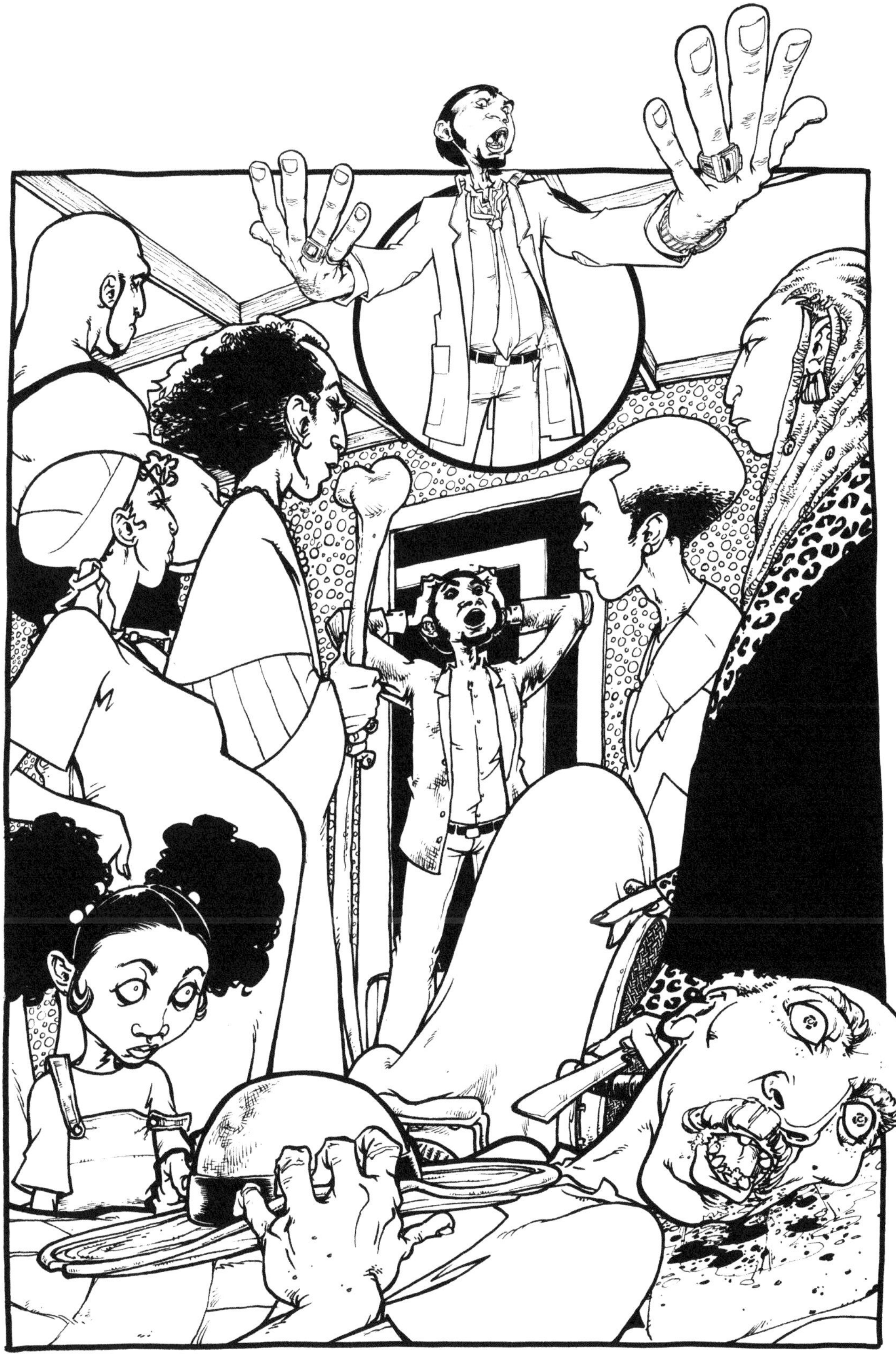

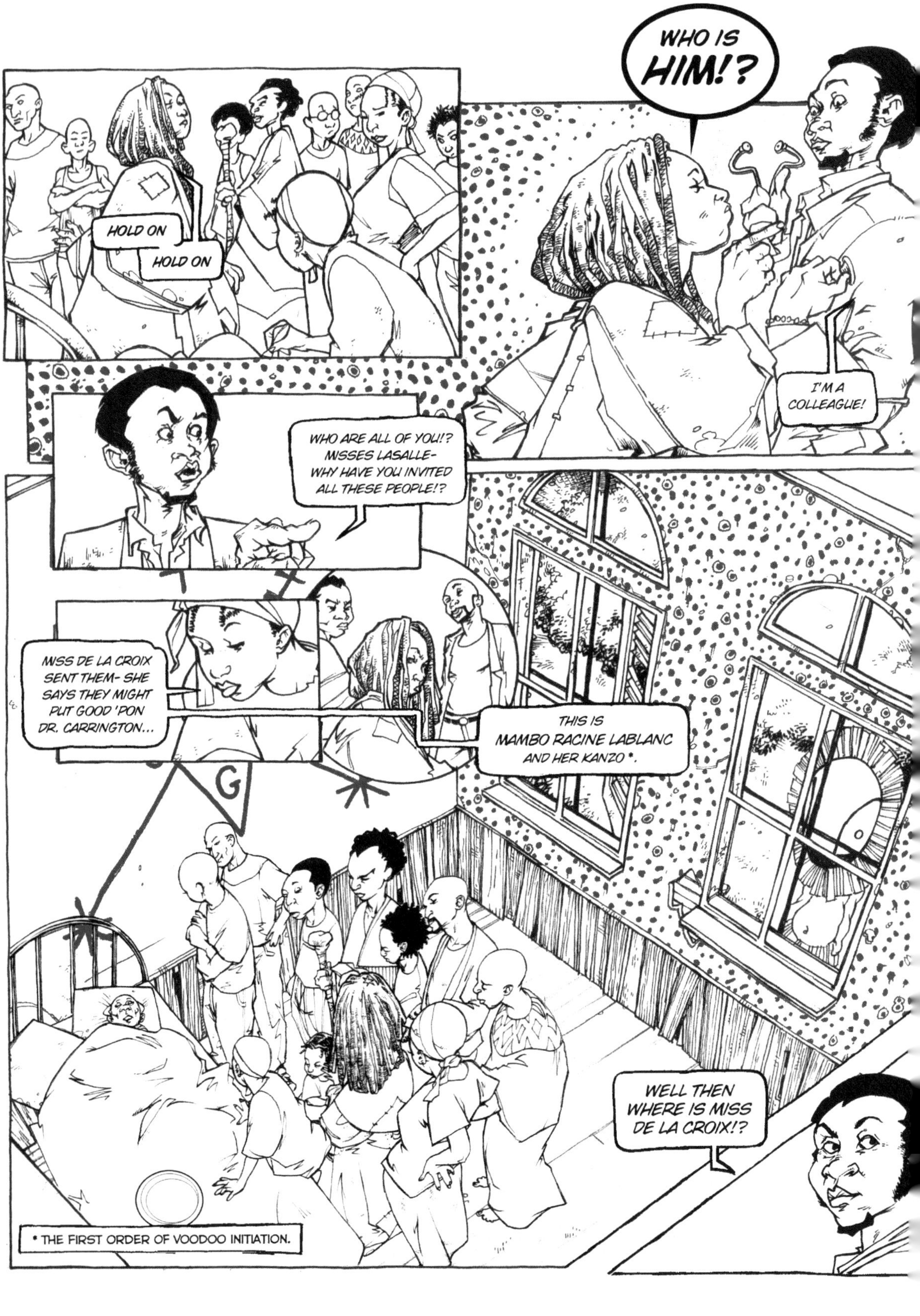
HOLD ON
HOLD ON
WHO IS HIM!?
I'M A COLLEAGUE!
WHO ARE ALL OF YOU!? MISSES LASALLE- WHY HAVE YOU INVITED ALL THESE PEOPLE!?
MISS DE LA CROIX SENT THEM- SHE SAYS THEY MIGHT PUT GOOD 'PON DR. CARRINGTON...
THIS IS MAMBO RACINE LABLANC AND HER KANZO *.
G
WELL THEN WHERE IS MISS DE LA CROIX!?
* THE FIRST ORDER OF VOODOO INITIATION.

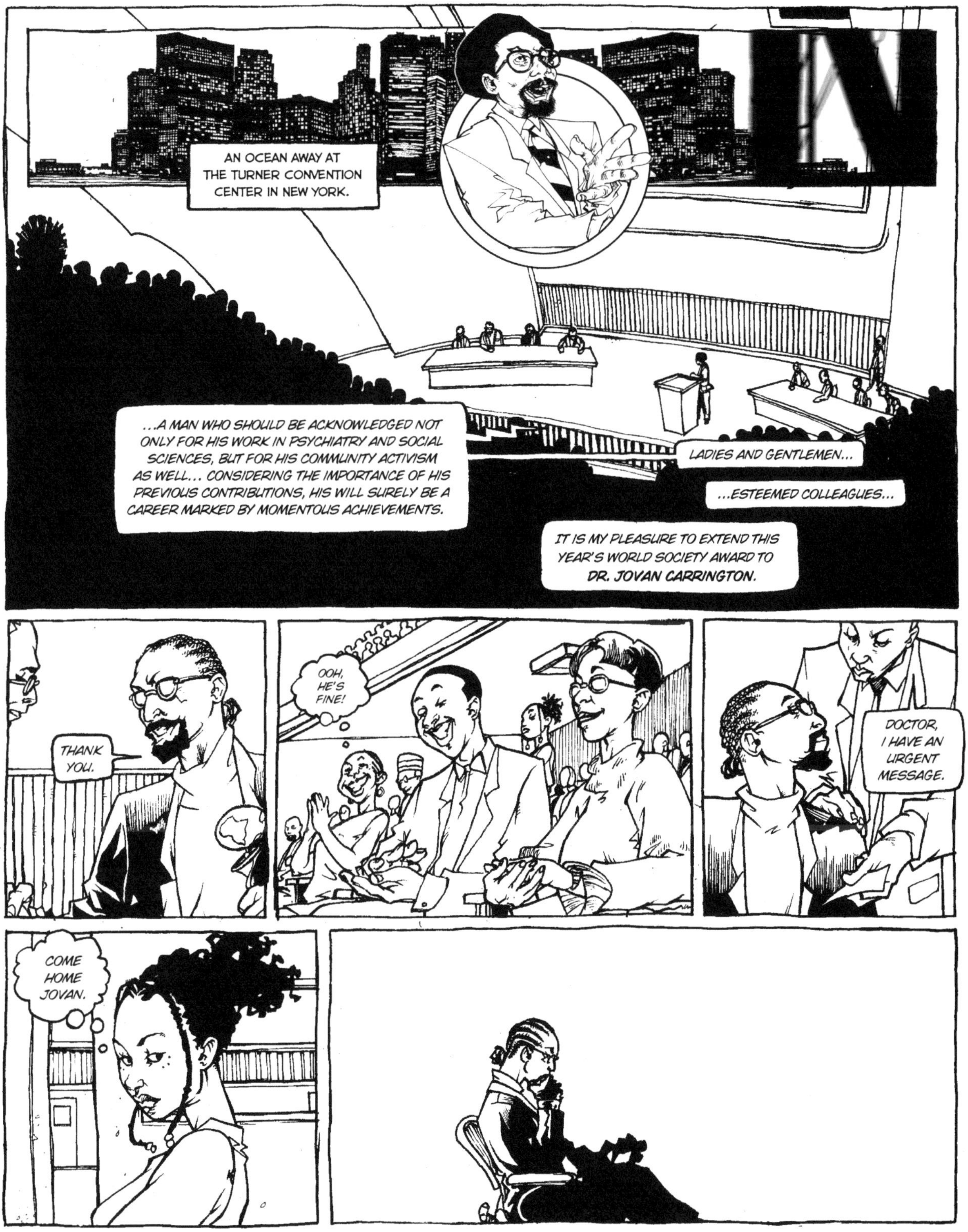
AN OCEAN AWAY AT THE TURNER CONVENTION CENTER IN NEW YORK.
...A MAN WHO SHOULD BE ACKNOWLEDGED NOT ONLY FOR HIS WORK IN PSYCHIATRY AND SOCIAL SCIENCES, BUT FOR HIS COMMUNITY ACTIVISM AS WELL... CONSIDERING THE IMPORTANCE OF HIS PREVIOUS CONTRIBUTIONS, HIS WILL SURELY BE A CAREER MARKED BY MOMENTOUS ACHIEVEMENTS.
LADIES AND GENTLEMEN...
...ESTEEMED COLLEAGUES...
IT IS MY PLEASURE TO EXTEND THIS YEAR'S WORLD SOCIETY AWARD TO DR. JOVAN CARRINGTON.
THANK YOU.
OOH, HE'S FINE!
DOCTOR, I HAVE AN URGENT MESSAGE.
COME HOME JOVAN.

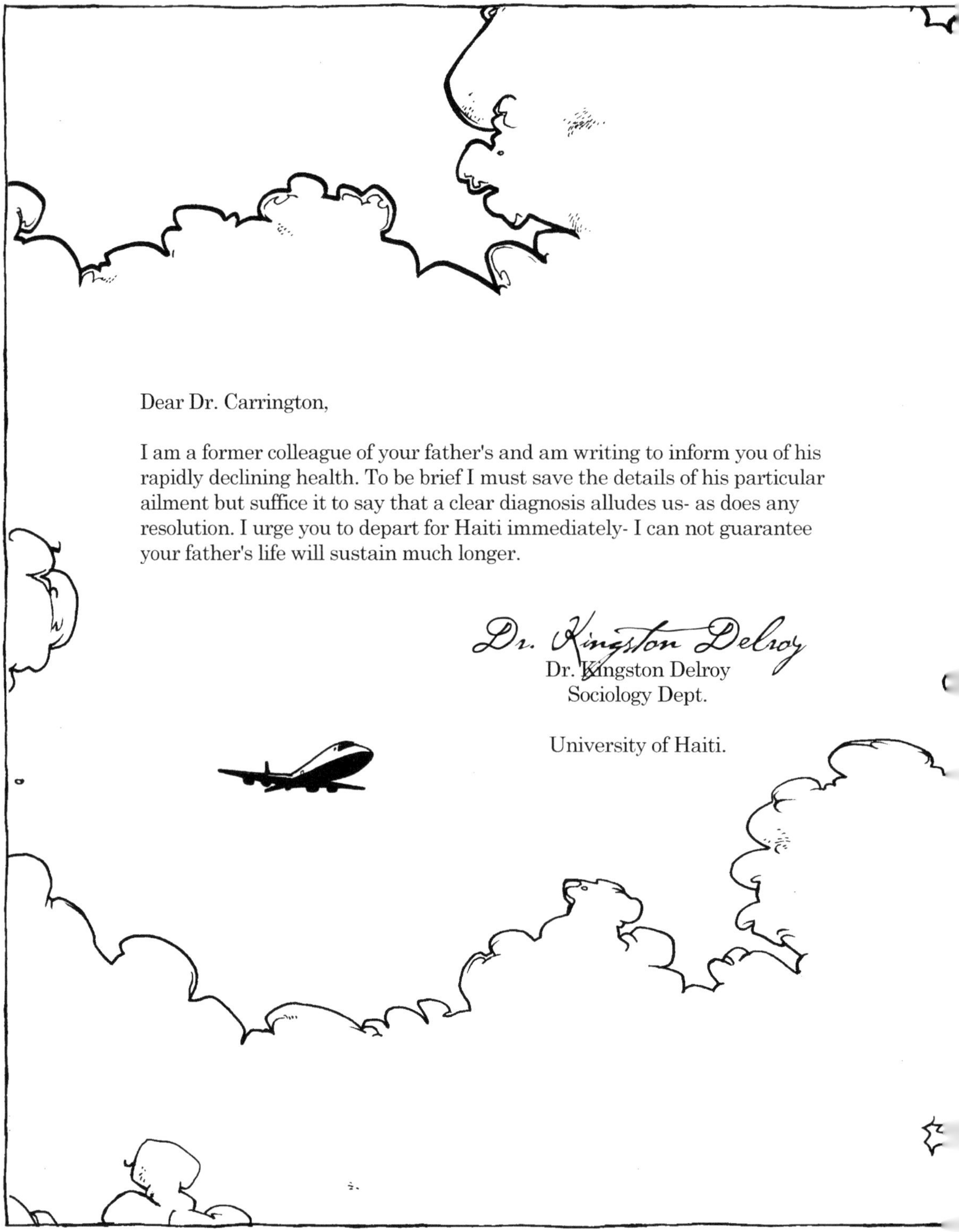
Dear Dr. Carrington,
I am a former colleague of your father's and am writing to inform you of his rapidly declining health. To be brief I must save the details of his particular ailment but suffice it to say that a clear diagnosis alludes us- as does any resolution. I urge you to depart for Haiti immediately- I can not guarantee your father's life will sustain much longer.
Dr. Kingston Delroy
Dr. Kingston Delroy
Sociology Dept.
University of Haiti.

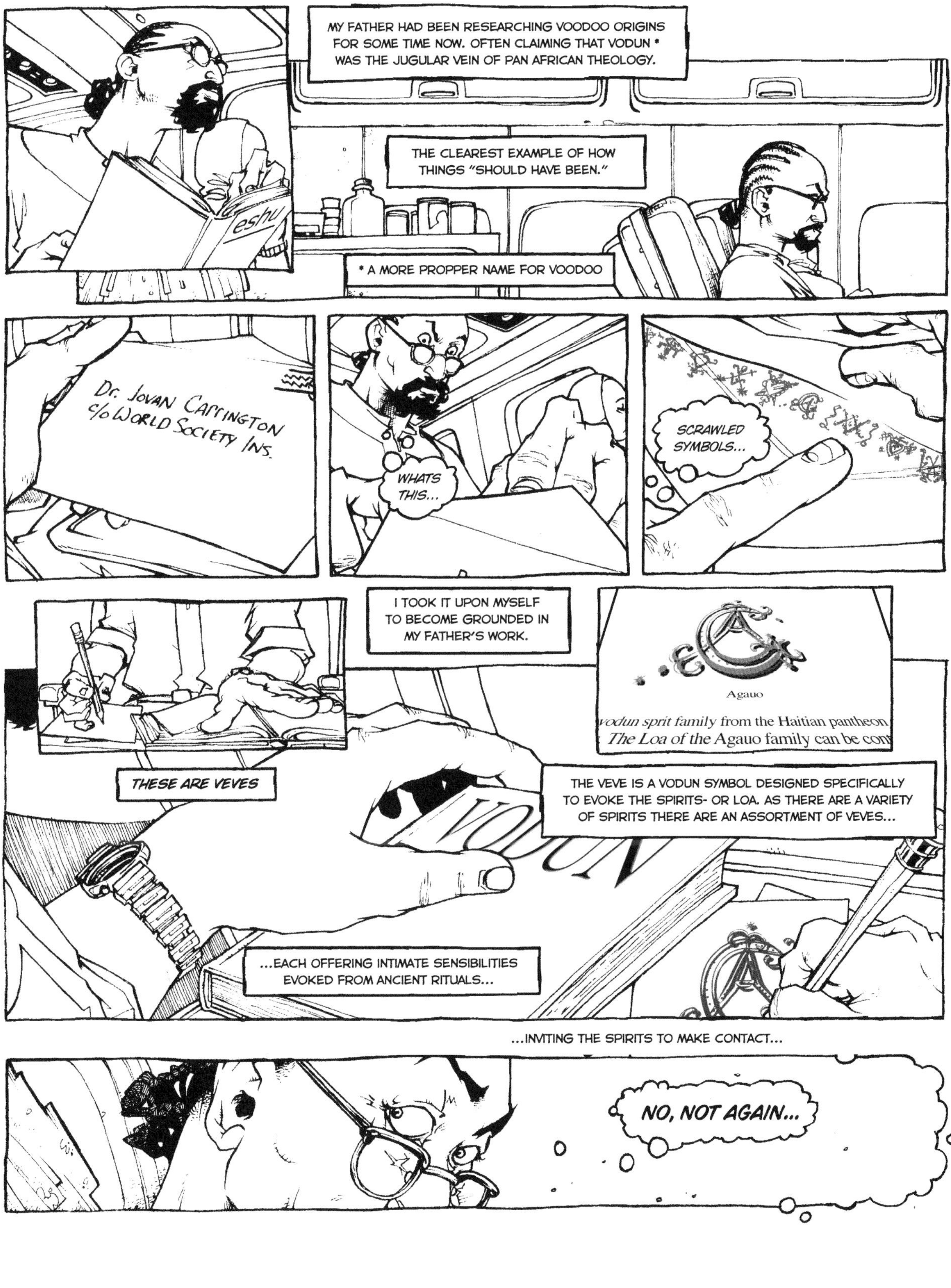
MY FATHER HAD BEEN RESEARCHING VOODOO ORIGINS FOR SOME TIME NOW. OFTEN CLAIMING THAT VODUN * WAS THE JUGULAR VEIN OF PAN AFRICAN THEOLOGY.
eshu
THE CLEAREST EXAMPLE OF HOW THINGS "SHOULD HAVE BEEN."
* A MORE PROPPER NAME FOR VOODOO
Dr. Jovan Carrington c/o World Society Ins.
WHATS THIS...
SCRAWLED SYMBOLS...
I TOOK IT UPON MYSELF TO BECOME GROUNDED IN MY FATHER'S WORK.
Agauo
vodun sprit family from the Haitian pantheon
The Loa of the Agauo family can be con
THESE ARE VEVES
THE VEVE IS A VODUN SYMBOL DESIGNED SPECIFICALLY TO EVOKE THE SPIRITS- OR LOA. AS THERE ARE A VARIETY OF SPIRITS THERE ARE AN ASSORTMENT OF VEVES...
VODUN
...EACH OFFERING INTIMATE SENSIBILITIES EVOKED FROM ANCIENT RITUALS...
...INVITING THE SPIRITS TO MAKE CONTACT...
NO, NOT AGAIN...

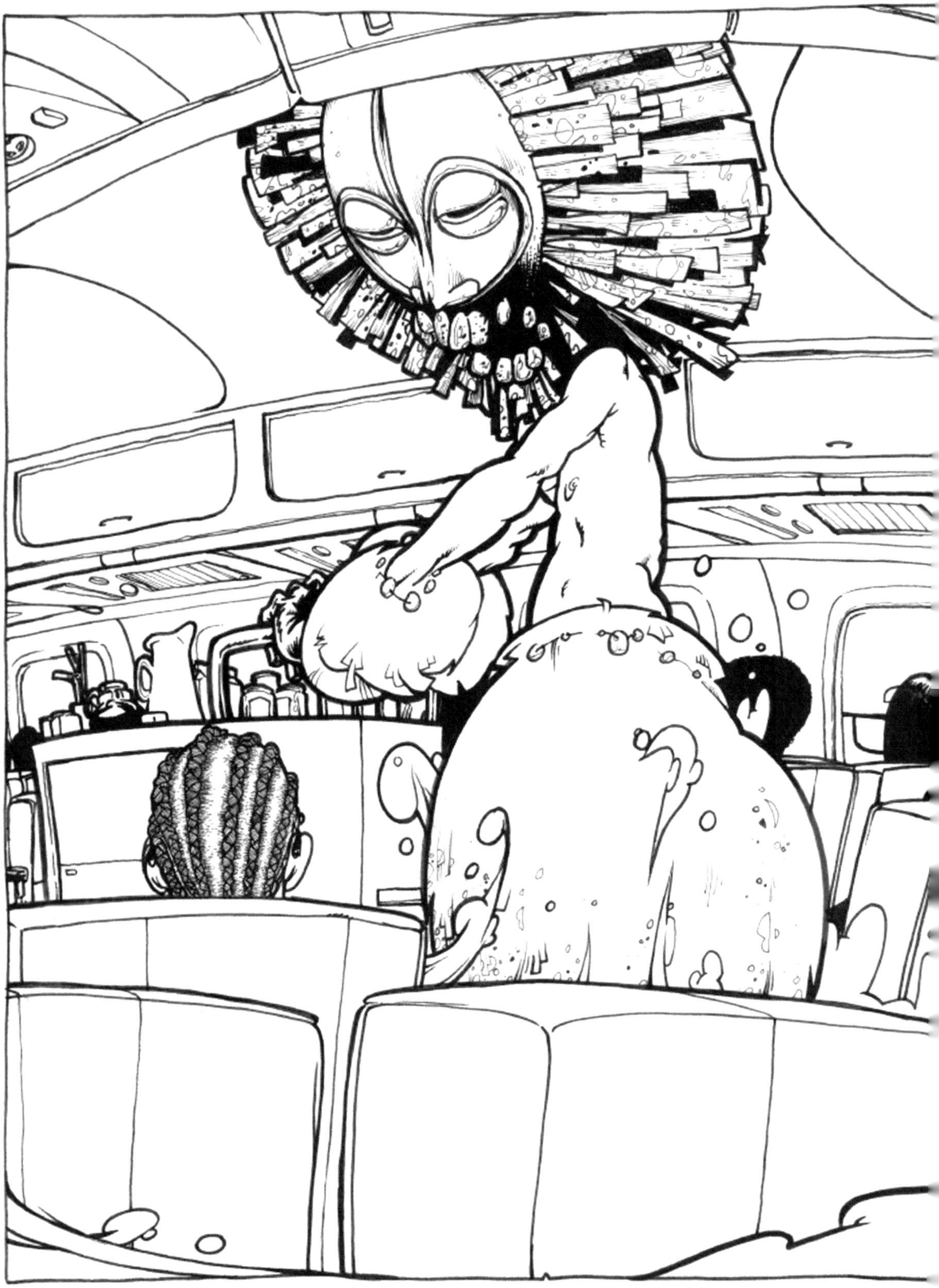

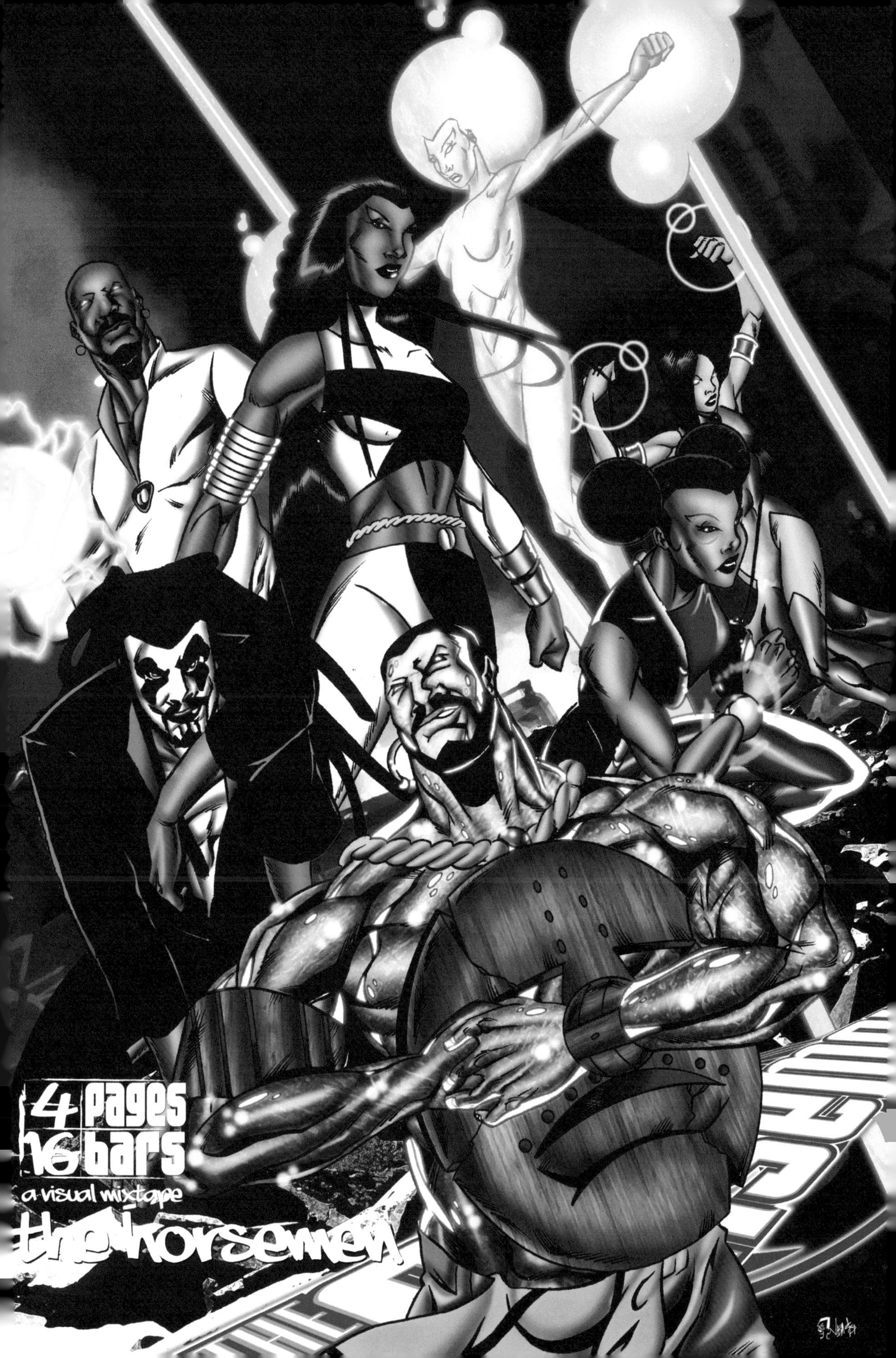
4 pages
16 bars
a visual mixtape
the horsemen

TYR SEGMENT ART BY
JACOB & JARED BYMERS

Jiba Molei Anderson is the owner of **Griot Enterprises** and creator
of its flagship property *The Horsemen* and *Outworld: Return of the
Master Teachers*. He has also written the educational text *Manifesto:
The Tao of Jiba Molei Anderson*. Anderson is also Creative Director
for **Cedar Grove Books** and maintains The Afrosoul Chronicles a blog
dedicated to the discussion of race, politics and the business
of popular culture.

Mr. Anderson is also a part of the fine art community having various
one-man and group shows including being featured in the book *Black Comix*
and guest lecturing at **The School of the Art Institute of Chicago** and
The **Smithsonian National Museum of African Art** with The Horsemen's
inclusion in The Smithsonian's permanent library.

Currently, Mr. Anderson is a Part-Time Lecturer at **Chicago State University**,
teaching courses in Animation, Multimedia and Video Game Design and
speaks across the country promoting comic books and graphic novels as
tools for education in the exploration of race, culture and identity. He recently
created ***The Song of Lionogo: An Indian Ocean Mythological Remix***
for the Smithsonian National Museum of African Art.

website: griotenterprises.com

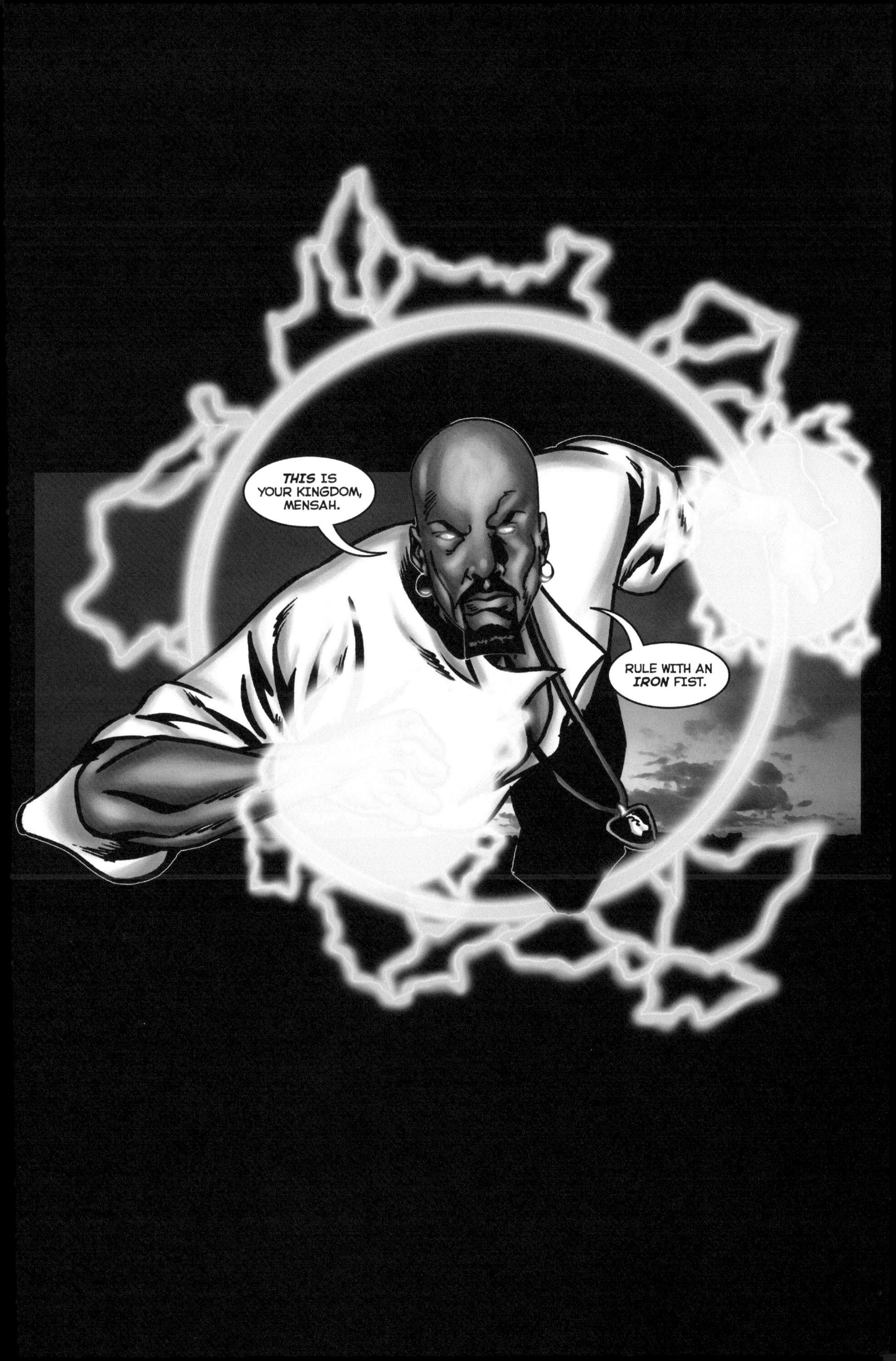
THIS IS YOUR KINGDOM, MENSAH.
RULE WITH AN IRON FIST.

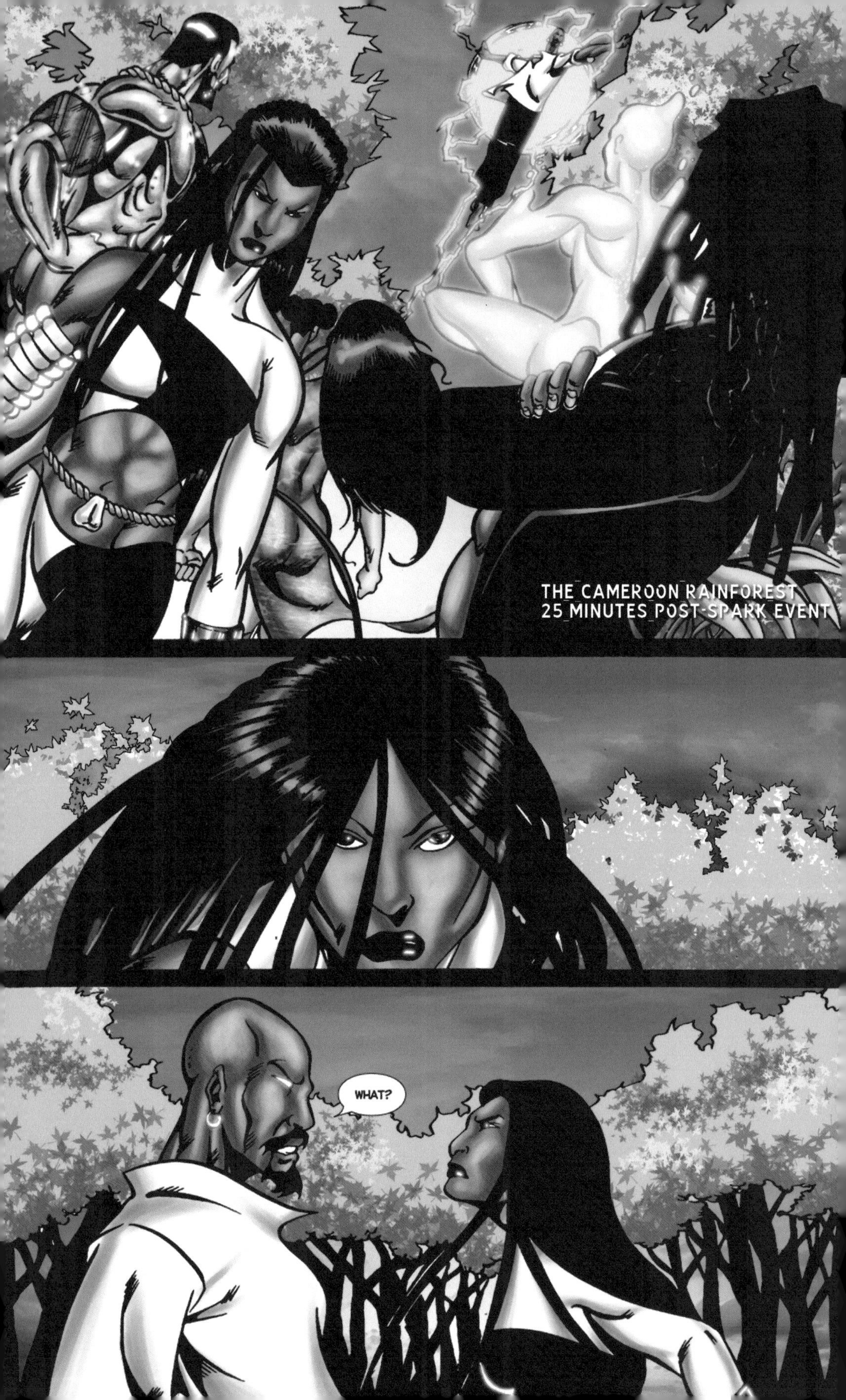
THE CAMEROON RAINFOREST
25 MINUTES POST-SPARK EVENT
WHAT?

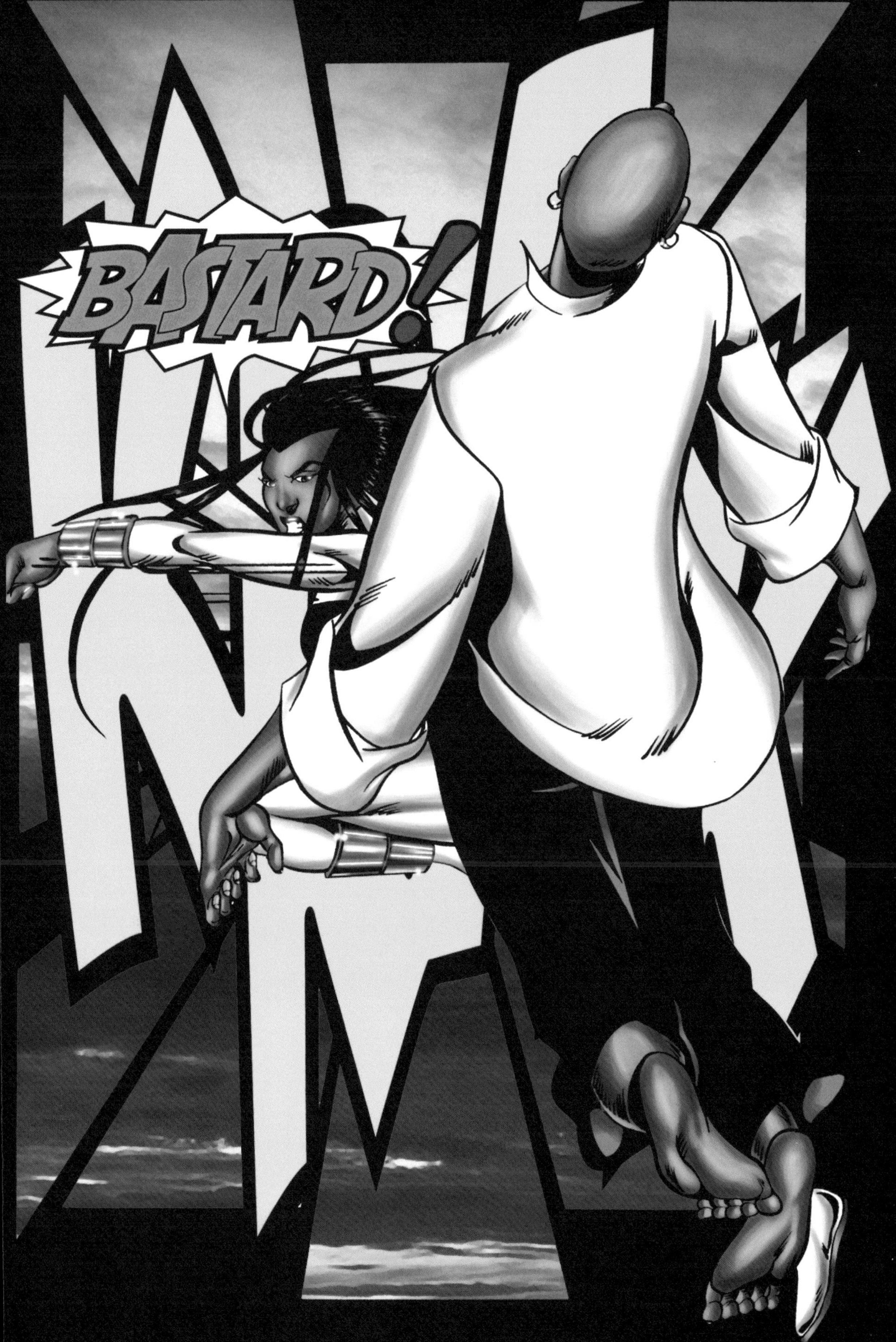
BASTARD!

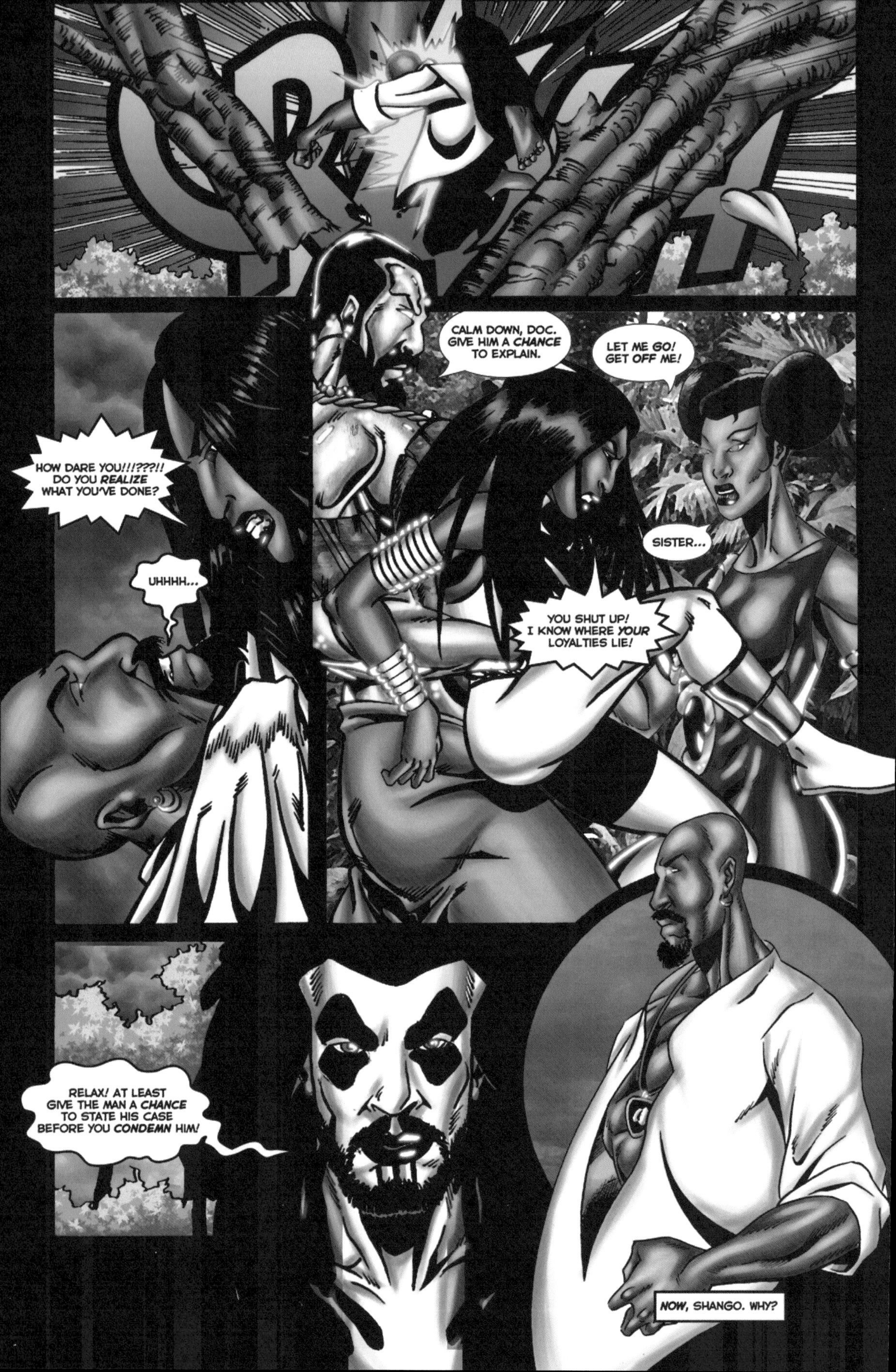
HOW DARE YOU!!!???!! DO YOU REALIZE WHAT YOU'VE DONE?
UHHHH...
CALM DOWN, DOC. GIVE HIM A CHANCE TO EXPLAIN.
LET ME GO! GET OFF ME!
SISTER...
YOU SHUT UP! I KNOW WHERE YOUR LOYALTIES LIE!
RELAX! AT LEAST GIVE THE MAN A CHANCE TO STATE HIS CASE BEFORE YOU CONDEMN HIM!
NOW, SHANGO. WHY?

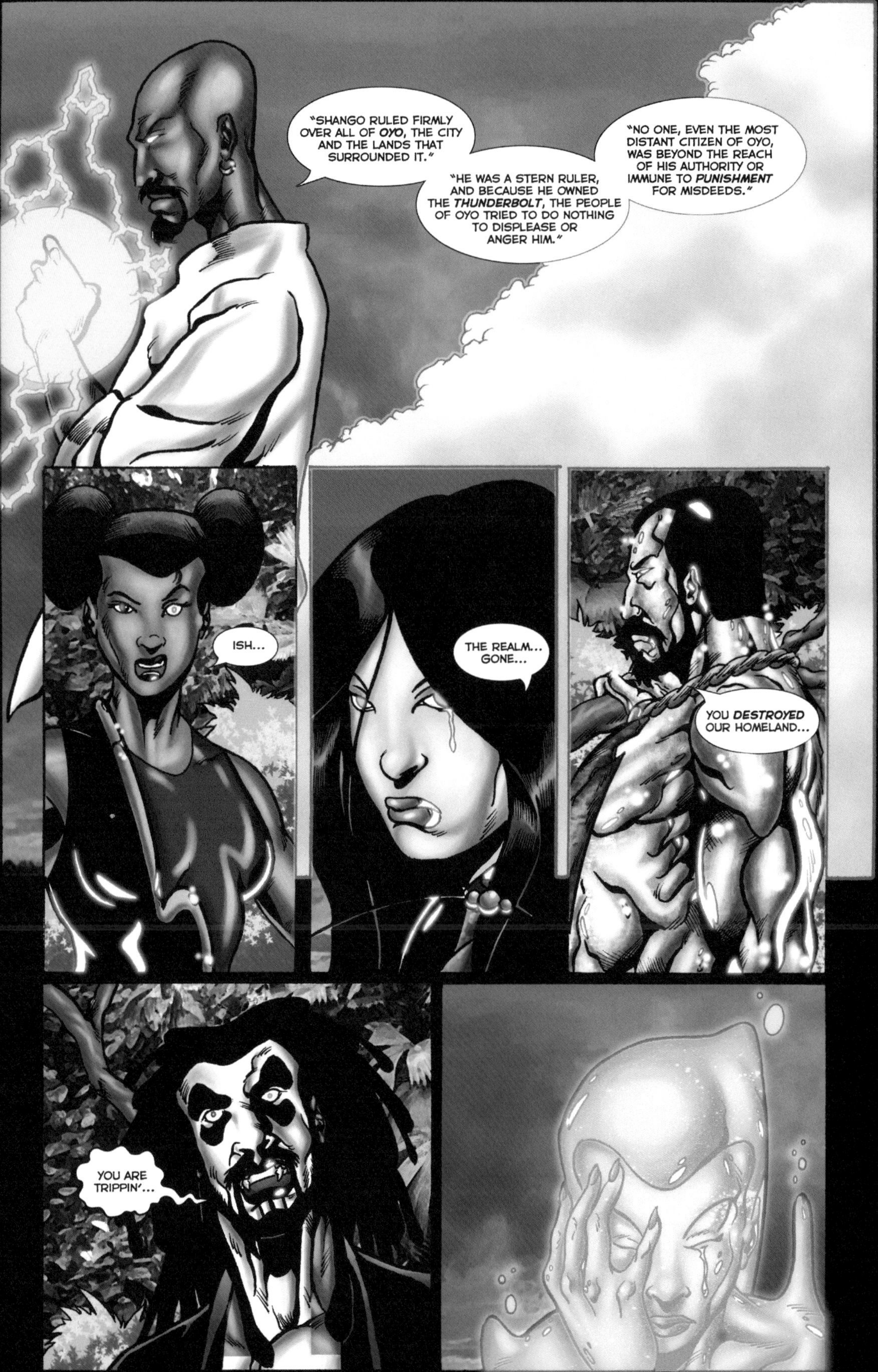
"SHANGO RULED FIRMLY OVER ALL OF *OYO*, THE CITY AND THE LANDS THAT SURROUNDED IT."
"HE WAS A STERN RULER, AND BECAUSE HE OWNED THE *THUNDERBOLT*, THE PEOPLE OF OYO TRIED TO DO NOTHING TO DISPLEASE OR ANGER HIM."
"NO ONE, EVEN THE MOST DISTANT CITIZEN OF OYO, WAS BEYOND THE REACH OF HIS AUTHORITY OR IMMUNE TO *PUNISHMENT* FOR MISDEEDS."
ISH...
THE REALM... GONE...
YOU *DESTROYED* OUR HOMELAND...
YOU ARE TRIPPIN'...

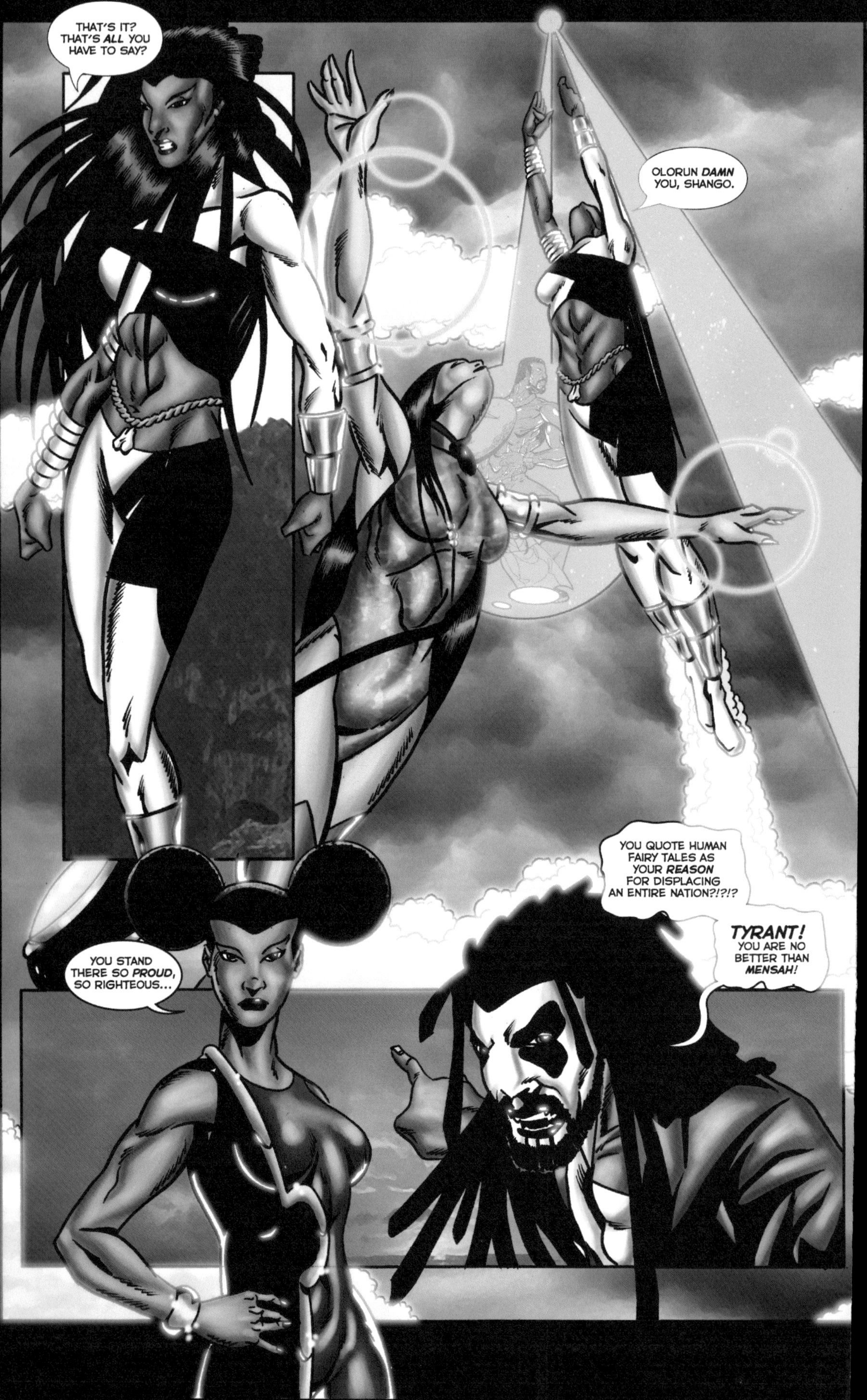
THAT'S IT? THAT'S *ALL* YOU HAVE TO SAY?
OLORUN *DAMN* YOU, SHANGO.
YOU QUOTE HUMAN FAIRY TALES AS YOUR *REASON* FOR DISPLACING AN ENTIRE NATION?!?!?
TYRANT! YOU ARE NO BETTER THAN *MENSAH!*
YOU STAND THERE SO *PROUD,* SO RIGHTEOUS...

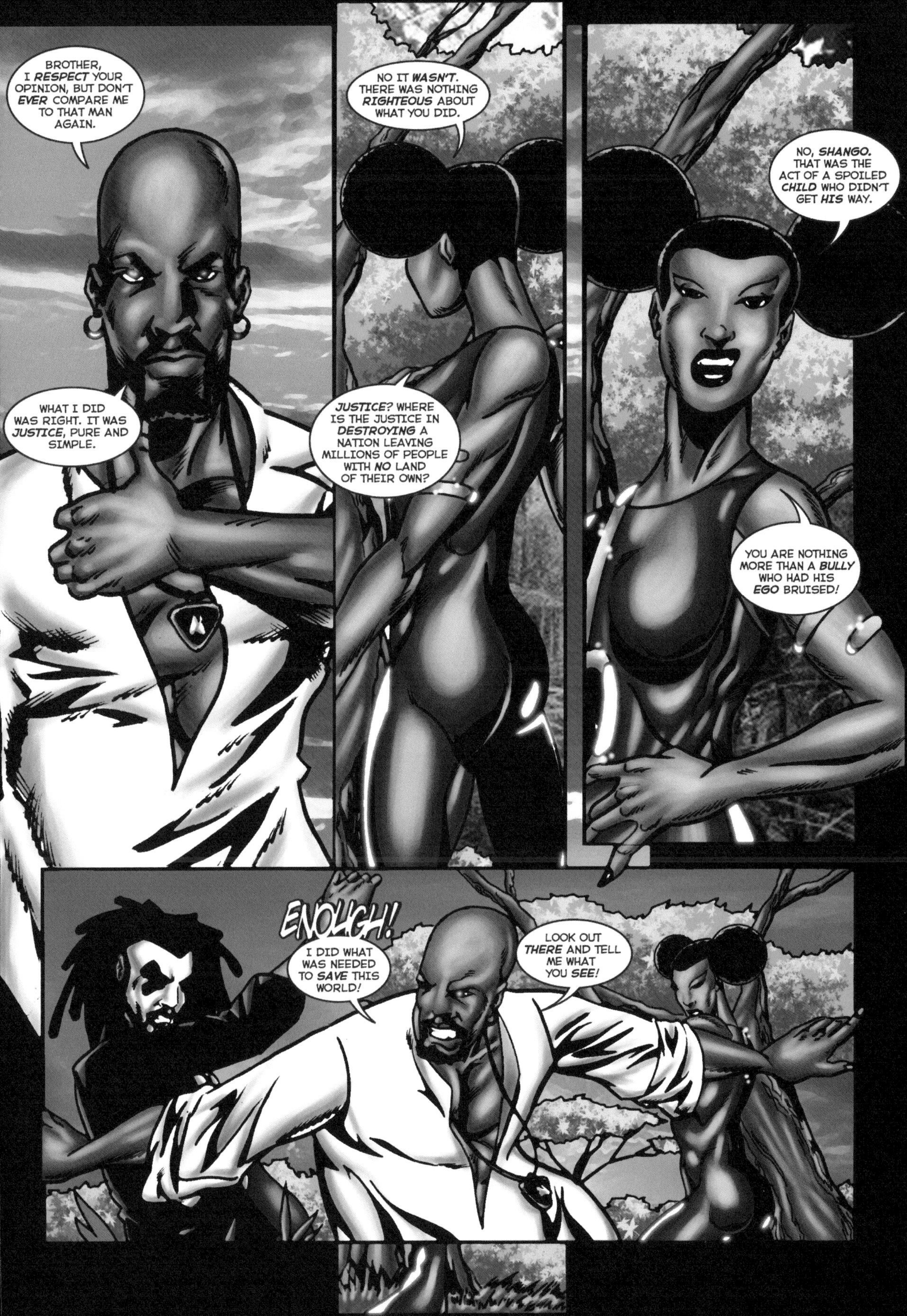
BROTHER, I RESPECT YOUR OPINION, BUT DON'T EVER COMPARE ME TO THAT MAN AGAIN.
WHAT I DID WAS RIGHT. IT WAS JUSTICE, PURE AND SIMPLE.
NO IT WASN'T. THERE WAS NOTHING RIGHTEOUS ABOUT WHAT YOU DID.
JUSTICE? WHERE IS THE JUSTICE IN DESTROYING A NATION LEAVING MILLIONS OF PEOPLE WITH NO LAND OF THEIR OWN?
NO, SHANGO. THAT WAS THE ACT OF A SPOILED CHILD WHO DIDN'T GET HIS WAY.
YOU ARE NOTHING MORE THAN A BULLY WHO HAD HIS EGO BRUISED!
ENOUGH!
I DID WHAT WAS NEEDED TO SAVE THIS WORLD!
LOOK OUT THERE AND TELL ME WHAT YOU SEE!

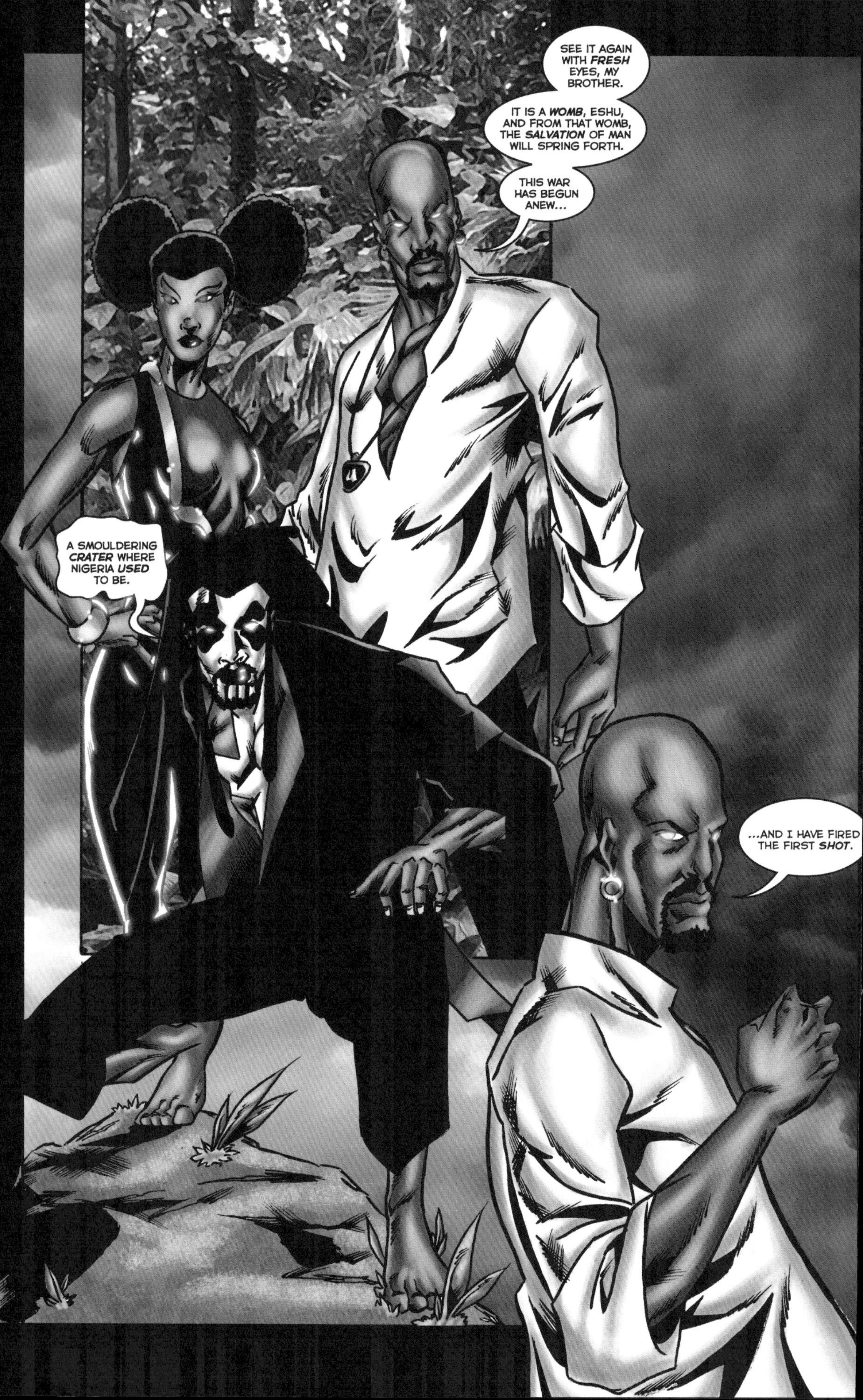
SEE IT AGAIN WITH FRESH EYES, MY BROTHER.
IT IS A WOMB, ESHU, AND FROM THAT WOMB, THE SALVATION OF MAN WILL SPRING FORTH.
THIS WAR HAS BEGUN ANEW...
A SMOULDERING CRATER WHERE NIGERIA USED TO BE.
...AND I HAVE FIRED THE FIRST SHOT.

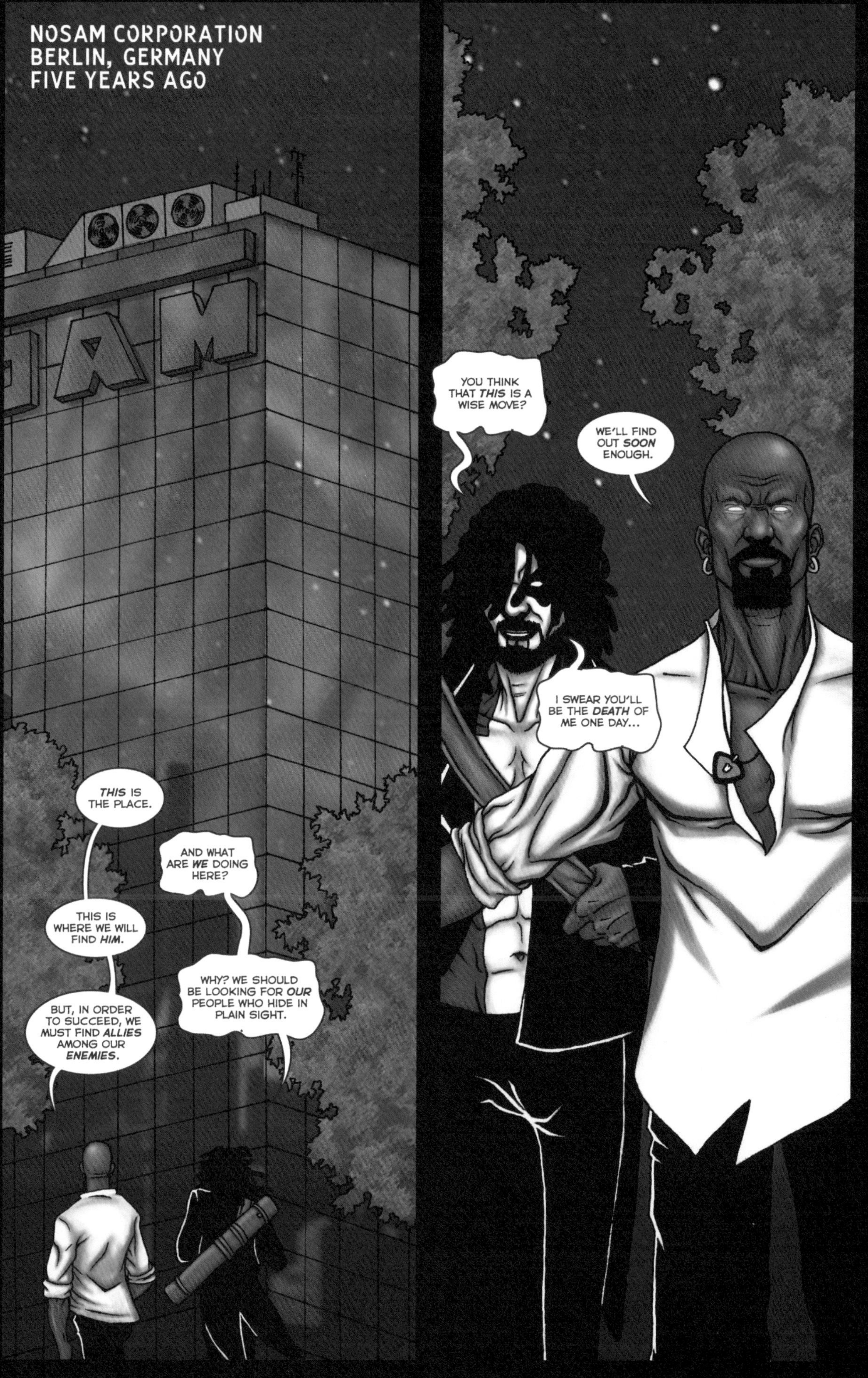
NOSAM CORPORATION
BERLIN, GERMANY
FIVE YEARS AGO
THIS IS THE PLACE.
THIS IS WHERE WE WILL FIND HIM.
AND WHAT ARE WE DOING HERE?
BUT, IN ORDER TO SUCCEED, WE MUST FIND ALLIES AMONG OUR ENEMIES.
WHY? WE SHOULD BE LOOKING FOR OUR PEOPLE WHO HIDE IN PLAIN SIGHT.
YOU THINK THAT THIS IS A WISE MOVE?
WE'LL FIND OUT SOON ENOUGH.
I SWEAR YOU'LL BE THE DEATH OF ME ONE DAY...

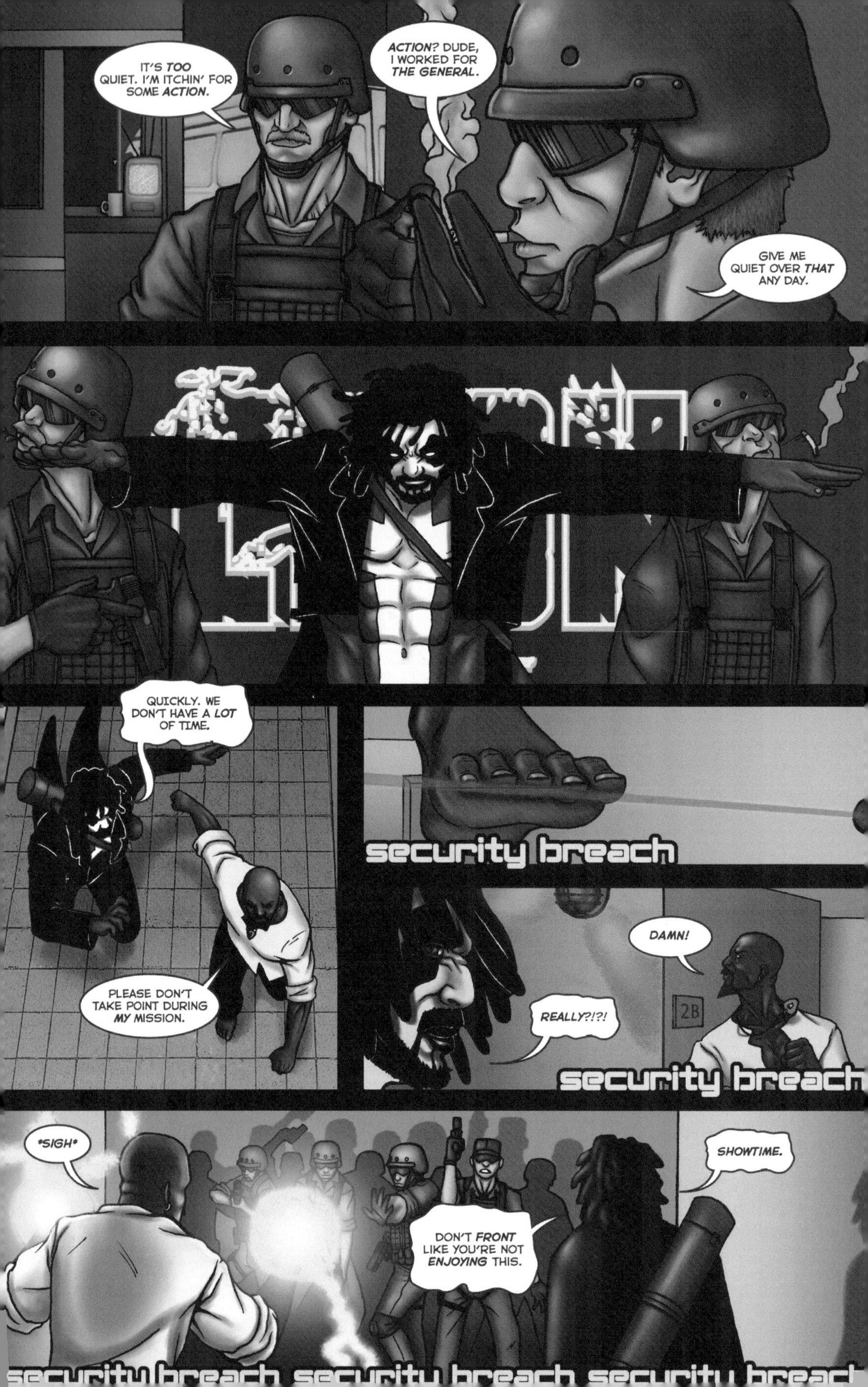
IT'S TOO QUIET. I'M ITCHIN' FOR SOME ACTION.
ACTION? DUDE, I WORKED FOR THE GENERAL.
GIVE ME QUIET OVER THAT ANY DAY.
QUICKLY. WE DON'T HAVE A LOT OF TIME.
PLEASE DON'T TAKE POINT DURING MY MISSION.
security breach
DAMN!
REALLY?!?!
2B
security breach
SIGH
SHOWTIME.
DON'T FRONT LIKE YOU'RE NOT ENJOYING THIS.
security breach security breach security breach

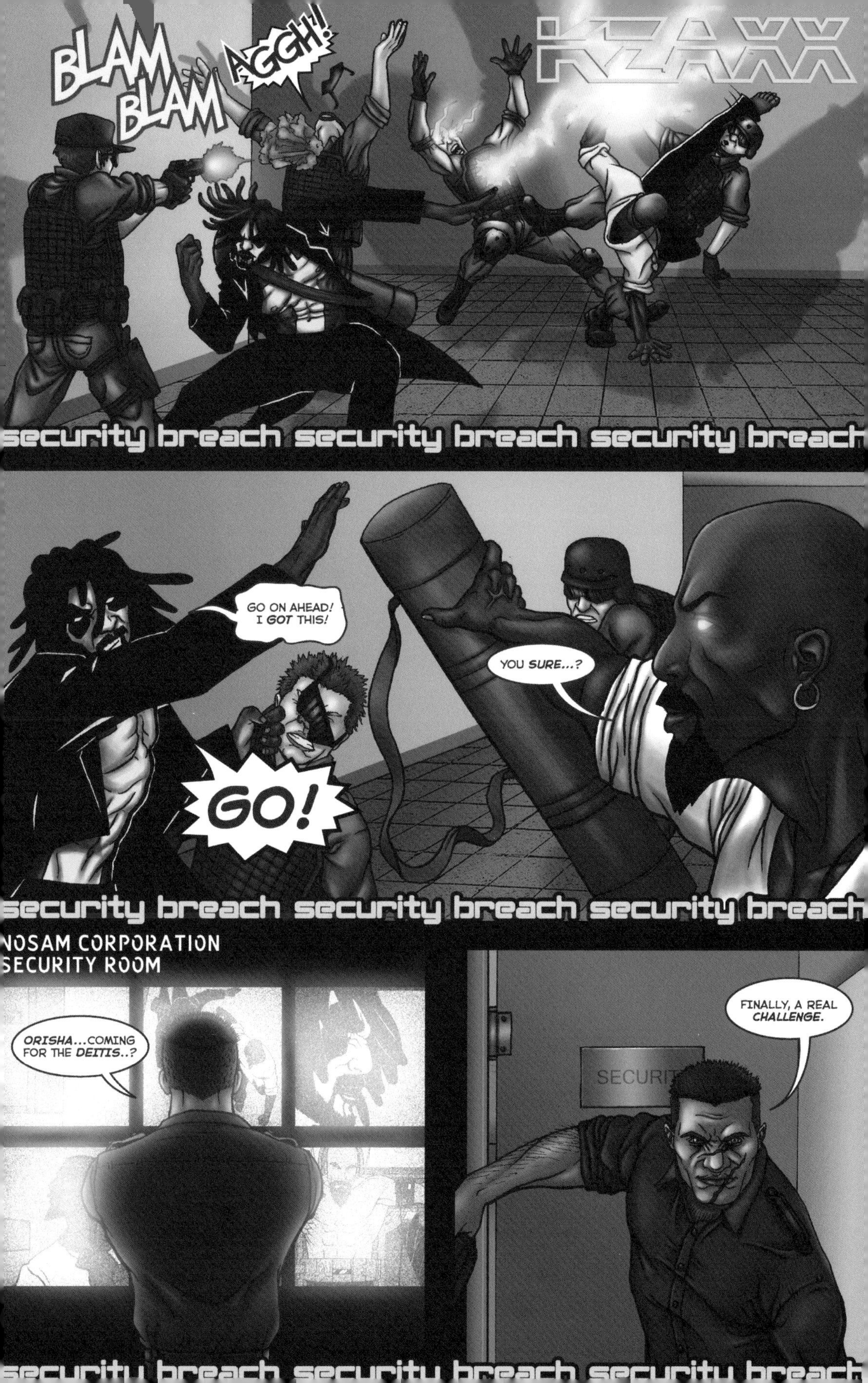
BLAM BLAM
AGGH!
security breach security breach security breach
GO ON AHEAD! I GOT THIS!
GO!
YOU SURE...?
security breach security breach security breach
NOSAM CORPORATION SECURITY ROOM
ORISHA...COMING FOR THE DEITIS..?
SECURIT
FINALLY, A REAL CHALLENGE.
security breach security breach security breach

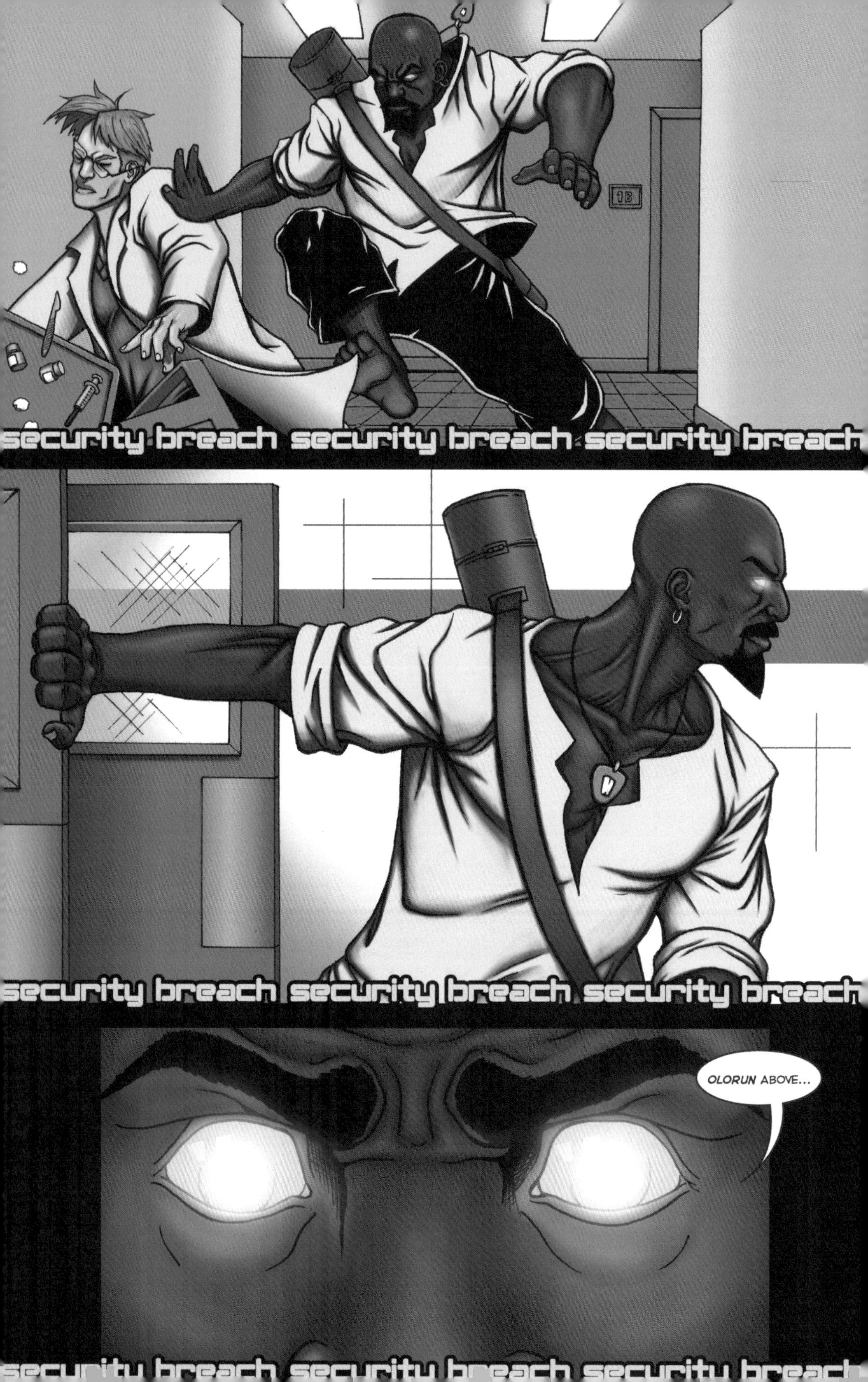
security breach security breach security breach
security breach security breach security breach
OLORUN ABOVE...

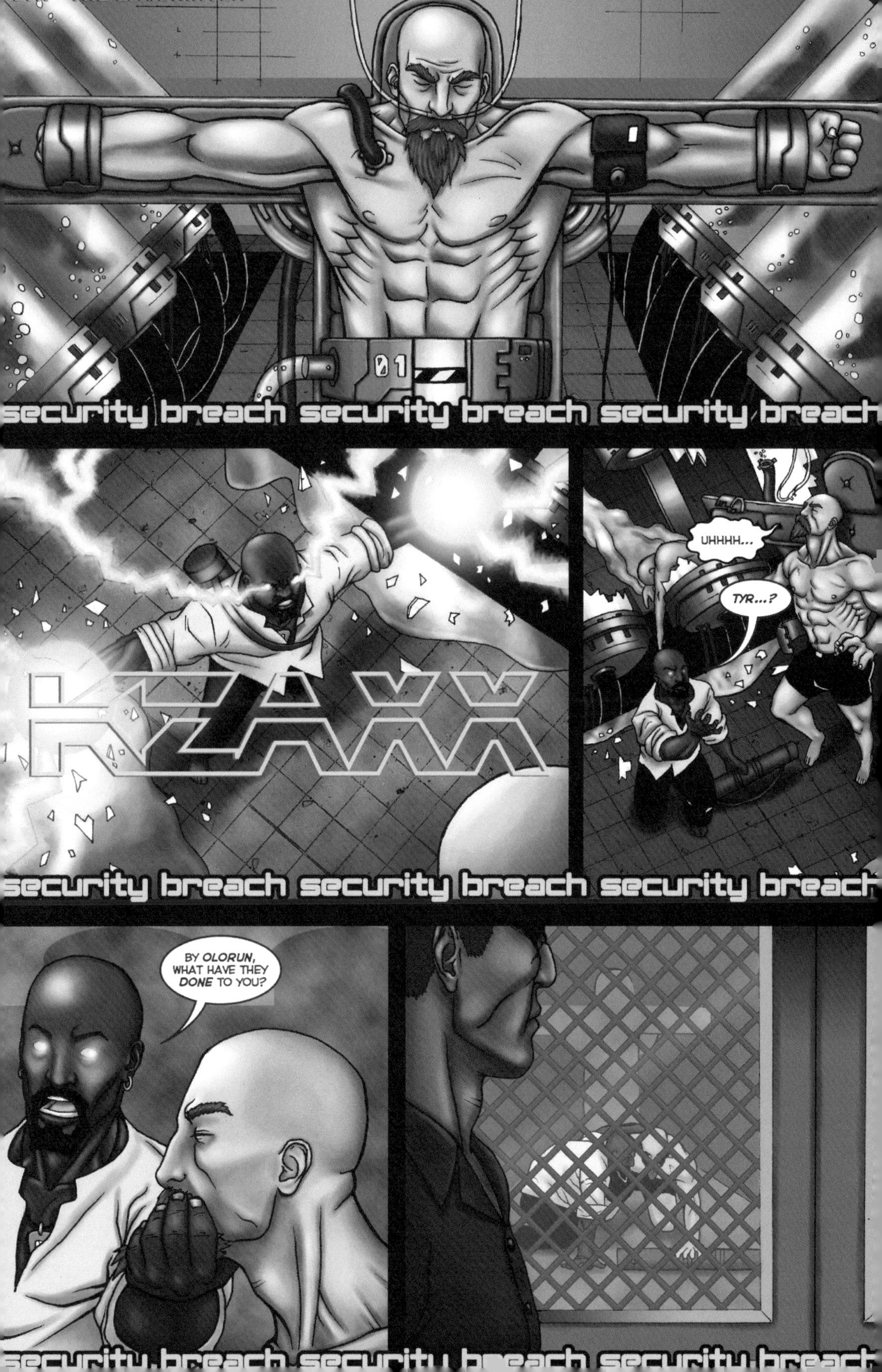
01
security breach security breach security breach
KZAXX
UHHHH...
TYR...?
security breach security breach security breach
BY OLORUN, WHAT HAVE THEY DONE TO YOU?
security breach security breach security breach

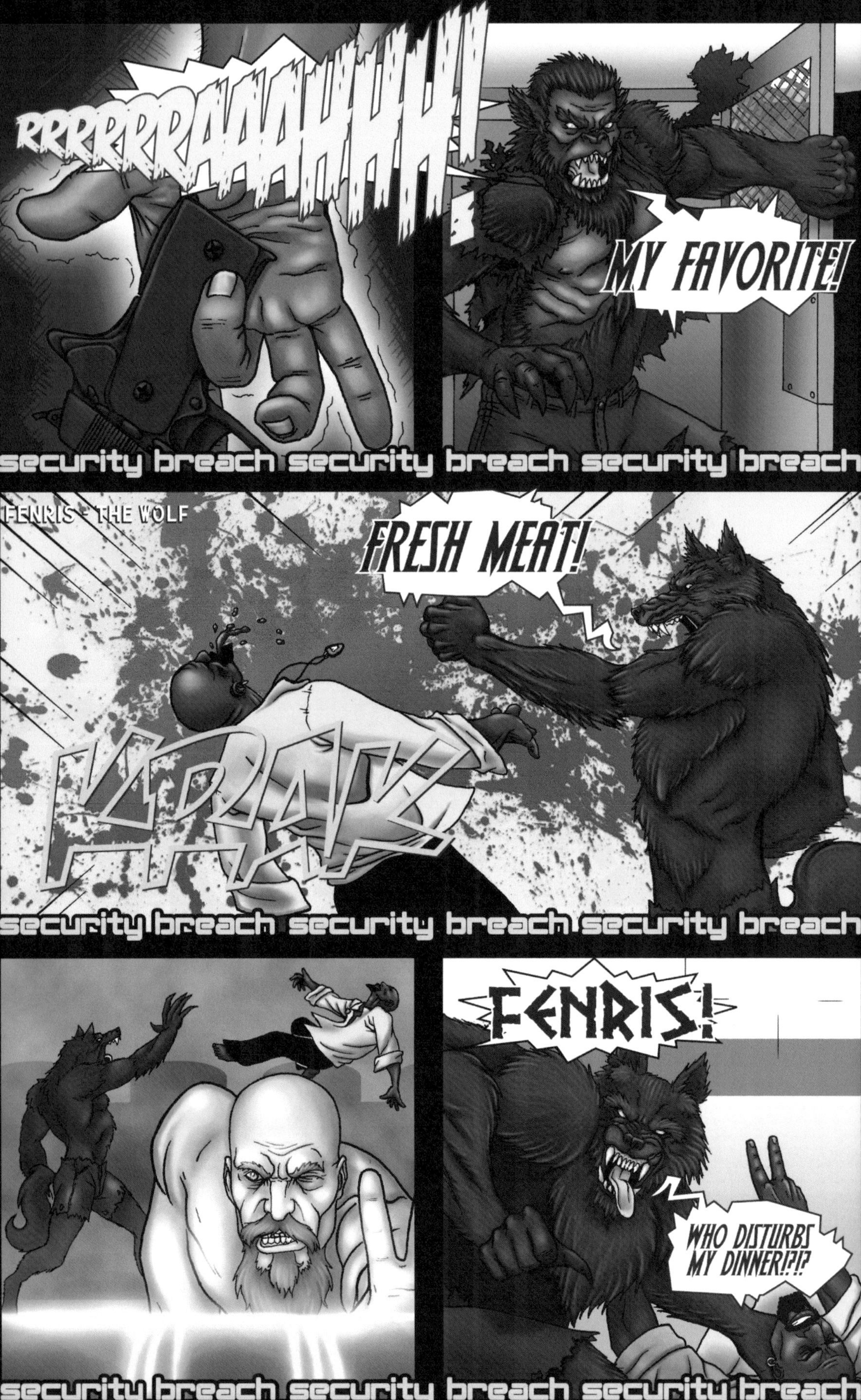
RRRRRAAAHHHH!
MY FAVORITE!
security breach security breach security breach
FENRIS - THE WOLF
FRESH MEAT!
security breach security breach security breach
FENRIS!
WHO DISTURBS MY DINNER!?!?
security breach security breach security breach

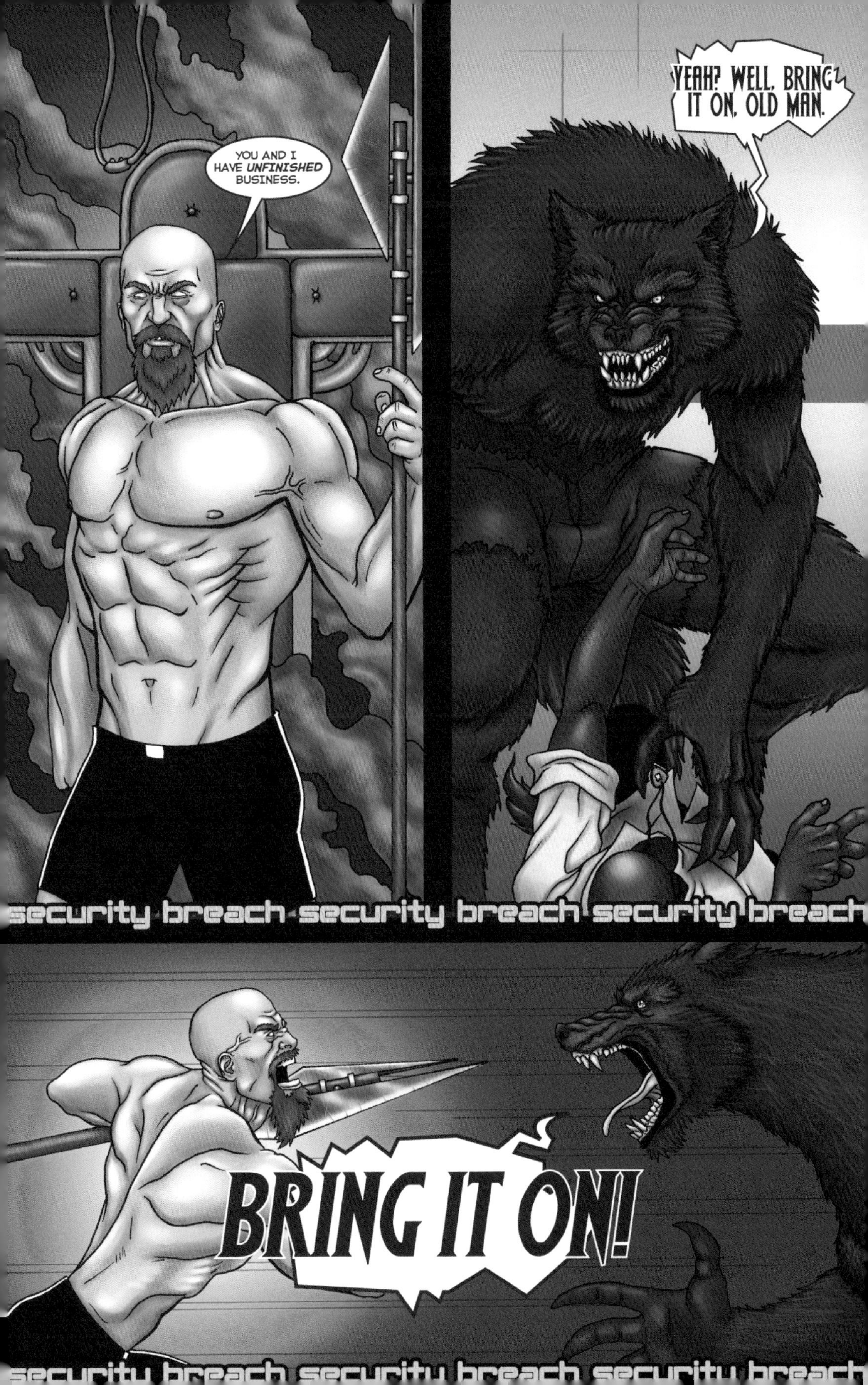
YOU AND I HAVE *UNFINISHED* BUSINESS.
YEAH? WELL, BRING IT ON, OLD MAN.
security breach security breach security breach
BRING IT ON!
security breach security breach security breach

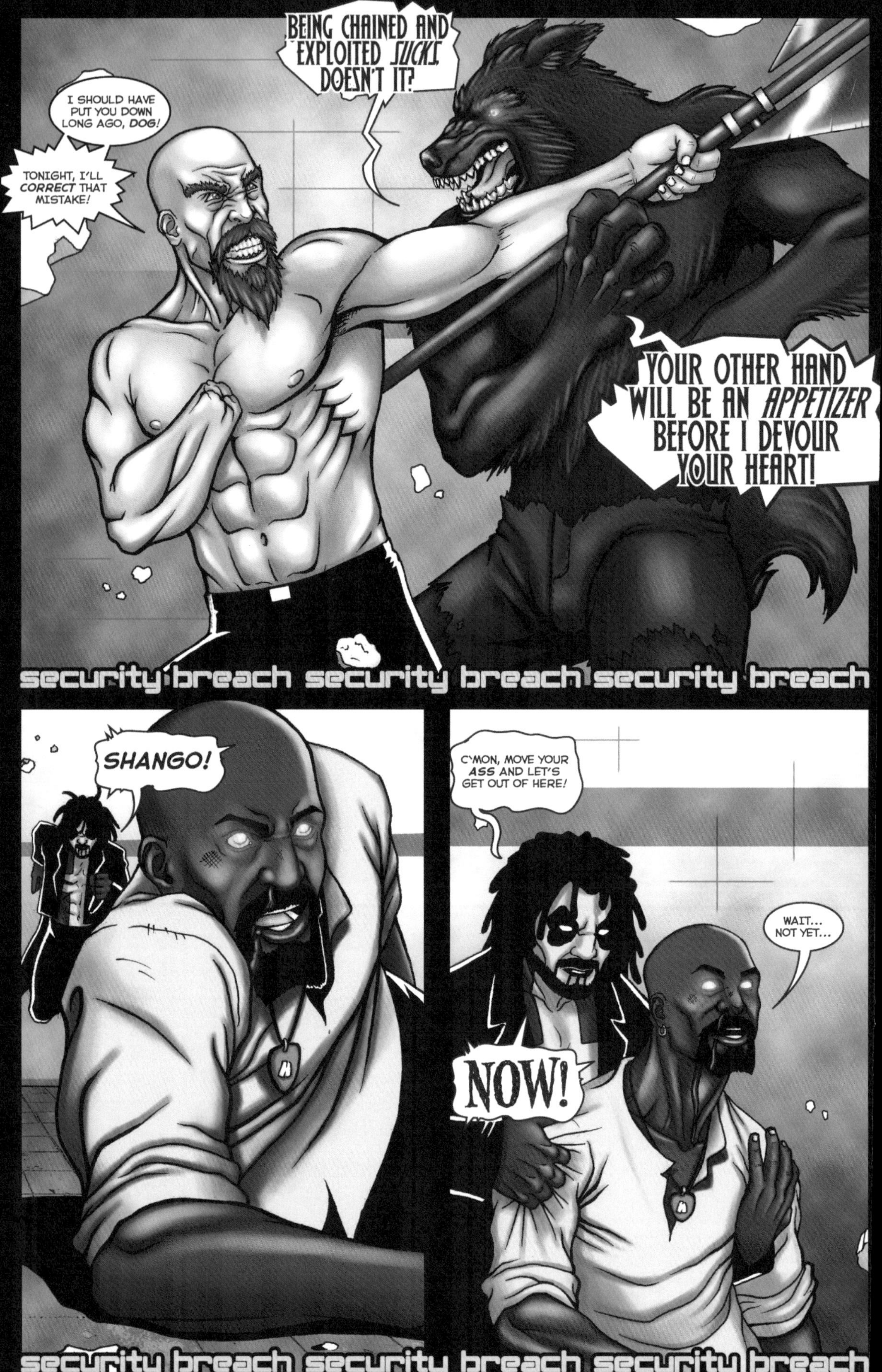
BEING CHAINED AND EXPLOITED SUCKS, DOESN'T IT?
I SHOULD HAVE PUT YOU DOWN LONG AGO, DOG!
TONIGHT, I'LL CORRECT THAT MISTAKE!
YOUR OTHER HAND WILL BE AN APPETIZER BEFORE I DEVOUR YOUR HEART!
security breach security breach security breach
SHANGO!
C'MON, MOVE YOUR ASS AND LET'S GET OUT OF HERE!
WAIT... NOT YET...
NOW!
security breach security breach security breach

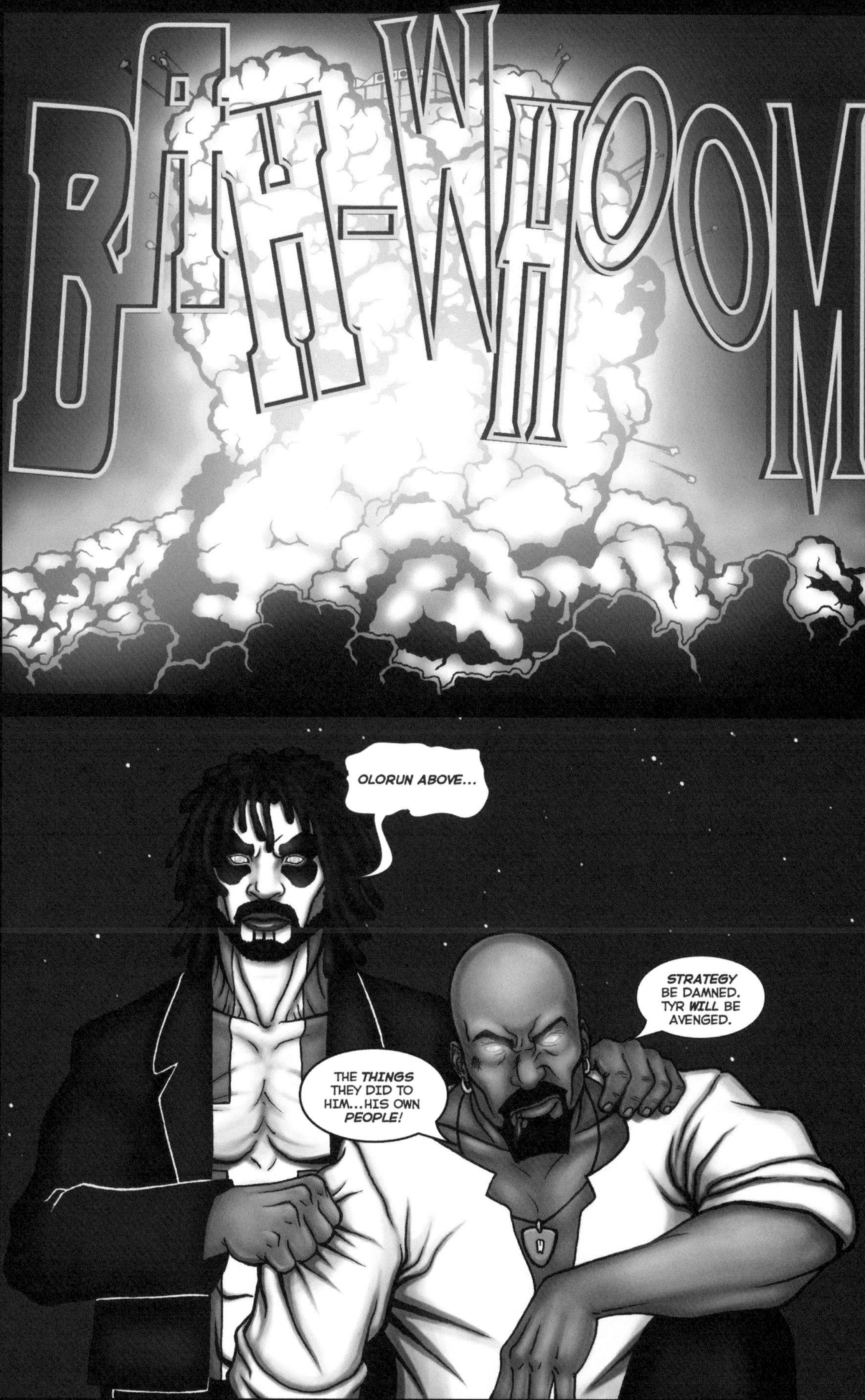
BAH-WHOOM
OLORUN ABOVE...
THE *THINGS* THEY DID TO HIM...HIS OWN *PEOPLE*!
STRATEGY BE DAMNED. TYR ***WILL*** BE AVENGED.

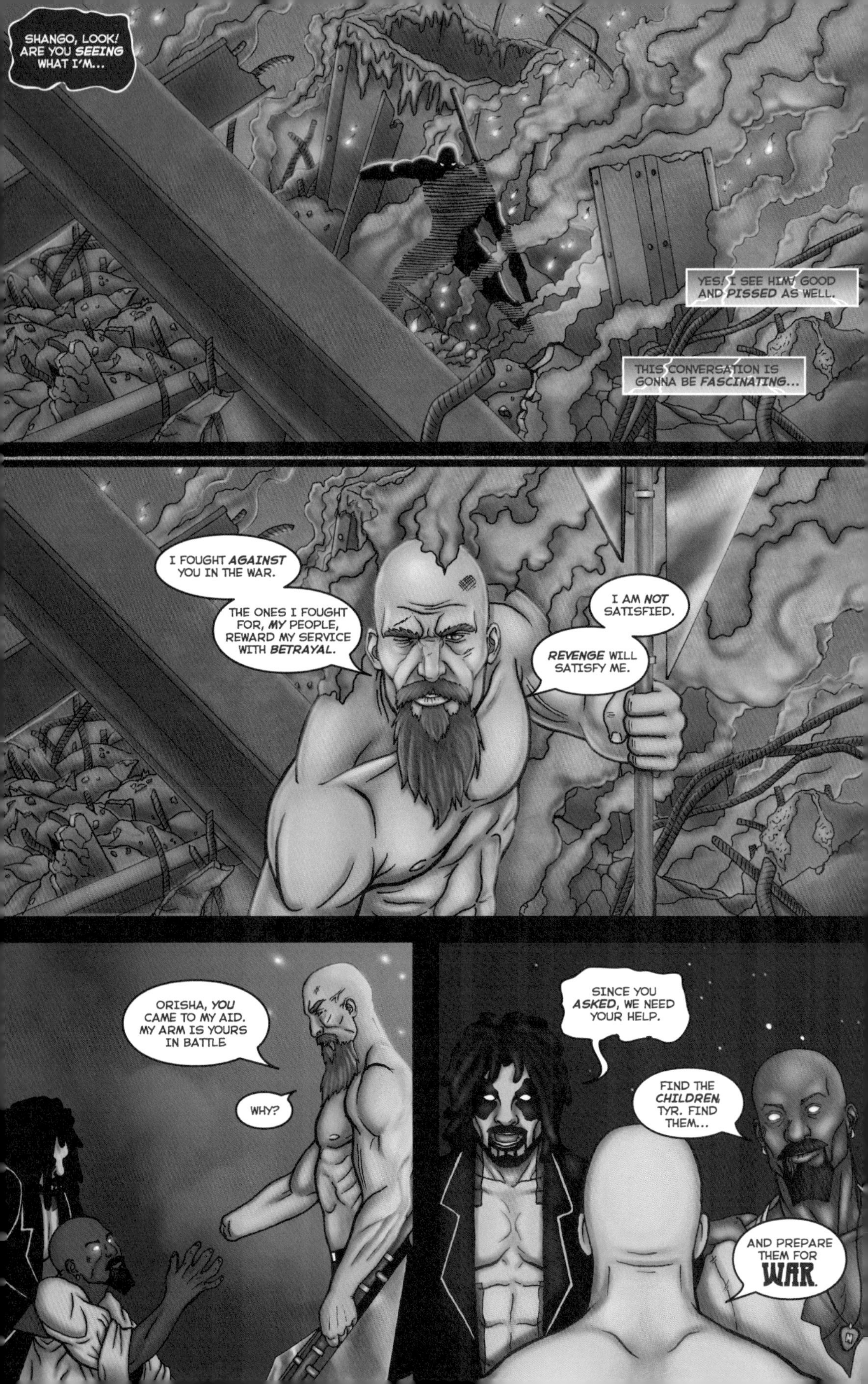
SHANGO, LOOK! ARE YOU SEEING WHAT I'M...
YES! I SEE HIM. GOOD AND PISSED AS WELL.
THIS CONVERSATION IS GONNA BE FASCINATING...
I FOUGHT AGAINST YOU IN THE WAR.
THE ONES I FOUGHT FOR, MY PEOPLE, REWARD MY SERVICE WITH BETRAYAL.
I AM NOT SATISFIED.
REVENGE WILL SATISFY ME.
ORISHA, YOU CAME TO MY AID. MY ARM IS YOURS IN BATTLE
WHY?
SINCE YOU ASKED, WE NEED YOUR HELP.
FIND THE CHILDREN, TYR. FIND THEM...
AND PREPARE THEM FOR WAR.

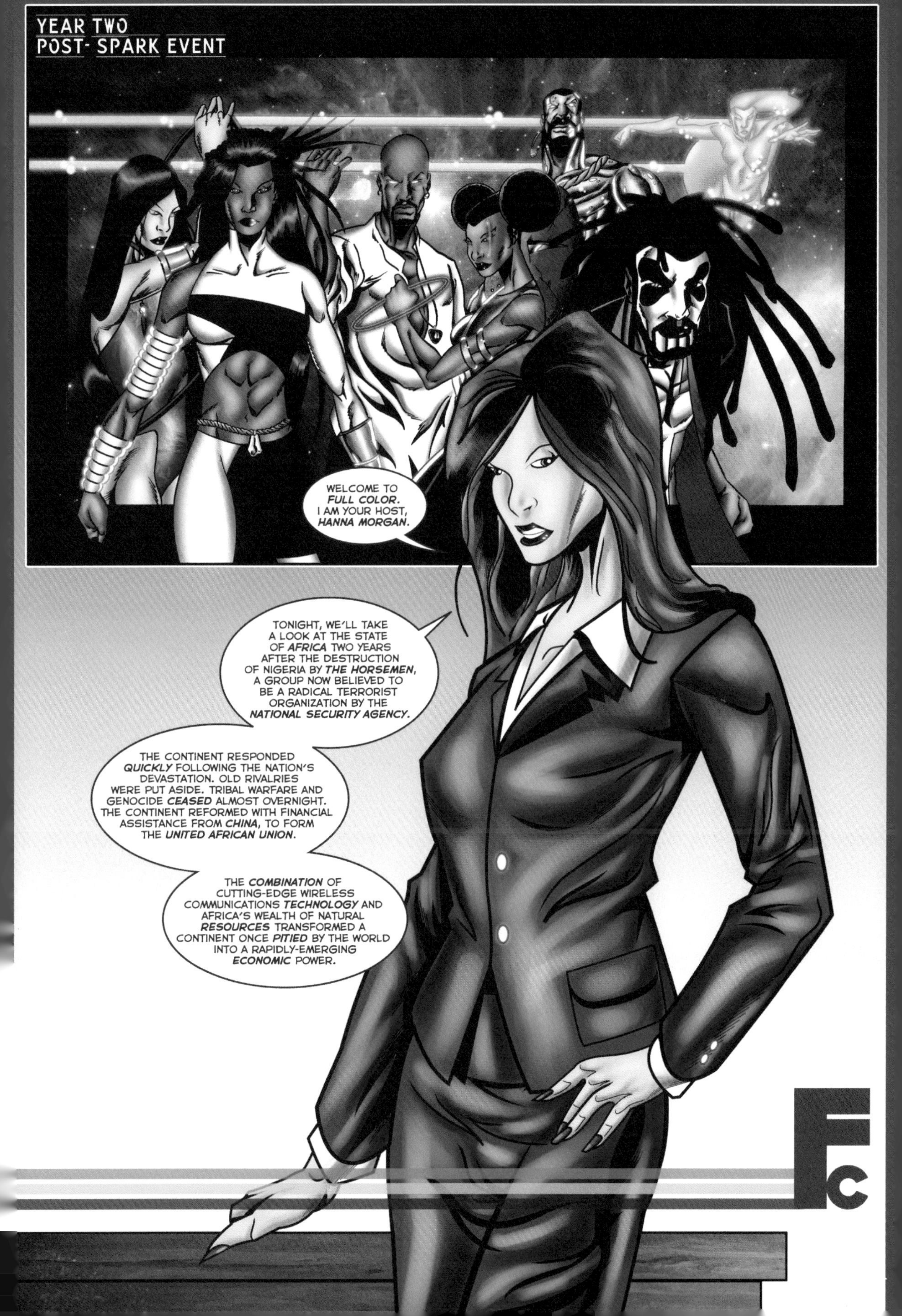
YEAR TWO
POST- SPARK EVENT
WELCOME TO FULL COLOR. I AM YOUR HOST, HANNA MORGAN.
TONIGHT, WE'LL TAKE A LOOK AT THE STATE OF AFRICA TWO YEARS AFTER THE DESTRUCTION OF NIGERIA BY THE HORSEMEN, A GROUP NOW BELIEVED TO BE A RADICAL TERRORIST ORGANIZATION BY THE NATIONAL SECURITY AGENCY.
THE CONTINENT RESPONDED QUICKLY FOLLOWING THE NATION'S DEVASTATION. OLD RIVALRIES WERE PUT ASIDE. TRIBAL WARFARE AND GENOCIDE CEASED ALMOST OVERNIGHT. THE CONTINENT REFORMED WITH FINANCIAL ASSISTANCE FROM CHINA, TO FORM THE UNITED AFRICAN UNION.
THE COMBINATION OF CUTTING-EDGE WIRELESS COMMUNICATIONS TECHNOLOGY AND AFRICA'S WEALTH OF NATURAL RESOURCES TRANSFORMED A CONTINENT ONCE PITIED BY THE WORLD INTO A RAPIDLY-EMERGING ECONOMIC POWER.
FC

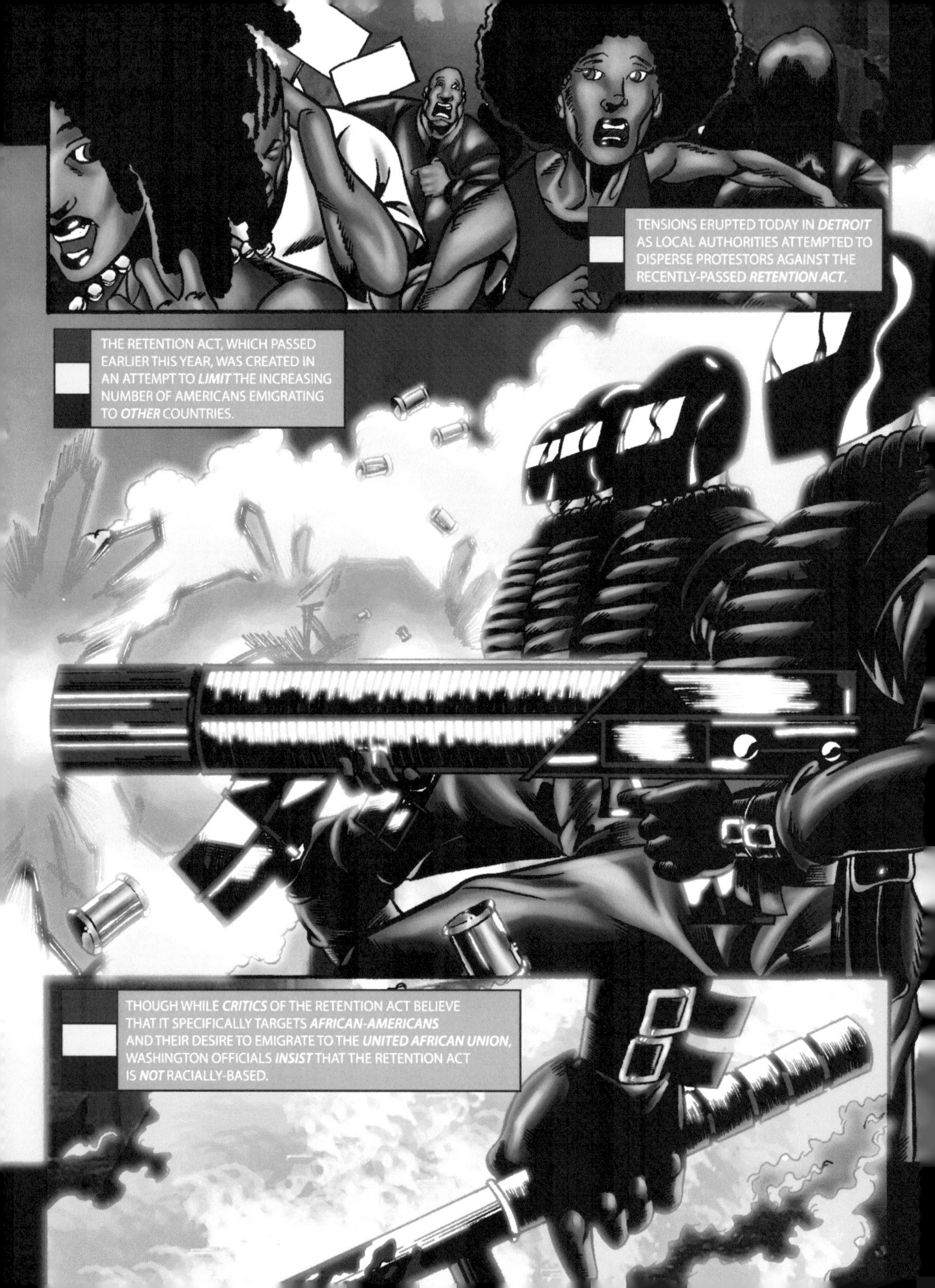
TENSIONS ERUPTED TODAY IN DETROIT AS LOCAL AUTHORITIES ATTEMPTED TO DISPERSE PROTESTORS AGAINST THE RECENTLY-PASSED RETENTION ACT.
THE RETENTION ACT, WHICH PASSED EARLIER THIS YEAR, WAS CREATED IN AN ATTEMPT TO LIMIT THE INCREASING NUMBER OF AMERICANS EMIGRATING TO OTHER COUNTRIES.
THOUGH WHILE CRITICS OF THE RETENTION ACT BELIEVE THAT IT SPECIFICALLY TARGETS AFRICAN-AMERICANS AND THEIR DESIRE TO EMIGRATE TO THE UNITED AFRICAN UNION, WASHINGTON OFFICIALS INSIST THAT THE RETENTION ACT IS NOT RACIALLY-BASED.

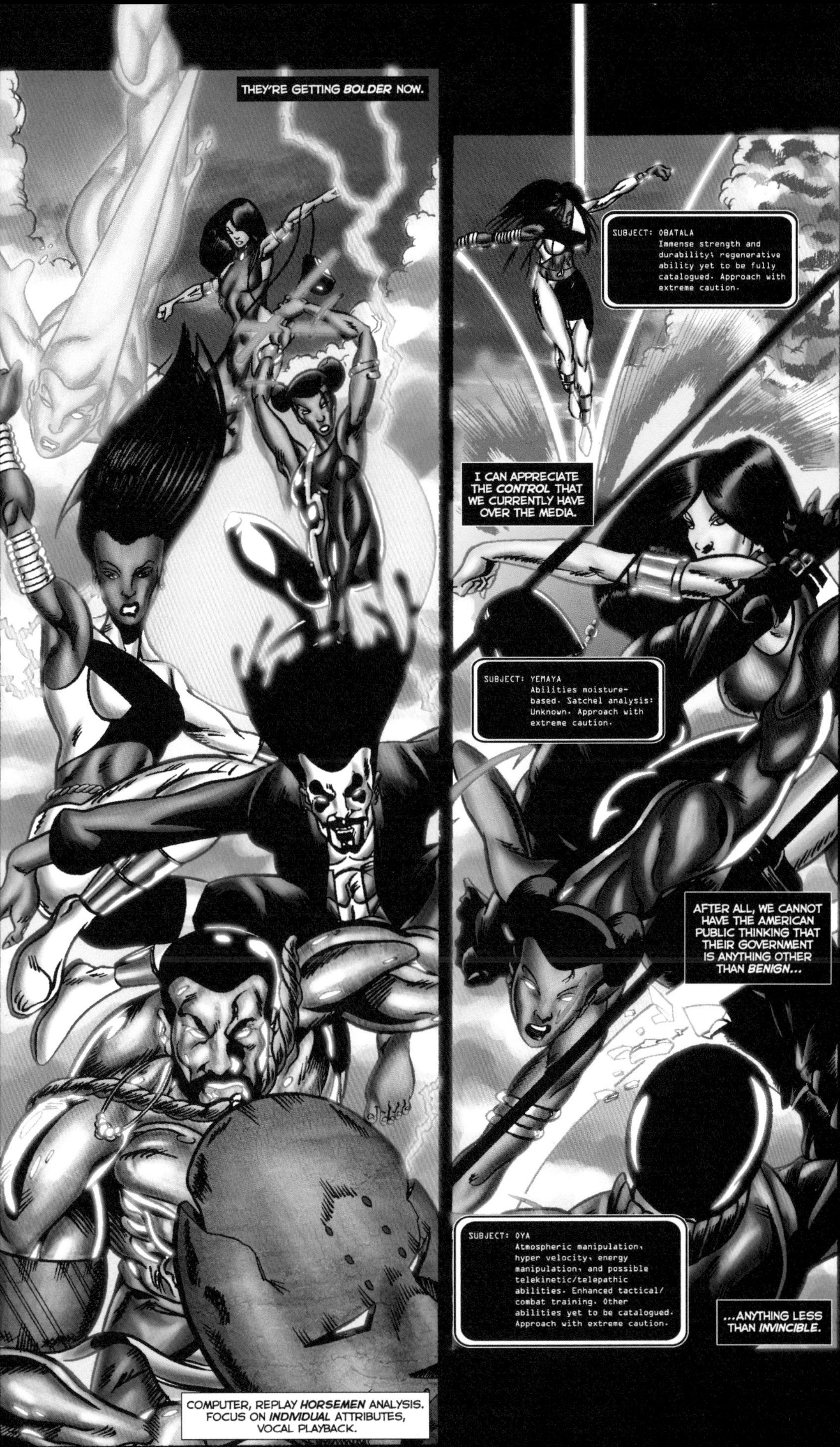

THEY'RE GETTING BOLDER NOW.
COMPUTER, REPLAY HORSEMEN ANALYSIS. FOCUS ON INDIVIDUAL ATTRIBUTES, VOCAL PLAYBACK.
SUBJECT: OBATALA Immense strength and durability; regenerative ability yet to be fully catalogued. Approach with extreme caution.
I CAN APPRECIATE THE CONTROL THAT WE CURRENTLY HAVE OVER THE MEDIA.
SUBJECT: YEMAYA Abilities moisture-based. Satchel analysis: Unknown. Approach with extreme caution.
AFTER ALL, WE CANNOT HAVE THE AMERICAN PUBLIC THINKING THAT THEIR GOVERNMENT IS ANYTHING OTHER THAN BENIGN...
SUBJECT: OYA Atmospheric manipulation, hyper velocity, energy manipulation, and possible telekinetic/telepathic abilities. Enhanced tactical/combat training. Other abilities yet to be catalogued. Approach with extreme caution.
...ANYTHING LESS THAN INVINCIBLE.

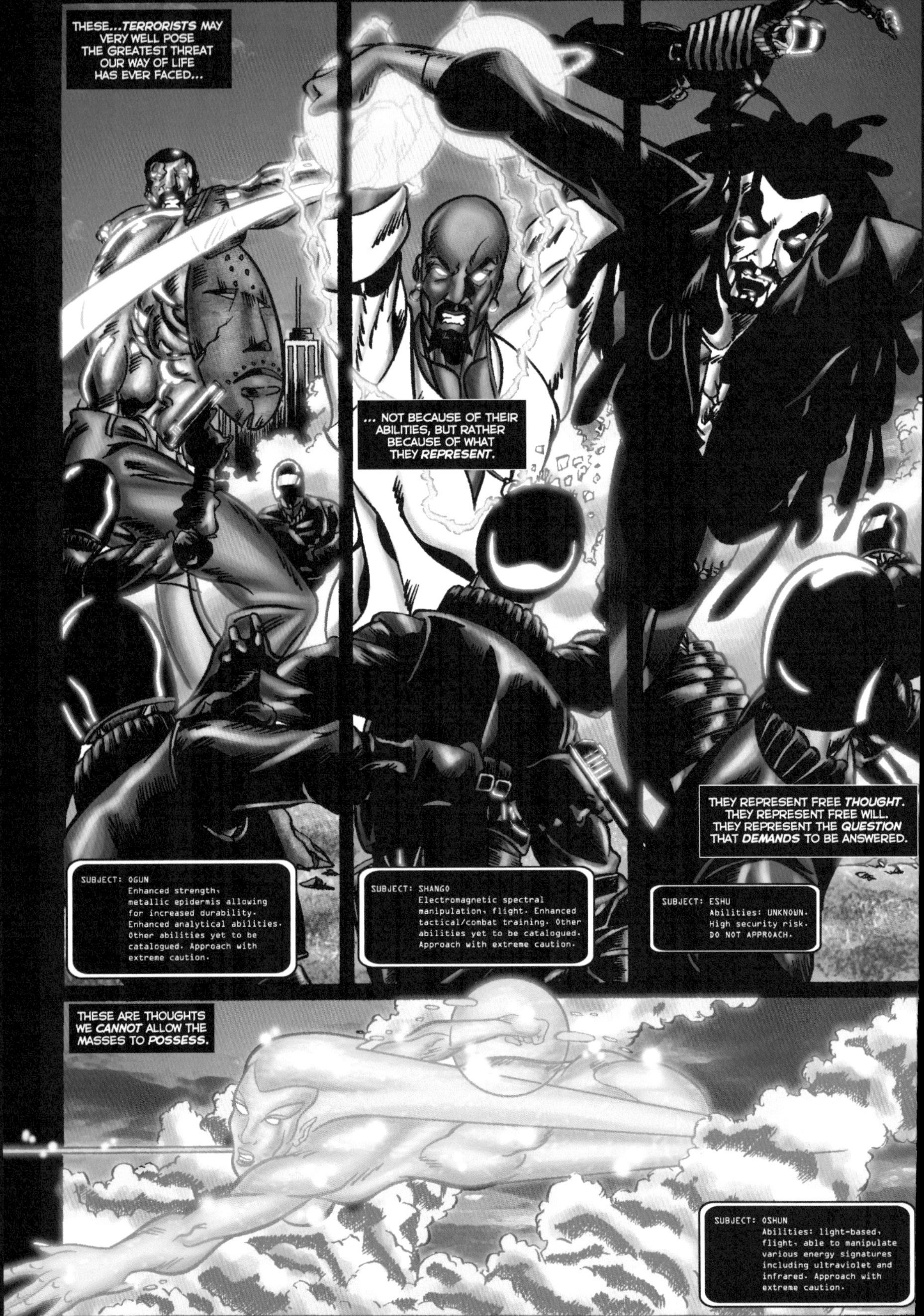
THESE...TERRORISTS MAY VERY WELL POSE THE GREATEST THREAT OUR WAY OF LIFE HAS EVER FACED...
... NOT BECAUSE OF THEIR ABILITIES, BUT RATHER BECAUSE OF WHAT THEY REPRESENT.
THEY REPRESENT FREE THOUGHT. THEY REPRESENT FREE WILL. THEY REPRESENT THE QUESTION THAT DEMANDS TO BE ANSWERED.
SUBJECT: OGUN Enhanced strength, metallic epidermis allowing for increased durability. Enhanced analytical abilities. Other abilities yet to be catalogued. Approach with extreme caution.
SUBJECT: SHANGO Electromagnetic spectral manipulation, flight. Enhanced tactical/combat training. Other abilities yet to be catalogued. Approach with extreme caution.
SUBJECT: ESHU Abilities: UNKNOWN. High security risk. DO NOT APPROACH.
THESE ARE THOUGHTS WE CANNOT ALLOW THE MASSES TO POSSESS.
SUBJECT: OSHUN Abilities: light-based, flight, able to manipulate various energy signatures including ultraviolet and infrared. Approach with extreme caution.

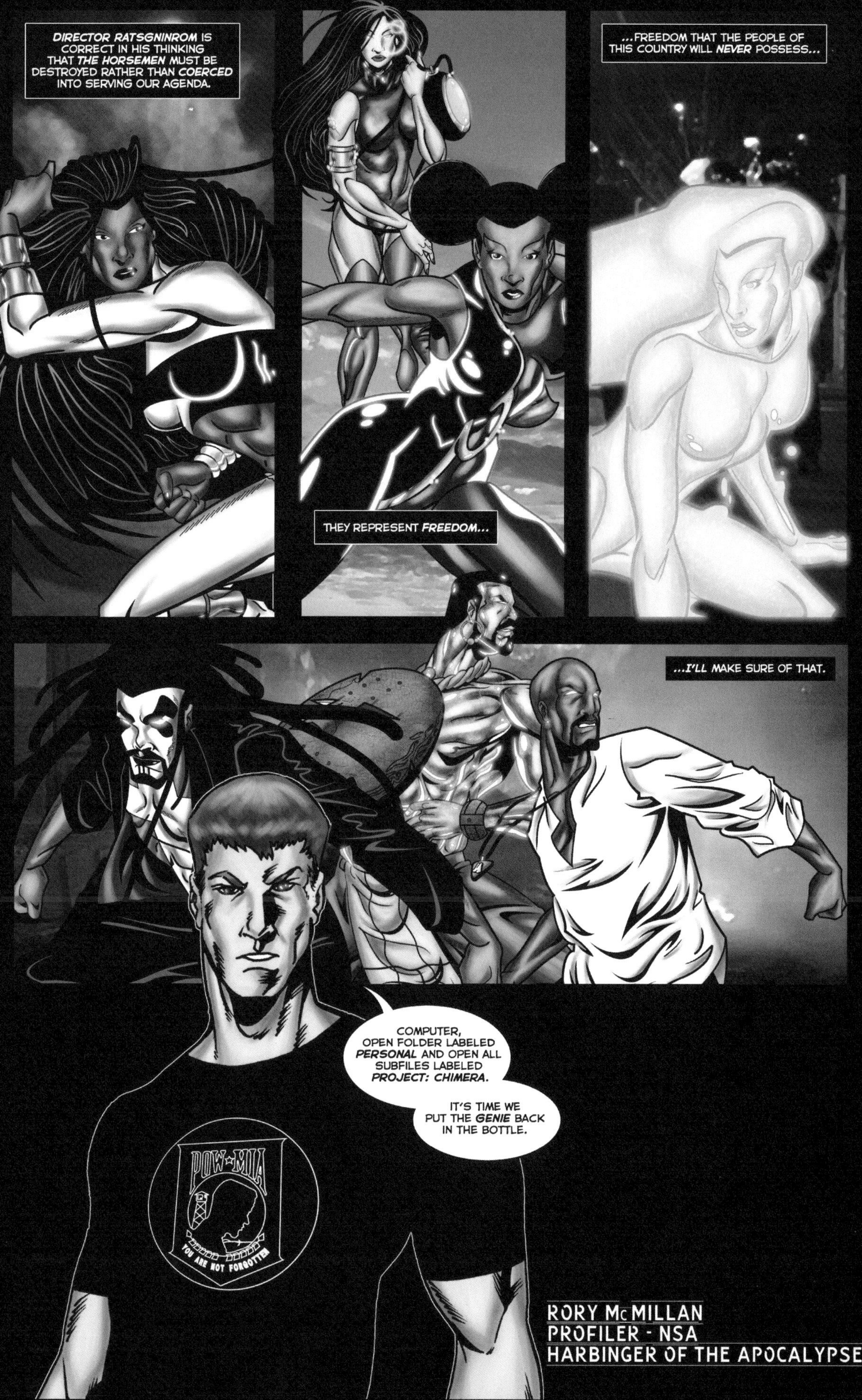

DIRECTOR RATSGNINROM IS CORRECT IN HIS THINKING THAT THE HORSEMEN MUST BE DESTROYED RATHER THAN COERCED INTO SERVING OUR AGENDA.
THEY REPRESENT FREEDOM...
...FREEDOM THAT THE PEOPLE OF THIS COUNTRY WILL NEVER POSSESS...
...I'LL MAKE SURE OF THAT.
COMPUTER, OPEN FOLDER LABELED PERSONAL AND OPEN ALL SUBFILES LABELED PROJECT: CHIMERA.
IT'S TIME WE PUT THE GENIE BACK IN THE BOTTLE.
POW★MIA
YOU ARE NOT FORGOTTEN
RORY McMILLAN
PROFILER - NSA
HARBINGER OF THE APOCALYPSE

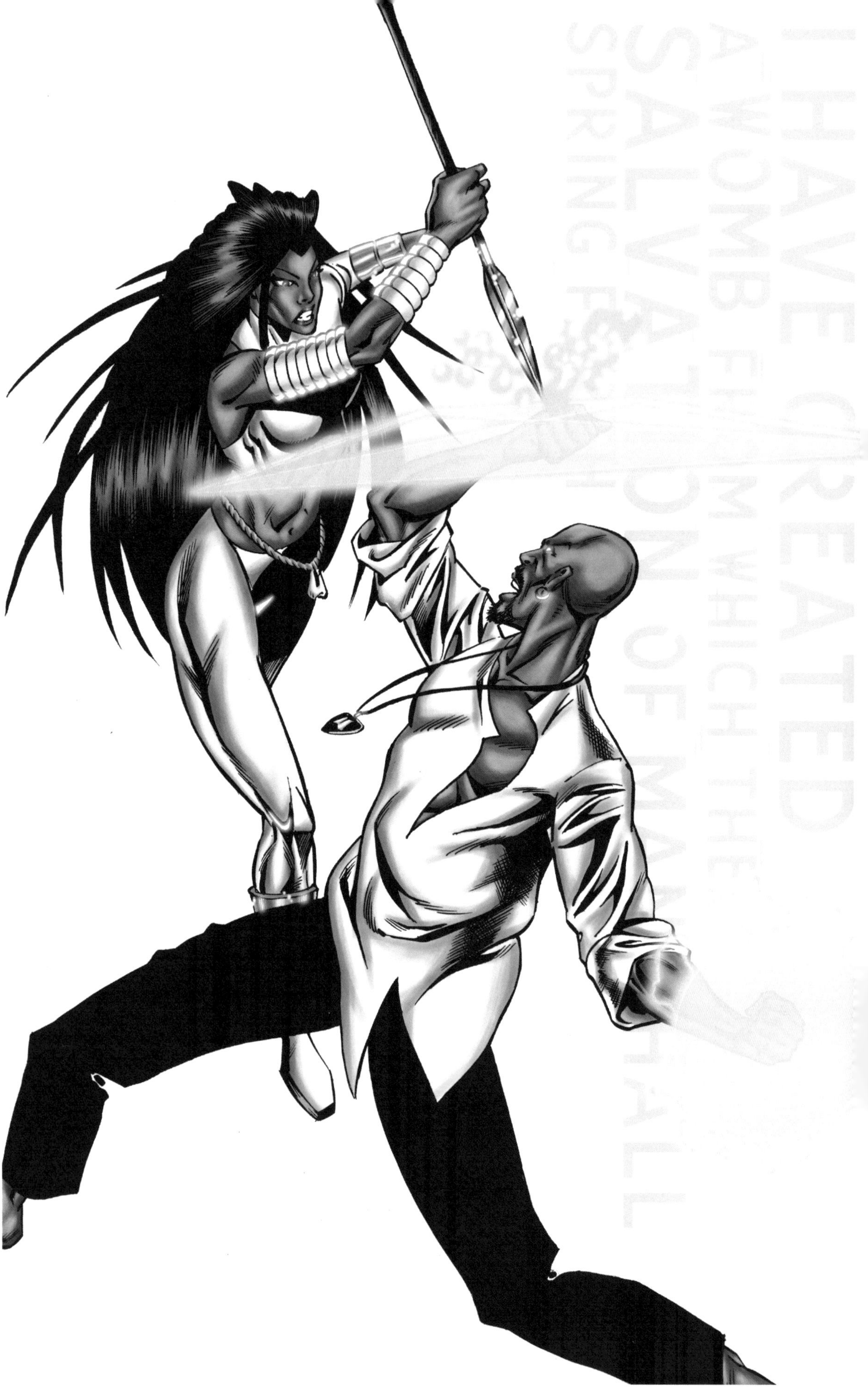
I HAVE CREATED
A WOMB FROM WHICH THE
SALVATION OF MAN SHALL
SPRING F

NEXT ON DECK:

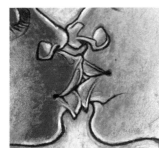

the big finish!

4 pages 16 bars

a visual mixtape

spring 2016

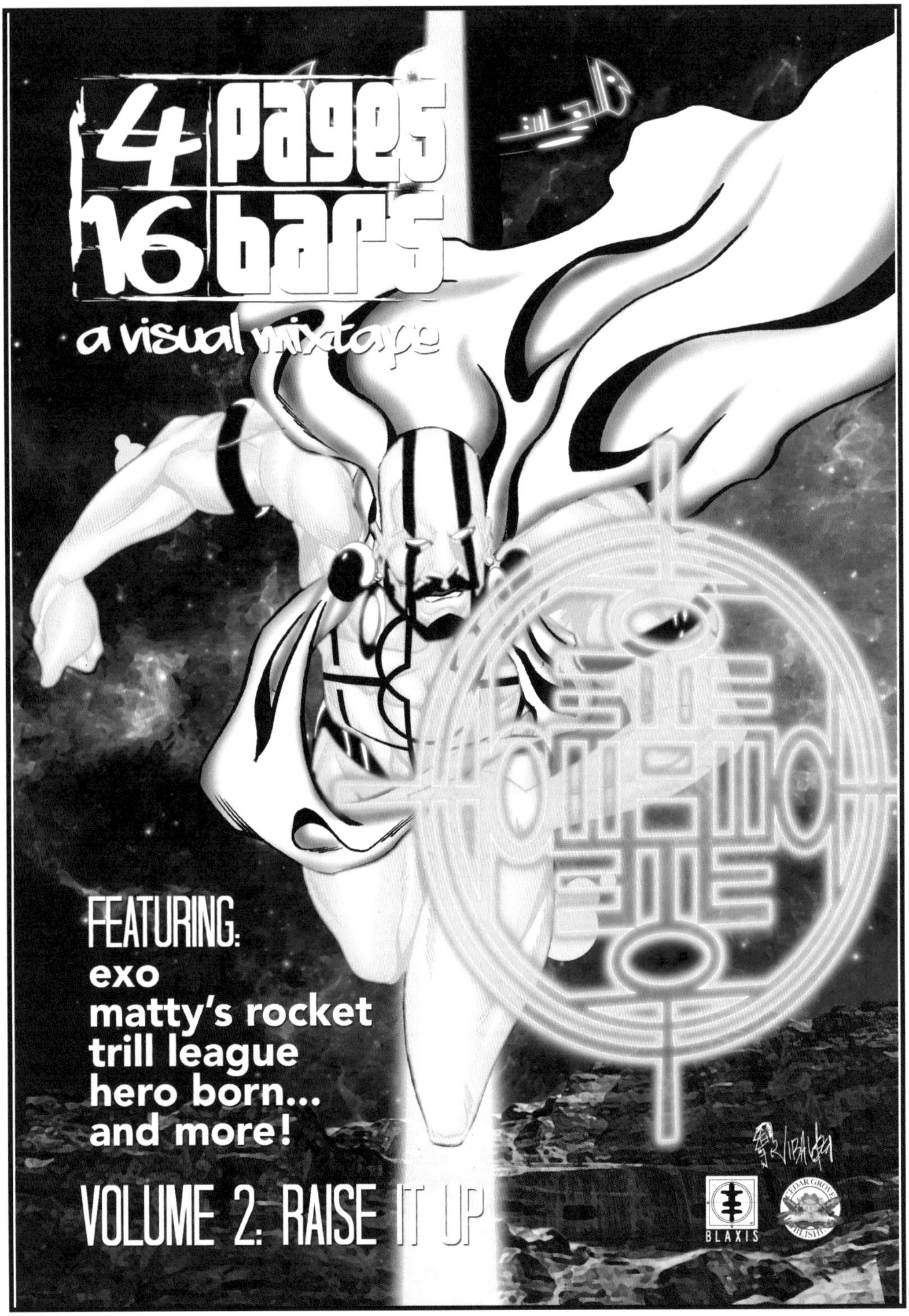
4 pages
16 bars
a visual mixtape
FEATURING:
exo
matty's rocket
trill league
hero born...
and more!
VOLUME 2: RAISE IT UP
BLAXIS

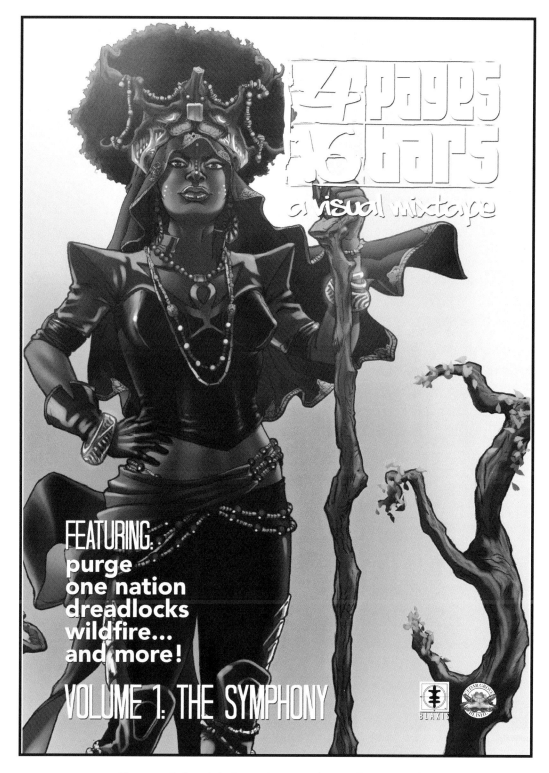

FEATURING:
purge
one nation
dreadlocks
wildfire...
and more!

VOLUME 1: THE SYMPHONY

The comic book industry is more than DC or Marvel.
The scene is more diverse than Image or Dark Horse. This is
visual Jazz, Rock, Funk, Hip Hop and electronic music.
This is art for the people.

on sale now!

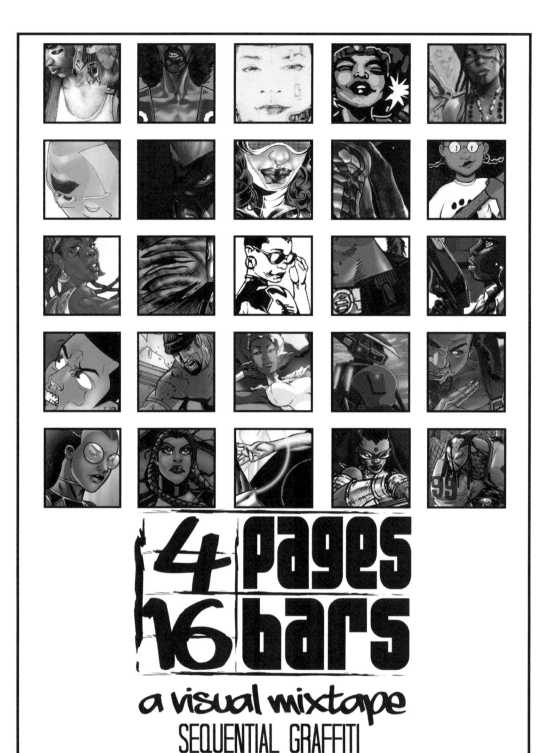

A poster book featuring some of the finest **Visual MCs** and **Literary DJs** comics, animation, and speculative fiction have to offer... This is the EP to the mixtape.

CPSIA information can be obtained at www.ICGtesting.com
Printed in the USA
LVIW01n2252180717
541839LV00005B/15

9 781941 958384